Nagauta

THE HEART OF
KABUKI MUSIC

*Recipient of the Monograph Prize
of the American Academy of Arts and Sciences
for the year 1959
in the field of the humanities*

by William P. Malm

GREENWOOD PRESS, PUBLISHERS
WESTPORT, CONNECTICUT

Library of Congress Cataloging in Publication Data

Malm, William P
  Nagauta: the heart of kabuki music.

   Reprint of the 1963 ed. published by C. E. Tuttle
Co., Rutland, Vt.
   1. Music, Japanese—History and criticism.
2. Kabuki. I. Title.
[ML340.M33 1973]   782.8   73-6260
ISBN 0-8371-6900-3

Originally published in 1963
by Charles E. Tuttle Company, Rutland, Vermont

Reprinted with the permission
of Charles E. Tuttle Co., Inc.

Reprinted by Greenwood Press, Inc.

First Greenwood reprinting 1973
Second Greenwood reprinting 1976

Library of Congress catalog card number 73-6260

ISBN 0-8371-6900-3

Printed in the United States of America

Table of Contents

List of Musical Examples and Tables

List of Illustrations

Preface

THE KABUKI theatre has long been admired for the artistry of its plays, the skill of its actors, and the brilliance of its decor. Its musical qualities, however, have generally been ignored. Writers on kabuki recognize the fact that the spectacular dramaturgical elements of kabuki float on a variegated but, for the Westerner, generally undifferentiated sea of music. Nevertheless, because of space or specialization, they have been unable to complete their discussions with actual musical analyses. This book is an attempt to fill in this gap by presenting an introductory study of one of its major musical elements, *nagauta*. In addition, it is hoped that a better understanding of this single form, as it is used both in and out of the theatre, will be a step toward a fuller appreciation of Japanese music in general. At present Japanese music tends to be viewed as a series of exotic pleasantries. With the gradual appearance of detailed studies in specific musics it may be possible to change such a picture to one of a group of historically connected art forms. As in Western music, each of these genres must obey certain general laws of musical logic. At the same time, each displays special solutions to its specific artistic problems. The discovery of how a particular music operates within such general and specific rules is one of the goals of music research. It has been a strong motivation for this work.

In a world as varied as that of Japanese music one could begin to study anywhere with intellectual and musical profit. I have chosen to begin with nagauta because it is a living tradition which grew out of the most recent flourishing period of Japanese music history, the eighteenth and nineteenth centuries. Perhaps more important than this is the fact that I like nagauta. I think it is beautiful, and beauty should be shared with others.

This book of necessity must be addressed to many different audiences; the musician, the Orientalist, the theatre devotee, and the intellectually curious. Because of this, it has been divided in such a way that those seeking specific knowledge can tell from the Table of Contents which sections of the book are germane. However, the book is designed primarily to be read straight through. The transcriptions have been printed separately so that the analytical sections of the book can be studied with the music in hand. I am sure that musicians join me in thanking the editors for providing this important convenience.

In presenting a study of nagauta to the Western reader several severe problems arise. Foremost of these is the lack in the West of a background of Japanese music in general and the kabuki music tradition in particular. Because of this it has been necessary to digress from the main topic at certain points and provide information of a type one could presume as common knowledge when writing about Western music. This problem also causes the study to be replete with Japanese technical music terms. Such a condition is unfortunate for the general reader but unavoidable. A glossary-index has been provided in order that one can follow the discussion without undue discomfort from unfamiliar terminology.

Another very important problem is the lack in the West of extensive listening experience in nagauta and its related genres. A partial solution to this has been provided by the fact that most of the major works discussed are available on Japanese LP recordings. Some of these recordings have been listed in Appendix I. For the fortunate few, of course, the ultimate source of musical experience is the kabuki theatre and the concert halls of Tokyo. In any event, it is strongly recommended that the reader listen to some recordings before entering this study.

In providing illustrative transcriptions several important decisions had to be made of which the reader should be aware. To the best of my knowledge, this is the first time any nagauta has ever been written down in score form. Part books have been the traditional method in Japan and even these are often only outlines or symbolic reminders of the specific music to be used in each instance. As will be seen in this study, each music guild plays each piece in a slightly different manner, and when there is a performance of mixed guilds the result is a compromise version of the piece. In other words, there is no one version of a composition. In making these transcriptions several sources were used. The shamisen and vocal parts are based almost entirely on the lessons and "corrected" part books of my teachers, Kikuoka Shinobu (shamisen) and Nishigaki Yūzō (voice).

Both men teach in the traditional music section of the music school in the Tokyo University of Fine Arts and are thus committed to upholding the nagauta tradition in as pure a form as possible. They are also excellent performing musicians and conscientious teachers. My drum teacher, Tanaka Denzaemon, is head of the Tanaka drum guild and chief percussionist for the Tokyo kabuki theatre. He is very seriously concerned with the purity of the guild style and thus was an excellent source of knowledge concerning unadulterated drum music. Other members of the guild, particularly Messrs. Tanaka Sadenji, Sashichirō, and Satōjirō, were most generous with information they themselves had acquired only through years of arduous apprenticeship.

In applying this knowledge to the transcriptions I was faced with the problem that a majority of recordings and my own tapes contain performances by musicians of the Mochizuki school. Though a few Mochizuki drum scores were found for sale, I had less opportunity for contact with the musicians of that guild because of my connections with the Tanaka group. Thus, in comparing the transcriptions with actual recordings one will find occasional discrepancies. The drum parts are basically Tanaka school, and the minor variations found in various recordings should not detract unduly from the basic structure of the music. The symbols used in the drum parts are explained in the front of the transcription volume.

A final point about the transcriptions concerns pitch level. The pitch of a performance is determined by the singer and therefore there is no special "key" for a piece. The basic pitch B has been chosen as typical rather the specific. The general interval distances are those of the tempered scale (for further discussion see page 117).

Turning to style problems, it should be noted that Japanese names have been written in the Japanese manner, surname first. The spelling and hyphenization of Japanese words is in general conformity with the style adopted in the previous Tuttle publication, *Japanese Music and Musical Instruments*. The names of shamisen genre, however, are not capitalized. Long marks do not appear on Japanese place names though they are used for all technical terms and proper names.

Since all the compositions mentioned are found in one of two types of native notation, these sources have been indicated by parenthetical abbreviations rather than footnotes. Thus, (Yoshizumi, III–2, p. 3) refers to a passage on page three of item two in Volume III of Yoshizumi Kosaburō's collection of nagauta pieces, *Nagauta Shin-keikobon* and (Bunka, 3334) refers to piece 3334 in the nagauta series of the so-called shamisen *bunkafu*, edited by Kineya Mishichi. Both notations are in print and can be purchased from the Hōgaku-sha (1 Nishikubo Sakuragawa-cho, Shiba, Minato-ku, Tokyo) or any of its outlets. For the reader's convenience, all pieces mentioned in the text are listed in Appendix I along with where they can be found in notation and in recordings.

With the aid of the various items mentioned above it is hoped that the reader will be able to follow this study and arrive at a deeper appreciation of the many merits of nagauta music.

The author wishes to thank Professors Laurence Petran, Mantle Hood, Jan Popper, Ensho Ashikaga, and Robert Wilson for their advice and guidance of this study in its dissertation form at the University of California, Los Angeles. Thanks also is due to Professor Kishibe Shigeo, who guided my studies during a two-year fellowship in Japan from the Ford Foundation. This study is deeply indebted to the foundation but does not necessarily reflect the opinions of the Ford Foundation or its officers.

Chapter I appeared first as an article in the *Journal of the American Oriental Society* and is printed in essentially the same form here with their kind permission. The drawings in this book are by Kuwata Masakazu. As noted on the title page, the publication of this study was made possible by a prize from the American Academy of Arts and Sciences to which I now extend my sincerest thanks. Finally, a word of thanks to Ogimi Kaoru, whose conscientious and imaginative editorship contributed so much to the style and usefulness of this book.

WILLIAM P. MALM

Nagauta

PART ONE

History and Theory

CHAPTER ONE
A Short History of Nagauta

JAPANESE music can be traced back historically some fifteen hundred years and is noted in legends of presumably greater antiquity. Over this long period one can see the gradual development of myriad genres of musical expression. Until approximately the thirteenth century Buddhist singing and court orchestral music were predominant. Between the thirteenth and the sixteenth centuries these musics were supplanted by lute narrations, the aristocratic noh-drama music, and the accompaniments for a host of folk theatricals. It was during the seventeenth and eighteenth centuries that the remaining "great" traditions of Japanese music were developed. These were zither (koto) music, the diverse forms for the three-stringed lute (shamisen), and the music for the kabuki theatre. The shamisen music form known as *nagauta,* literally "long song,"[1] stands at the center of this last purely Oriental (pre-Western-influenced) period of Japanese music history. The eclectic nature of its growth makes it an ideal research subject for the exposition of certain basic Japanese concepts concerning music. Beyond its synthetic value, nagauta merits study by virtue of its position as one of the many art music forms of the Orient about which the Western world has little knowledge.

Since the history of nagauta is intimately connected with the general growth of shamisen music, it is necessary first to consider the early forms of shamisen music in order to place nagauta in its proper historical matrix. When the shamisen first came to Japan from the Ryukyu Islands (*circa* 1560) it seems to have been used as a substitute for the larger *biwa* lute used by the storytellers in the Osaka-Kyoto district.[2] Traditionally it

[1]The term *nagauta* is used in the ancient anthology of poetry, the *Manyōshū* (*circa* A.D. 760) to indicate poems of greater than usual length. However, this term has no known historical connection with the music under consideration in this study.

[2] Tanabe Hisao, *Nihon no Ongaku* (Tokyo: Bunka Kenkyū-kai, 1954), p. 288.

is said that around 1610 Sawazumi Kengyō and/or Ishimura Kengyō, both biwa musicians, began to play *kumiuta* music on the shamisen.[3] In view of the fact that kumiuta consists of a suite of short lyric pieces and is not a narrative form and the fact that biwa musicians for several centuries have been primarily concerned with narrative music, it seems likely that either these were not the first Japanese shamisen players or that the first shamisen music was not kumiuta. An alternative possibility is that the shamisen was first used in folk music. On the basis of existing historical sources, however, the traditional version of the origin of shamisen music in Japan can be accepted as at least part of the early history of the instrument.

Whatever the origins may have been, the earliest developments in shamisen music grew out of the lute narrative tradition. The ancient lute-accompanied tales of the glory and demise of the Heike clan have been in existence since the thirteenth century.[4] In the fifteenth century, however, a new story dealing with a Princess Jōruri appeared to rival the popularity of these so-called Heike-biwa tales. It should be mentioned that Takano Tatsuyuki,[5] noted authority on the history of Japanese songs, has placed the possible origin of this new style of narrative as far back as 1444, with the appearance of a tale called the *Yasuda Monogatari*. He also lists the word *jōruri* as appearing in the 1537 manuscript, the *Moritake Senku*.[6] It is generally held, however, that the sixteenth-century romance, the *Jōruri-hime Monogatari Jūnidan Zōshi* (The Tale of Princess Lapis Lazuli in Twelve Sections), represents the real founding of a new narrative form. This form goes under the name of the princess of whom it first spoke, *jōruri*.

In the district around the port city of Sakai near present-day Osaka there was a special group of lute narrators who sang a music known as *sekkyō-bushi*. Between the twelfth and fourteenth centuries this term referred to a form of Buddhist ballad drama which may have developed out of the sermons *(saemon)* of the traveling itinerant priests prevalent after the late Heian period (858–1185).[7] These folk morality ballads developed contempo-

---

[3] Iba Takashi, *Nihon Ongaku Gairon* (Tokyo: Koseikaku Shoten, 1928), p. 806. For details concerning *kumiuta* see page 31 of this study.

[4] Iba, *op. cit.*, p. 432. Singing of the Heike story dates traditionally from 1197 and is connected with the *biwa* by 1308.

[5] Takano Tatsuyuki, *Nihon Kayōshi* (Tokyo: Shūju-sha, 1926), p. 610.

[6] Ibid., p. 608.

[7] Nakagawa Aihyō, *Sangengaku-shi* (Tokyo: Dainippon Geijitsu Kyōkai, 1941), p. 63. See also Donald Keene, *The Battles of Coxinga* (London: Taylor's Foreign Press, 1951), p. 13. *Saemon* later became a type of low-class folk narrative.

raneously with jōruri and eventually became known as *sekkyō-jōruri,* one of the earliest predecessors of shamisen narrative music.

Another folk narrative form called *oku-jōruri* developed in the Mikawa district. This music did not use the lute for accompaniment, but instead, the narrator beat a fan against the hand. This genre and sekkyō-jōruri merged into the so-called shamisen-jōruri. Though a separate sekkyō-jōruri form remained until about 1680,[8] the main stream of shamisen history flowed from the new shamisen-jōruri tradition. With the advent of this form the history of a truly independent shamisen music can be said to have begun.

TABLE 1 : *Schools of shamisen music*

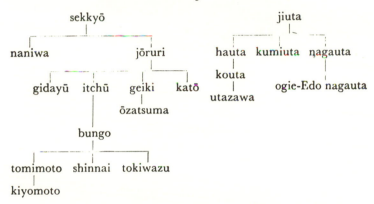

Japanese scholars usually divide the schools of shamisen music into two categories, *katarimono* and *utamono.* Those styles of music listed under katarimono are basically concerned with narration while those under utamono emphasize the music rather than the words. Within the repertoire of each school many pieces can be found in either style. The general classification of shamisen music along these two basic orientations, however, is most useful in organizing an overall understanding of the history of a music which is split into so many schools. Table 1 shows the basic styles of shamisen music. For every name on the table there are a dozen smaller independent schools which do not appear. Only the forms listed, however, are of real significance in the history of nagauta. It is not necessary here to go into a detailed

[8] "Sekkyō-bushi," *Ongaku Jiten* (Tokyo: Heibon-sha, 1955 57), 6 (1956), p. 1. The sekkyō tradition was carried on by *naniwa-bushi,* a form of folk narrative usually done to shamisen accompaniment. It can be heard daily on the Japanese radio and has a rural popularity comparable to hillbilly music in America.

history of each school.[9] However, the table may be helpful in placing the various forms when they are mentioned.

In addition to the early narrative styles of shamisen music already mentioned, there were various lyric forms. Kumiuta, the first known shamisen music, was one of these. This form consisted of the setting of a collection of short songs whose poems usually had no common topic. From the traditional kumiuta extant today it would seem that the musical settings of these poems were also independent. However, it is difficult to know for certain about the old forms, because the earliest shamisen notation, the third volume of the *Shichiku Shoshinshū* of 1664,[10] contains no kumiuta. It is only with the appearance in 1685 of the shamisen volume, the so-called *ōnusa*, of the *Shichiku Taizen* collection that we have a notation of kumiuta. Thus, one can only vaguely imagine the sound of shamisen music in the first hundred years of its existence.

One might wonder why the shamisen developed no notation when the much more ancient gagaku court orchestra and, to some extent, the noh drama tradition both had some written form of preserving their music. One answer is that the shamisen, along with its predecessors the biwa and the koto, were traditionally a means of livelihood for the blind. These blind musicians learned their music by rote and taught it by the same method. The strength of traditional pedagogy was such in Japan that even non-blind musicians used this method. Actually, it was not until the twentieth century that any concentrated efforts were made to create an accurate shamisen notation. Despite this lack we can form some idea as to the popularity of early shamisen music and learn of the names under which it was classified from the collections of song texts.

Though kumiuta was mentioned as the earliest name for shamisen music, there is another word which more properly can be considered as the generic term for early shamisen music of the Osaka-Kyoto district. This word is *jiuta*, literally "district or local songs." Under the term *jiuta* one finds all the other lyric forms, *hauta, kouta,* and the first nagauta (see Table 1).

[9] A short history of most of these forms can be found in Chapter VIII of the author's book, *Japanese Music and Musical Instruments* (Tokyo: Tuttle, 1959). See also Nakagawa, *op. cit.*

[10] "Shichiku Shoshinshū," *Ongaku Jiten*, 4 (1955), p. 261. A reprint of this book can be found in Kanetsune Kiyosuke's *Nihon no Ongaku* (Tokyo: Hattori Shoten 1913), pp. 161–214. The word *kumi* is used at the head of the table of contents but the music is referred to as *zokugaku*, common music, or *hayari*, popular music. The author also consulted a microfilm of the original, courtesy of Dr. Richard Lane.

As in the history of early Baroque instrumental music in Europe, the seventeenth-century shamisen nomenclature in Japan was highly flexible and uncodified. By the middle of the eighteenth century the terms jiuta and kumiuta usually referred to pieces in the koto repertoire while hauta, kouta, and nagauta were shamisen genres. In the seventeenth century, however, all these terms were used in a very cavalier manner and no clear distinctions can be made.

In the second volume of the 1703 collection, *Matsu no Ha*, one finds a list of fifty pieces called *jiuta no nagauta*. This is said to be the first direct reference to the term nagauta in relation to shamisen music.[11] There is no notation in this collection. Therefore, we cannot make clear distinctions between these fifty nagauta songs and the other types of music found in the *Matsu no Ha* except that the poems of the nagauta tend to be longer than the other texts. Actually, there are some long poems attached to other songs classified as hauta.[12] When one views the entire collection the general term for all the poems is found to be kumiuta. The same is true for the slightly later collection of texts, the *Wakamidori*.[13] All this information only serves to point up the futility of attempting to make any strict differentiation between the early shamisen musical styles beyond the general distinction of narrative or lyric musics.

By the early eighteenth century there was a new distinction that could be made. This was between the *kamigata* music of the Osaka-Kyoto district and the newer style of the Edo (Tokyo) area. It is reasonable to presume that shamisen music developed first in the south and then gradually moved northward, since the shamisen entered Japan in the Osaka area. The early Edo styles were probably direct imitations of the Osaka-Kyoto traditions. The social and cultural atmosphere of each of these two centers, however, was enough different to reflect a distinct change in music styles, Edo being the city of the new and gaudy while the south, particularly Kyoto, was the land of tradition and quieter living. Thus, there grew up an Edo kouta in contrast with the so-called kamigata-kouta, an Edo jiuta, an Edo hauta, etc. Most important to this study was the appearance of an Edo nagauta. Before we can discuss this music in detail, we must retrace our steps slightly and follow the progress of one of the most important elements in the history of nagauta, the kabuki theatre.

[11] Ikeda Kojirō, *Nagauta Shōshi*, Vol. 1 of *Hōgaku Sōsho* (Tokyo: Nagauta Ginreikai Shuppanbu, 1930), pp. 18–19. The titles of the fifty pieces are listed here.
[12] "Matsu no Ha," *Ongaku Jiten*, 10 (1957), p. 96.
[13] Ikeda, *op. cit.*, p. 19.

Kabuki first appeared at the end of the sixteenth century. It began as one of a host of popular entertainments of that time and grew to become the major traditional popular theatre of Japan. Looking first at the environment in which it was born, one sees, through the eyes of the genre painters of the Momoyama period (1568–1615), a charming picture of colorful pageantry and theatrical enthusiasm. In addition to the public and private performances of the aristocratic noh plays there was an endless variety of folk theatricals. The comic *kyōgen, sarugaku,* and *dengaku* performances were common additions to every public affair. The Buddhist and Shinto shrines had their own brand of entertainment. Saints' days often were accompanied by morality-play performances spiced with comic interludes or by special dances.[14] The New Year's *ennen* dances at the Buddhist temples had become so popular by the Momoyama period that they were given weekly instead of annually.[15] Special priests were assigned to the performance of such theatricals while others traveled the streets singing revival hymns or doing propitiatory dances for the benefit of those wishing to buy a bit of salvation. The gay *fūryū* street festivals and the Shinto *kagura* dances also added theatrical spectacle to the life of the cities.

Out of this swirl of people and activities arose the name of a Shinto priestess Okuni of the Izumo shrine. Her performance around 1596 of a Buddhist *nembutsu-odori* on the banks of the Kamo River in Kyoto is said to be the origin of kabuki. One must not be led to believe, however, that kabuki was a form of religious entertainment. We have already seen how thin was the distinction between secular and sacred in things theatrical in sixteenth-century Japan. Indeed, the origin of the word kabuki seems to be the old verb *kabuku,* meaning "to incline." In this period the word had the connotation of sexual debauchery.[16] The present written characters used for the word kabuki mean music, dance, and acting. However, when viewing the early history of kabuki one can see that the first meaning was appropriate. For example, the early kabuki troupes, called *onna* (women's) *kabuki,* consisted to a large extent of male and fe-

[14] The annual pantomimes in April at the Mibu Temple in Kyoto, the so-called *Mibu-kyōgen,* are direct descendents of this tradition. See further, René Sieffert, "Mibu-kyōgen," *Bulletin de la Maison Franco-Japonaise,* New Series 3 (1953), pp. 119–51.

[15] See *Ongaku Jiten,* 1 (1956), p. 282.

[16] Earle Ernst, *The Kabuki Drama* (New York: Oxford University Press, 1956), p. 10.

male prostitutes playing roles of the opposite sex. Women were banned from the stage in 1629 but the competing homosexual troupes *(wakashū-kabuki)* were allowed to continue until mid century. After this time men's troupes *(yarō-kabuki)* became the dominant form. The history of kabuki makes for lively reading as it treads the narrow path between government censorship and the demands of public taste.[17] Our concern, however, is with the music of this tradition, not the growth of the entire system.

One of the first paintings of a kabuki performance is the early Tokugawa-period scroll, the *Kunijo Kabuki Ekotoba* (Plate 2). In it Okuni can be seen dancing on an outdoor shrine stage. She is holding a small gong used traditionally as accompaniment for the Buddhist nembutsu-odori. Three of the five men seated at the rear of the stage are playing drums of the noh theatre. While a flute is never shown in this scroll, one can guess that one of the remaining men is probably a noh-flute player and the other is a singer.[18]

The flute is seen actually being played in the second scene of another early Tokugawa scroll, the *Kabuki Sōshi Emaki* (Plates 3–4). Atsumi Seitarō calls this instrument merely a *takebue,* a bamboo flute, and does not specify a noh flute *(nōkan)*.[19] It does look rather thin for a noh flute but it has the proper number of holes (seven) and shows the characteristic wrappings of cherry bark between the holes found on a noh flute but not on a common bamboo flute. When the flute is not being played it can be seen placed in a case between the front folds of the player's robe in exactly the same manner as the noh flute is placed. Considering these various factors it seems very likely that the flute seen in this scroll is indeed a noh flute.

To sum up, the early kabuki music was basically that of the noh drama plus some form of singing, probably regional popular songs.[20]

In another section of the *Kabuki Sōshi Emaki* one sees that two priests have set up concessions outside the entrance of the theatre (Plates 5–6). One (not shown here) is busy repeating

[17] For an interesting account of this see Donald H. Shively's "Bakufu versus Kabuki," *Harvard Journal of Asiatic Studies,* XVIII (1955), pp. 326–56.

[18] Support for this is found in the seating arrangement, which is exactly that of the noh stage except for one curious fact, everything is reversed. The noh singers sit on stage left at a right angle to the instrumentalists who from stage left should be in the order of flute, shoulder drum, hip drum, and stick drum. The runway from the greenroom is also on the wrong side of the stage by usual noh standards.

[19] Atsumi Seitarō, *Kabuki Nyūmon* (Tokyo: Tōkai Shobō, 1949), p. 271.

[20] See "Kabuki," *Ongaku Jiten,* 2 (1956), p. 304.

formulas of salvation to the accompaniment of a small gong.[21] Across the road stands a lecturer who is apparently moving his audience to remorse by the powers of his speech, accompanied by the beats of two split bamboo sticks *(sasara)*. Among his listeners is a blind man dressed in white. In his right hand he holds his staff to guide him and under his left arm is tucked his means of livelihood, his shamisen. This scene is important historically in that it shows that the shamisen was a common street instrument *outside* the kabuki theatre in the seventeenth century.

The exact date at which the shamisen came inside the kabuki is unknown. Japanese scholars give dates ranging from 1634 to 1702, their choice depending on whatever ancient source they are inclined to believe. Iba says that the shamisen was used before 1688, while Tanabe and Nakagawa would seem to indicate that it was not used until 1702.[22] While it may never be possible to answer this question definitely, a review of several sources may help us to arrive at a closer approximation.

The first kabuki, as shown in early scrolls, used basically a noh ensemble for its music. At the same time, manuscripts such as the *Shichiku Shoshinshū* of 1664 indicate that there was a great deal of popular music for shamisen to be heard in the local party houses. The connection between such brothel districts and the kabuki remained strong even after the banning of the prostitute kabuki. Brothel songs were incorporated into the kabuki often under new names.[23] In addition, many plays centered around brothel life or the selling of a loved one to a procurer. It is interesting to note further that two of the early kabuki dance forms, *komai* and *odori-kudoki,* were also known as special party dances.

One of the forms popular with the young boys' (wakashū) kabuki, which was contemporary with the prostitutes' kabuki, was the comic pantomime known as *saruwaka-kyōgen.* A text from a kabuki saruwaka-kyōgen dated between 1624 and 1652 contains the words "kouta sounds and the shamisen is played."[24] Also, in the *Manzaigaku* collection of 1687, there is a picture of three kabuki members playing the shamisen, *kokyū* (a bowed instrument), and a *hitoyogiri* (an end-blown flute) to accompany

---

[21] The Jōdo sect of Buddhism believes in the absolute efficacy of repetitions of the Buddha's name as means to salvation. This concept spread through many sects and thus wandering *nembutsu* priests were common in Japan. The tradition is still strong.

[22] Iba, *op. cit.,* p. 816. Tanabe Hisao, *Edo Jidai no Ongaku* (Tokyo: Bunkyō Shoin, 1928), p. 255. See also *Ongaku Jiten,* 3 (1956), p. 72. Nakagawa, *op. cit.,* p. 67.

[23] See "Yūri to ongaku," *Ongaku Jiten,* 11 (1957), p. 20.

[24] 「小歌にのせて三味をひく」. See Takano, *op. cit.,* p. 716.

PLATE 2: *Scene from the* Kunijo Kabuki Ekotoba. *One of the earliest kabuki records, showing Okuni, the foundress of the kabuki genre, on stage.*
        —*Courtesy Kyoto University Library.*

PLATES 3–4: *Scene and detail from the Kabuki Sōshi Emaki. . Another early Tokugawa scroll showing the prototype kabuki hayashi. The flute has the same construction as the noh flute used today.*
—*Courtesy Tokugawa Reimeikai.*

PLATES 5–6: *Scene and detail from the* Kabuki Sōshi Emaki. *Outside the kabuki theatre various types of storytellers thrived. The shamisen had apparently become a common street instrument early in its history.* —Courtesy Tokugawa Reimeikai.

the odori-kudoki of three female impersonators.[25] Both the words of the first example and the picture of the second refer to party situations, but it seems quite possible that a similar music would be used by these same people when on stage.

Dr. Donald H. Shively writes of a passage in the *Keichō Kemmonshū*, presumably dated no later than 1644, which tells of the shamisen in use within the kabuki.[26] In this case the shamisen is said to be used to accompany the dancing of a large number of people on stage. At the same time, Anda Hiroshi states that the shamisen was used around 1648 by Kineya Rokusaburō, but he gives no source.[27] On the other hand, Nakagawa claims that in 1657 Rokusaburō's father, Kisaburō, first used the shamisen to accompany *saruwaka-komai* at the Nakamura kabuki theatre in Edo.[28] This man Kisaburō changed his name to Kangorō. Under that name we find a man who is said to have come with the Nakamura Kanzaburō troupe from Kyoto to Tokyo and played in Tokyo first around 1702.[29] Kangorō, however, is listed as dead in 1634 in an early Kineya lineage chart,[30] though this date is regarded with suspicion by modern scholars. Clarification of this problem depends partly on which Kisaburō and which Kangorō one is speaking of in each case. Under the guild system in Japan certain names are passed on to qualified successors. For example, in 1894 the second Kineya Eizō was advanced to the title of the eleventh Kisaburō and in 1902 he was made the fifth Kangorō.[31] As long as the Japanese do not give generation numbers or quote the sources of their information, it is nearly impossible to state clearly the relationship between these various names. However, if we view all these disparate sources, we can hazard a guess that the shamisen must have entered the kabuki before 1650. This estimate is based on the following facts:

1. Shamisen music was flourishing by the early seventeenth century, especially among female impersonators.

2. It is plausible that the shamisen could have entered the kabuki along with forms such as komai and odori-kudoki, which used the shamisen for accompaniment in party situations and which are listed as kabuki forms before 1650. This is possible

[25] *Ibid.*, pp. 724–25.
[26] Shively, *op. cit.*, p. 328.
[27] Anda Hiroshi, "Sangengaku," in *Geinōshi no Kenkyū*, Ema Tsutomu, ed. (Tokyo: Hoshino Shoten, 1934), p. 112.
[28] Nakagawa, *op. cit.*, p. 68.
[29] Tanabe, *Edo Jidai no Ongaku*, p. 255.
[30] *Ongaku Jiten*, 3 (1956), p. 72.
[31] *Loc. cit.*

especially in view of the eclectic manner in which kabuki developed.

3. The shamisen appears in the text of kabuki songs dated not later than 1658. At least one notice indicates that it may have been present before 1644.

4. The name Kineya has always been associated with kabuki shamisen, not with noh ensembles. Since the Kisaburō of 1702 in Edo is known as the fourth generation of this name it is reasonable to assume that the previous Kisaburōs were connected with the Kyoto kabuki. Allowing only twenty years for the existence of each one of the persons with such a name there would be a Kineya Kisaburō in the Kyoto kabuki by at least 1642. If one of the Kangorōs died in 1643 as stated, it is possible that the Kineya name reaches back even further.

By the beginning of the eighteenth century the shamisen had become a regular part of the kabuki ensemble. This was the period of the Genroku kabuki during which the world of entertainment enjoyed a dazzling popularity unprecedented in previous Japanese history. One of the contributing factors to the growth of kabuki at this time was the improvement of its dramatic quality. This was due in part to the influence of the great playwright of the Takemoto puppet theatre in Osaka, Chikamatsu Monzaemon (1653–1724). Many of the famous kabuki plays were adaptions of his puppet dramas while others were created in emulation of his style.

Though there was a greater emphasis on drama in eighteenth-century kabuki, dance and, hence, music were still an important part of every performance. These dances were at first accompanied by short songs (kouta) on the shamisen or by noh ensemble music.[32] As the kabuki productions became more elaborate a need was felt for longer dances and hence more extensive music. Thus, kabuki nagauta was created. The first known use of the term Edo nagauta is said to be found on an Edo kabuki poster of 1703.[33] Its list of musicians is as follows: four Edo shamisen, two Edo kouta singers, one jōruri singer, and three Edo nagauta musicians. These last three seemed to have been singers. With the appearance of this reference we can move more surely and quickly through the remaining history of our topic.

---

[32] The shamisen and noh ensemble were said to have been combined first by Kineya Rokuzaemon around 1650. See Tanabe, *Edo Jidai no Ongaku*, p. 258. However, the source for this claim is not given, and the early history of kabuki would seem to indicate that initially they were used to accompany separate dances.

[33] Takano, *op. cit.*, p. 946. Terms usually appear in print later than use, so it may have been created earlier.

Though nagauta was firmly established in Edo by the eighteenth century, it was not without its rivals. We have mentioned earlier the growth of the narrative jōruri forms, their use in the puppet theatres, and the influence of jōruri plays on kabuki. This dramatic influence was soon accompanied by a musical one. Naturally, first reports of such importations come from the kabuki of the Osaka-Kyoto area. The term *chobo* which refers to the kabuki jōruri team of a singer and a shamisen player appears as early as 1715.[34] It was mentioned that the term jōruri was used on the 1703 Edo poster advertising Edo nagauta. By mid century the existence of such noted kabuki jōruri playwrights as Namiki Shōzō (1730–73) of Osaka indicates that jōruri had become an important part of the kabuki tradition.

At first the functions of nagauta and the various jōruri genres in kabuki seem to have been different. Jōruri provided music for the narrative portions while nagauta accompanied dances or provided reflective interludes *(meriyasu)* within the dramas. However, there were considerable interpenetrations of musical styles as well as exchanges of functions between the two musics.

As can be seen in Table 1, jōruri split into a host of different styles. Most of them appeared in the kabuki at one time. At present only *gidayū, kiyomoto, tokiwazu,* and occasionally *shinnai* are used. As each of these other styles passed across the boards of the kabuki, however, it left an influence in the music of nagauta. Thus, as one studies the nagauta repertoire in detail, traces are found of *ōzatsuma, itchū, katō, geiki,* and other old musics.[35]

In summary, it can be said that the eighteenth century saw the establishment of nagauta as a permanent element in the kabuki. During this period the basic forms and classifications of this music were also crystallized. Finally, the beginning of a continuing influence of various narrative forms can be noted at this time.

The era of the composition of the great nagauta classics of today lies approximately within the boundaries of the nineteenth century. Reading through the history charts of this period one can find a galaxy of nagauta stars.[36] One of the

[34] Kawatake Shigetoshi, "Kabuki no Ongakuteki Enshutsu," in *Taō Ongaku Ronsō,* Kishibe Shigeo, ed. (Tokyo: Yamaichi Shobō, 1944), p. 180.

[35] *Bungo* and *tomimoto* are shown in Table 1 as links between other forms which bear closer relations to nagauta. *Naniwa* is listed because of its continued popularity though it is independent of the kabuki movement. It should also be noted that there are two types of gidayū, *onna-gidayū* sung by women and the *gidayū* music of the puppet theatre which is often referred to by the generic term jōruri.

[36] See the nagauta composition chart in the back of Asakawa Gyokuto's *Nagauta no Kiso Kenkyū* (Tokyo: Hōgaku-sha, 1955), 288 pp. Note that nagauta composers are always performers as well.

earliest was the ninth Kineya Rokuzaemon (died 1819), who wrote such famous dance pieces as *Echigojishi* and *Oharame*. The tenth Rokuzaemon (1800–59)[37] is noted for such favorites as *Shakkyō, Tsuru-kame*, and *Aki no Irogusa*. The eleventh Rokuzaemon (1829–77) produced the popular pieces *Tsunayakata, Funa Benkei*, and one of the many *Dōjōji* compositions. Rokuzaemon was not the only famous name of the period. Kineya Shōjirō (1828/9–1896) wrote many famous dance pieces such as *Ise Ondo, Kanjinchō, Renjishi*, and *Genroku Hanami-odori*. The second Kineya Katsusaburō (1820–96) was the composer of *Miyakodori, Utsubozaru*, and *Kimi no Niwa*. In addition, the other famous nagauta guilds like the Yoshizumi and Yoshimura singers produced some of their greatest artists at this time.

Through the efforts of these and many other men nagauta matured into one of Japan's major music genres. The kabuki dance-form pieces developed certain specific musical traits while the influence of jōruri and the noh ensemble made the music more dramatic and colorful. It was during this period that the musical patterns of the now defunct ōzatsuma-jōruri music began to play a significant role in nagauta music.

In the nineteenth century two important new tendencies appeared in nagauta. First, there was a movement toward concert music, the so-called *ozashiki-nagauta*. This music was not composed for the kabuki but for separate non-dance performances. In such pieces the importance of the instrumental interludes and the concomitant exploitation of virtuosity are more highly developed than in previous kabuki forms. The two classic examples of this type of nagauta are *Azuma Hakkei* (1818) and *Aki no Irogusa* (1845). One interesting aspect of the latter piece is that it uses no percussion at all. Though the subject matter (the colors of the autumn foliage) is conducive to pastoral, non-percussive music, the exclusion of the drums may be a reaction against the traditional kabuki dance-music sound.

The second tendency in nineteenth century nagauta was the extensive composition of pieces based on noh-drama texts and music. Of course, many kabuki dramas were based on noh plays before, but there was a rash of revivals and rewriting of these themes. Titles such as *Kanjinchō, Hashi Benkei, Oimatsu*, and *Tsuru-kame* are representative of the trend. Folk music also

[37] It was mentioned that musicians changed names as a symbol of rank. Rokuzaemon is the final grade of a series which begins with Saburōsuke and goes to Kangorō up to Rokuzaemon. Thus, composers have different names during various periods of their careers. I have tried to use only their final names here regardless of what they were called at the time of the composition mentioned.

appears as a deliberate mood-setting device in nineteenth-century nagauta. The beautiful boatman's song in the piece *Kibun Daijin* is one of the lovelier examples of this technique.

By the end of the nineteenth century nagauta had reached its zenith. All its forms were fully developed and its position in both the theatre and concert life was secure. New composers arose in the twentieth century who tried to incorporate Western ideas into nagauta music. This usually meant playing the shamisen faster in violin cadenza style or augmenting the size of the ensemble with the unfortunate idea that sounding louder was synonymous with sounding better in the Western art music concept. Thus, though there was a great deal of music composing and polemic article writing in the twentieth century, little really new has happened in nagauta in the last fifty years. The Tōonkai, a group of teachers and graduates from the University of Fine Arts in Tokyo, contains the most active and enthusiastic protagonists for new nagauta. The talented nagauta composers of today, however, tend to produce replicas of the nineteenth-century classical style with a few fast passages added in hopes of capturing the attention of the modern ear.

There is one innovation in twentieth-century nagauta that should be mentioned. This is the development of accurate notation systems. Thanks to these systems the preservation of the standard repertoire is now assured. We can only hope that such systems will penetrate more deeply into the realm of shamisen music so that the basic compositions of lesser forms will also be preserved.

Nagauta can be said to be a closed circuit whose main current runs through the eighteenth and nineteenth centuries. It is a product of the Edo period (1615–1867) and best represents musically the dance facet of the Edo theatrical world. Unlike many of the other Edo shamisen forms, it has managed to hold its own in the modern world through the support of the kabuki and an extensive development of an amateur and professional concert life. Its musical style has been so highly and subtly developed that there seems little hope of its finding a new direction without destroying itself in the process. This is the big problem that lies before the modern professional nagauta musician. For the Western scholar the problem is to understand its past and investigate the contributions it has already made to the musical and cultural life of Japan. On the basis of these accomplishments alone it should find a significant place in the general history of Japan.

CHAPTER TWO

Classifications of the Nagauta Repertoire

FROM TIME to time Japanese scholars have tried to arrange the nagauta repertoire into various categories. As a rule, these categories are not mutually exclusive, so that one piece may be listed in several places. The importance of some of these classification systems to the understanding of nagauta is questionable. However, they do illustrate certain Japanese attitudes toward the music and therefore should be noted.

Machida Kashō (born 1888) was the first twentieth-century writer to make extensive use of categorical distinctions in nagauta.[1] Later, Asakawa Gyokuto published in his *Nagauta no Kiso Kenkyū*[2] a compendium of all the different distinctions. The following study is based primarily on these two sources.

The first major division of nagauta is made between compositions that are primarily dance pieces and those which are lyric works. These categories can be further subdivided into compositions which have a plot and those which are more poetic. The former are classified as *danmono* and the latter are called *hamono*. These divisions of nagauta are shown in Table 2[3] along with some typical pieces in each category.

TABLE 2: *Dance and lyric nagauta pieces*

DANCE PIECES		LYRIC PIECES	
HAMONO	DANMONO	HAMONO	DANMONO
Gorō	*Ataka no Matsu*	*Matsu no Midori*	*Utsubozaru*
Echigojishi	*Funa Benkei*	*Azuma Hakkei*	*Tsunayakata*
Renjishi	*Dōjōji*	*Aki no Irogusa*	*Yuya*
Tomoyakko	*Tsuchigumo*	*Tokiwa no Niwa*	*Kibun Daijin*
	Kanjinchō		

[1] Machida Kashō, *Nagauta no Utaikata to Hikikata* (Tokyo: Hōki Shoten, 1930), p. 14 ff.

[2] (Tokyo: Hōgaku-sha, 1955), p. 13–21.

[3] Derived from Machida, *op. cit.*, p. 15.

The category of lyric, non-narrative pieces is fairly easy to distinguish. Most of the compositions listed therein are *ozashiki*, concert pieces rather than stage works. By the same token, the danmono dance pieces can be recognized as famous dance dramas from the kabuki. The hamono distinctions in the dance literature require more background knowledge concerning each composition. For example, *Gorō* is part of the saga of the Soga brothers,[4] but the section presented in this piece does not concern an entire episode from the story. Instead, it is a tableau, catching a moment or a mood in the story which is well-known to the audience. In the appreciation of nagauta music and dance the significance of such previous knowledge will be seen to be of the greatest importance as this study progresses.

The placing of pieces in the danmono section of the non-dance category also requires some explanation. For example, one will find a dance piece called *Utsubozaru* in the modern repertoire of the kabuki. However, the music for this dance is based on an 1838 tokiwazu-style composition and not on the 1869 nagauta piece of the same name, which is not used for dance accompaniment.[5] Other pieces like *Kibun Daijin* (1911) are based on jōruri narrative style and hence have more evolved plot lines. Such pieces are good examples of the mixture of the utamono and katarimono traditions discussed in Chapter I.

The next most common classification of nagauta is that of historical forms. These have been adumbrated in the previous historical chapter. It remains only for us to set them in an outline form. Asakawa lists seven basic forms ; 1) *meriyasu*, 2) *shosa*, 3) *jōruri*, 4) *ozashiki*, 5) *ōzatsuma*, 6) *yōkyoku*, and 7) *shinkyoku*.[6]

1. Meriyasu-nagauta are very simple, short forms of reflective music used within kabuki plays at times when the actor is called upon to express his inner emotions through pantomime or through thinking out loud. In both cases, the actual singing is done by a professional musician, not the actor himself. Meriyasu are one of the earliest forms of nagauta. The first known meriyasu, called "Mugen no Kane," appeared in 1731 within the Nagoya kabuki play, *Keisei Fukibiki*.[7] The origin of the term meriyasu is uncertain.[8] However, the music seems to have grown

[4] See Aubrey S. and Giovanna M. Halford, *The Kabuki Handbook* (Tokyo: Tuttle, 1956), pp. 462–63.

[5] Atsumi Seitarō, *Hōgaku Buyō Jiten* (Tokyo: Fuzambō, 1956), p. 420.

[6] Asakawa, *op. cit.*, pp. 16–21.

[7] Takano, *op. cit.*, p. 947.

[8] See Asakawa Gyokuto, "Meriyasu Godai," *Nihon Ongaku*, No. 84 (May, 1956), pp. 13–15.

out of the kamigata (Osaka-Kyoto) short-song tradition. In addition to the simple, rather melancholy kamigata quality found in meriyasu, one can also note a high prevalence of kamigata shamisen tunings (ni-agari and san-sagari, see page 59).

2. Shosa refers to the posturing of kabuki dancers. The use of this term in relation to nagauta also refers to dance pieces. This is a major category and has enjoyed the most extensive exploitation and development. Pieces in the so-called kabuki dance form (to which space will be devoted later) are shosa music. *← Based on story about Peruvian joruri*

3. Jōruri-nagauta refers, of course, to pieces derived from or based on previous jōruri pieces or styles. As nagauta gradually developed from a basically lyric music toward a more narrative style, the influence of jōruri became stronger. This influence is sometimes to be found in the formal outlines of a piece as, for example, in *Kibun Daijin*. At other times, it is a "lifting" of an entire section from a jōruri piece and the placing of it in a nagauta composition. In nagauta nomenclature, any such borrowing from another form of music is known as *kakari* (sometimes pronounced *gakari*). Such borrowings need not necessarily remain intact in their new settings, but they are recognized as historically, if not thematically, related.

4. The fourth classification is ozashiki. Little need be said about this concert form of nagauta since it was discussed earlier (see page 18). While this music is specifically non-dance music, much of it shows a strong influence from its theatrical predecessors. The main difference is in the freedom granted the composers in arranging the order of the moods and tempos of the compositions and in their choice of form.

5. The next class, ōzatsuma, should really be included under jōruri because ōzatsuma is the name of an old narrative music form. However, the special series of patterns derived from that music and used in nagauta appear so frequently that they are set off as something special. These patterns may be seen in the transcriptions (Part IV, pp. 331–38). They are discussed in detail in Chapter V.

6. Yōkyoku pieces are those derived from noh drama stories or musical styles. Some influence of noh singing style, known as yōkyoku, crept into nagauta through the early influence of kamigata singing. However, in pieces such as *Shakkyō* or *Funa Benkei* one can find long sections of direct imitation. These sections may be labeled *yōkyoku-gakari*, using the term mentioned above. In such pieces one also finds noh terminology used in

relation to the formal structure. Other characteristics of such pieces are discussed in Chapters III and IX.

7. Shinkyoku are new pieces. One finds that this term is not clearly distinguished from ozashiki except for the fact that new pieces can be composed for theatrical as well as concert use. Shinkyoku refers to the twentieth-century experimentations. Such pieces are built on many different formal structures usually related to some older form. Such cases are discussed in the mixed-forms section of Chapter III.

Nagauta music is also classified according to subject matter. While this classification has only an indirect relation to the music, it must be included to complete our discussion of the Japanese view of this genre. Asakawa lists the following fifteen topics which are found in nagauta.[9]

1. The first type are pieces dealing with the "Dōjōji" legend, for example, *Musume Dōjōji* and *Kishū Dōjōji*. This story deals with the love of a girl for a priest. It ends with the famous scene in which the priest hides beneath the temple bell while the girl, now turned into a demon, stands atop of it with the temple in flames around her. The popularity of this story in Japan has recently been attested to by its use as the basis of a musical revue. On one occasion it was even used as the *pièce de résistance* of a nude show.

2. The next type are pieces built on the idea of the noh drama *Shakkyō*. Since the finale of the second scene of this play contains a dance for two lions, many of the famous kabuki lion dances are placed in this classification such as *Renjishi* and *Kagamijishi*.

3. Pieces involving demented people such as *Shizu Hata Obi* and *Ninin Wankyū* are considered as another common type. This classification is also found in the dramatic divisions of noh dramas.

4. The next classification is called *tanzenmono*. This refers to a series of pieces which derive their mood from the popular music and *fūryū* dance festivities of Edo. *Takasago Tanzen* and *Sukeroku* are good examples. The derivation of the term is rather interesting.[10] In the middle of the seventeenth century there was a large bathhouse opposite the manor of Matsudaira Tango no Kami in Edo. In Japan, bathhouses serve as much a social function as a sanitary one, and in the Edo period they were often lavishly appointed with lovely scrubbing girls and adjacent restaurants and hotels. The fops and dandies of Edo would often

[9] Asakawa, *Nagauta no Kiso Kenkyū*, pp. 13–15.
[10] See *Geinō Jiten* (Tokyo: Kokugeki Kōjōkai, 1954), p. 421.

meet at this bathhouse. It became so well known that certain music and mannerisms were associated with it. In much the same way that a San Franciscan says, "Meet you at the top of the Mark," the Edo period man-about-town would say, "Meet me in front of Tango no Kami's." The written character for the word "before" can be pronounced *zen* or *mae*. Therefore, this expression became abbreviated from "Tango no Kami no mae" to simply "tanzen." Thus, all the music and atmosphere of that neighborhood was known thereafter as *tanzenmono,* tanzen things. This classification of nagauta illustrates nicely the importance of a cultural-historical background to the full appreciation of nagauta as theatre music.

5. Among the most ancient types of music are the "Sambasō" pieces. These works are used to accompany dances which originally were used at the beginning of each day of kabuki performances. These dances came from the noh tradition, which in turn developed them out of Shinto ceremonial dances. Today "Sambasō" dances are used in the kabuki and the noh theatres only in January, though one may see them at other times of the year in geisha and amateur performances. The original function of these dances was to purify the Shinto shrine, thus, they were done always at the beginning of ceremonies. A vestige of this tradition is seen in the fact that even in amateur performances "Sambasō" is placed at the opening or immediately after an intermission as a kind of dedication dance.

The best-known nagauta "Sambasō" piece is *Ayatsuri Sambasō* in which the dancer pretends to be a hand puppet. The dancer is handled by three men in the Japanese puppet theatre fashion. Another well-known " Sambasō" is named for its outstanding choreographic gesture. It is called *Shita-dashi Sambasō,* tongue-sticking-out Sambasō.[11]

6. Besides the opening pieces mentioned above there are other nagauta that are considered appropriate for beginning festive occasions. The best known of these so-called congratulatory pieces is *Tsuru-kame* (discussed in greater detail in Chapter IX). Its title refers to the good-luck symbols of the tortoise and the crane. The music of such pieces tends to be influenced by the more ceremonial noh style.

7. As was mentioned earlier, one of the famous stories in the kabuki is that of the saga of the Soga brothers, who were sworn to revenge their father's death. This classification of stories, known as the *kusazuribikimono,* contains such nagauta pieces as *Gorō* and *Sukeroku.*

[11] A picture of this gesture is seen opposite page 346 in Atsumi, *op. cit.*

8. Ghost stories are common in kabuki, particularly in the summer when their chilling effect is said to distract one from the heat. *Sagi Musume* and *Momiji Gari* are two well-known examples of nagauta ghost stories.[12]

9. The next category contains *shirabyōshi* stories. Shrabyōshi were female dancers attached to the court or to a shrine. Many of them became the mistresses of famous warriors or even emperors (see also page 39). It is natural, then, to find some nagauta, for example *Hanaguruma,* concerned with the life and loves of these doubly talented women.

10. Asakawa, in one of those all-too-common moments of redundancy in Japanese scholarship, adds a category for nagauta derived from noh plays though this was already mentioned in a previous division *(yōkyokumono)*. *Hashi Benkei* and *Kanjinchō* are two good examples of such pieces.

11. The music from off-stage or nagauta used in the opening of plays *(deha)* only is called by Asakawa *dokkin,* solo music. Under this class he includes such pieces as *Tsui no Amigasa* and *Miyakodori.*

12. Ōzatsuma, discussed earlier, is listed once more by Asakawa as a content classification, though pieces using ōzatsuma patterns are found in many different categories already listed.

13. The next class is called *hengemono* (変化物), changing pieces. This term refers to dance compositions in which the actor, usually a female impersonator, does a series of dances, each in a different mood and costume.[13] Part of the enjoyment of these performances is watching the skill with which the stage assistants rip out the small threads that hold one costume together over the next one. Hengemono date back as far as the late seventeenth century. During that time five- and seven-change dances often appeared on kabuki programs.[14] The oldest henge piece still in existence is actually a tanzen piece as well. It appeared in 1755 at the Ishimura theatre in Edo. This piece, *Suisen Tanzen,* originally used nagauta music, though the present composition is found in the *ogie-bushi* repertoire.[15] Hengemono became extremely popular during the first half of the nineteenth century and many new pieces were written. Because of the length of these dances and the variety of moods involved, these

[12] A description of the kabuki version of *Momiji Gari* can be found in Malm, *op. cit.,* Chapter IX

[13] This form should not be confused with *henkeimono* (変形物) in which the person changes from a human being to a ghost.

[14] "Hengemono," *Ongaku Jiten,* 9 (1957), p. 288.

[15] *Ogie-bushi* is a derivative of nagauta. See *Ongaku Jiten,* 1 (1955), p. 293.

pieces tended to use music from many different sources. Thus, within one performance there might be several forms such as tokiwazu, kiyomoto, or some other narrative form, each used for a separate change. Nagauta, of course, was used also. These full-length hengemono[16] are seldom performed today even in the kabuki. However, the individual selections often appear both in the theatre and on the concert stage. Two good examples of nagauta derived from this tradition are *Urashima* and *Echigo-jishi*. A certain number of changes can be seen in the "Dōjōji" pieces discussed above.

14. Asakawa repeats the ozashiki classification, the pure concert-music style.

15. The final classification is also redundant. It is narrative style.

Japanese scholars go on indefinitely arranging and rearranging the nagauta repertoire into such divisions as, for example, songs suitable for children and songs suitable for adults,[17] or songs using direct or indirect imitations of natural sounds. However, the three big divisions mentioned above; the distinction between dance and non-dance music, the division into historical forms, and the classification by content, are all one needs to know in order to study nagauta. The primary source of knowledge concerning nagauta still lies ahead in the music itself.

[16] The *tour de force* in this genre is a twelve-sectioned dance in which each section represents a month of the year.

[17] This presents a definite problem, as many of the song texts are quite erotic.

CHAPTER THREE

Form in Nagauta

THE JO-HA-KYŪ CONCEPT

There are certain aesthetic theories underlying every music culture which are referred to whenever an explanation is sought for various compositional processes. Thus, the concept of question and answer appears often in Western music as a theoretical fulcrum upon which the musical expressions of each age are balanced artistically. In a similar way, the theory of *jo-ha-kyū* is used as a frame of reference for the aesthetical explanation of Japanese musical form.

In their broadest meaning these three words can be interpreted as follows: jo signifies the introduction, ha is the scattering or breaking apart, and kyū is the denouement or rushing to the end. Japanese court dances *(bugaku)* are given credit as being the earliest form to use these terms extensively.[1] Here they refer to the three-part division of the dances. During the jo the dancer walks from the greenroom onto the dance platform. The ha occurs at the true beginning of the dance, and the kyū is the last half of the dance which is faster in tempo. The famous piece, *Gojōraku* is an example of such a form. As the dance repertoire evolved this form became more complex, but for our purposes it is necessary merely to note the fact that the theory existed in Japan by at least the seventh century. It is possible that it may have existed in China even before that time.

The terms jo-ha-kyū also appear in the terminology of ancient Buddhist chanting *(shōmyō)*. Present opinion[2] claims that they were borrowed from the court-dance terms, though extensive research on this question has yet to be done. As used in this religious singing these terms referred first to three different

[1] See "Jo-ha-kyū," *Ongaku Jiten,* 5 (1957), p. 159.
[2] *Loc. cit.*

rhythms or tempos in which the chants were sung. In the Kama-kura period (1186–1333) they referred to three types of pieces. Thus, within the contemporary repertoire of the Buddhist chant one finds the jo rhythm appearing in many introductory pieces[3] while the ha and kyū rhythms are found in the main body of the chants.[4]

The great philosophical refinement of this concept occurred in the writings of the famous noh playwright and theorist, Zeami (born 1363). In his *Kadensho*[5] he uses the terms jo-ha-kyū to represent not only the overall structure of entire plays but also the form of each act, the sections within the acts, and the individual phrases which make up the music as well as being indicative of tempo. This all-encompassing view of jo-ha-kyū led to its further application in other art forms from tea ceremony and flower arrangement to painting and poetry. Thus, it is not surprising to find its influence in the art of nagauta music.

NOH-DRAMA FORM[6]

In the fourteenth century the formal elements of noh as well as its aesthetic theories were codified. Since noh is the predecessor of kabuki, its dramaturgical and musical formal elements influenced the structure of nagauta strongly. Therefore, it is necessary to outline briefly the fundamental structure of the noh drama in order better to understand the form of the later nagauta.

The classic noh play is organized into five main units or *dan*. These are usually placed within a two-act framework with four units in the first act and one in the second. Each of these dan are further subdivided into dramatic or musical sections. In a theatre form of such a large repertoire and long history one can expect many exceptions and variations as to the method with which these many divisions and subdivisions are handled, but as a point of departure the following information can be considered as representative of standard procedure. It should be noted that there is considerable confusion in Japanese writings on this subject due to the lack of a clear distinction between terms which represent formal units of the play and those which apply to types of music that can appear in several different

[3] See "Jokyoku," *Ibid.*, 5, p. 150.
[4] See "Teikyoku," *Ibid.*, 7, p. 8.
[5] Zeami, *Kadensho*, Iwanami Bunko No. 171 (Tokyo: Iwanami, 1927), p. 28.
[6] The formal outline that follows is essentially the same as the one in the author's previous book, *Japanese Music and Musical Instruments*. It is repeated here for the convenience of the reader.

formal units within the play. In this discussion a distinction has been attempted between these two types of nomenclature.

Following the jo-ha-kyū division of the play as mentioned above, the classic noh play is organized as follows:

1. Jo: the introduction

This unit is the first dan. It contains the introductory music, the appearance of the secondary actor (waki), and the general setting of the scene and preparation for the entrance of the principal actor (shite), who has not as yet appeared. Before this unit there is a warm-up piece played by the hayashi ensemble (one flute and three drums). This so-called *oshirabe* is often imitated in kabuki dramas drawn from noh plays.

Within the jo unit the most important musical section is the *shidai*. This music is meant to represent the character of the secondary actor. Originally, there were many types of shidai, but today only one is used, the *sō-shidai*, the priest entrance music.

2. Ha: the exposition

Theoretically this unit has three dan. The first contains the entrance of the principal actor and his first song. It has two important musical sections, the *issei* and the *michiyuki*. It may also contain its own introductory music (shidai). The word issei in this connotation (it has others) means "first song." Issei sections are found sometimes in the introductory part of the play sung by the supporting actor.

The michiyuki section occurs when the principal actor travels from the greenroom to the stage via a covered walk that connects them. The music is dependent on the personality of the character. Often there is no music at all when the actor first appears. The silent, stately measure of such entrances is very powerful when experienced as part of a professional performance. When the michiyuki is sung, one of two types of song *(uta)* is used. These are the *sageuta*, which is relatively short and low in range, and the *ageuta*, which is longer and higher. These two terms apply to various songs throughout the play as well as to those used in the michiyuki.

Another musical term that appears in different sections but especially during this second dan of the play is *sashi*. This is a type of heightened speech. It is like an opera recitative in that it serves as a bridge between more lyrical sections.

In the third dan of the piece (the second of the exposition) the plot is furthered by means of questions and answers between the two actors. This section is called the *mondō*. Much of it is done in a recitative style. The drums often provide a rhythmic background for this conversation. The chorus commonly completes this section with a commentary on the dialogue. This is done in a more melodic style.

There are several special sections that may appear at this time depending on the plot. One of the most common is the *kudoki,* a section appearing during tender, feminine scenes.

The fourth dan of the play (the final dan of the exposition) brings the first act to its climax. It contains two basic sections, the *kuri* and the *kuse.* The kuri is significant musically because it has the highest note in the composition. The pitch itself is called kuri. During this section the basic emotional tension of the plot is revealed.

The kuse is a dance and is considered to be the center of the play. It is meant to be a full exposition of the spirit of the principal character. The musical accompaniment of this dance is also one of the most evolved sections of the music, and independent instrumental or choral concerts of noh music are often drawn from such music.

The fourth dan of the play is closed by means of a section called the *rongi,* which is again a period of exchanges between the two actors either in heightened speech or in song. The chorus frequently ends the act with a song known as the *nakairi.* This is also used as an interlude between the acts.

Other units may be used to fill in the time between the acts while the main actor is changing costume. For example, a short comic interlude called a *kyōgen* is common. These are performed by special kyōgen actors who come on stage at this time. Like the *intermezzi* of eighteenth-century Italian opera, their style of declamation is more in the vernacular and their subject matter is often unrelated to the theme of the main play. The word kyōgen actually represents a whole genre of plays and folk theatricals whose influence on later kabuki music is somewhat independent from that of noh music.

3. Kyū: the denouement

A transition into the final dan is formed by a song called the *machiuta,* the waiting song. Soon thereafter the main actor reappears in a new role, usually that of some supernatural being. A first song (issei) and a dialogue (mondō) similar in style to those found in the first act are used. The highlight of the second act, however, is also a dance. This is called the *mai.* Its music is dependent on the character of the dancer. The accompaniment may be the instrumental group (hayashi) alone, the chorus alone, or more often both, at least at the end. One should note that when the hayashi is used alone the music for both this dance and the kuse of the first act is drawn from a group of some twelve set pieces.[7] Such a use of extended musical units, usually of specific emotional or dramatic connotation, is an idiomatic technique found in kabuki, particularly in the off-stage *(geza)* music.

After the dance there is usually a short poem called a *waka,* the name of a Japanese poetic genre. The play ends with a final commentary by the chorus called the *kiri.*

Putting the above information into an outline, the classic noh form looks as follows:

JO: INTRODUCTION
First dan: shidai
HA: EXPOSITION
Second dan: issei, michiyuki
Third dan: mondō
Fourth dan: kuri, kuse, rongi
INTERLUDE
nakairi: kyōgen, machiuta
KYŪ: DENOUEMENT
Fifth dan: (issei, mondō), mai, waka, kiri

There is great variety in the use of this form as it is applied to the various types of plays. The "mad" plays and those about devils are particularly varied. However, for the purpose of understanding the relation between noh form and kabuki and nagauta forms, the above outline can be considered as basic. The strength of noh-form influence will become more apparent as this study progresses.

KUMIUTA FORM

The earliest known shamisen music that has come down to us is a set of six songs known as the "Ryūkyū-gumi."[8] These songs date from the late seventeenth or early eighteenth century and are the beginning of the so-called kumiuta form.

At this early stage kumiuta form consisted simply of a number of poems set to music and strung together. There was no connection between the theme of the poems nor the melodies of the music at that time. The rather vague outlines of this form were further blurred by a confusion in terms. Since most of these songs were created in the Osaka area they were also called jiuta, local songs, or kamigatauta, songs from the Kansai dis-

[7] For a complete list see Komparu Sōichi, *Komparu-ryū Taiko Zensho* (Tokyo: Hinoki Shoten, 1953), p. 253 ff.
[8] Takano, *op. cit.*, pp. 727–32.

trict. The term jiuta took precedence as shamisen music developed but the two terms remained mixed to the present day.

As more kumiuta collections were made the form took on new aspects. The most important musical change was the addition of short introductions and endings. Together with the koto musicians, the shamisen composers developed a standard jiuta or kumiuta form. In its simplest style it consisted of an instrumental introduction *(maebiki)*, a first song *(maeuta)*, an instrumental interlude *(tegoto)*, and a final song *(atouta)*. The extension of the instrumental interludes is espcially noticeable in eighteenth century koto music. At that time the interludes (tegoto) were expanded so that there was a transitional passage from the previous song to the interlude proper *(tsunagi)*, an introduction to the interlude *(makura)*, the interlude itself *(tegoto)*, and a finale and transition to the next song *(chirashi)*.

The form continued to accrete new songs and interludes so that the standard form became as follows: introduction (maebiki), first song (maeuta), interlude (tegoto), middle song (naka-uta), interlude (tegoto), and last song (atouta).

At the same time, the interludes became more extensive, so that they might consist of the following sections: transition (tsunagi), introduction (makura), interlude (tegoto), middle climax (naka-chirashi), interlude (tegoto), true finale (hon-chirashi).

The further refinements of this form lie within the realm of research into koto music. What is important to notice here is the precedent set by this form for an alternation of songs and instrumental interludes. This is of great importance to shamisen music, especially when nineteenth and twentieth century composers were searching for forms other than the kabuki dance form in which to set their pieces. Its influence on kabuki dance form itself is considerable.

JŌRURI FORM

In the survey of shamisen music history in Chapter I the narrative tradition of jōruri was mentioned as one of the most vital genres. This being the case one would expect the formal organization of this music to be of equal importance to the general development of form in shamisen music.

Gidayū-bushi, as the leading style of jōruri music, is considered to exemplify the basic jōruri formal concept. Since the music is so closely allied with the story there needs to be a certain amount of flexibility in the form to suit the particular situation of each plot. However, the stories were often written expressly for the puppet theatre, so that they tended to conform in structure with the requirements of the stage and music. The strength of this theatrical influence was felt even when playwrights wrote novels not meant for stage production.[9]

The classic jōruri form as used in gidayū-bushi is organized into five parts or dan. Within these five parts the music is further subdivided into eight sections which in their normal order are: the oki, the michiyuki, the kudoki, the monogatari, the uta, the odori, the miarawashi, and the chirashi or seme.

There is considerable variation in the manner in which these eight sections fit into the larger five-part scheme. All the sections need not appear in one play. In truth, there is much yet to be discovered about the specific relations of music, text, and form in jōruri. This form, however, has a very close relation to both the noh drama form which preceded it and the kabuki dance form which developed contemporarily with it. A description of the content of these eight sections will reveal some of these relations.

The oki or okiuta is the introductory song which sets the mood and scene. It serves the same function as the first unit of the noh form. The michiyuki introduces the characters in a manner similar to the michiyuki of the noh form. Since the number of *dramatis personnae* is, however, more extensive in most puppet plays the use of the michiyuki is more flexible than in noh. We find in both forms the use of a tender section, the kudoki, sometimes after the michiyuki. The monogatari or story section can be compared with the mondō of the noh form, for both concentrate on advancing the plot so that it will reach a climax suitable for musical treatment. The song (uta) and dance (odori) provide opportunities for the singer and puppeteers respectively to display their talents. These sections also reflect the noh dramatic form orientation in which the kuri and kuse sections provide similar vocal and terpsichorean opportunities for the principal actor. Since plot lines as such are more highly developed in puppet plays, there is need for more exposition of the story than is normally required in a noh drama. Hence, there is the miarawashi section in which the central problem of the plot is brought to its climax. As in the noh, this second climax occurs most often in the second act of the play, thus affording the singer and puppeteers an opportunity to build once more to the type of climax they achieved in the first act.

---

[9] Richard Lane, "Saikaku's Five Women," in Saikaku, *Five Women Who Loved Love*, Wm. Theodore de Bary, trans. (Tokyo: Tuttle, 1956), p. 259.

The word chirashi in jōruri, as in kumiuta form, indicates a finale. In practice there are several small chirashi before the final denouement is accomplished.

With the introduction of jōruri form we are confronted with a full-blown dramatic form comparable to those forms known in the West. The noh has elements of these same dramatic outlooks, but the extensive use of allusion in the stories makes their dramatic appeal more specialized. Jōruri was built for a general audience and hence was forced to become more obvious and melodramatic in its structure. Since kabuki also vied for this same audience one can expect to find a similar orientation in the formal articulations of that art. The corroboration of this expectancy is evident in the section that follows.

KABUKI DANCE FORM

Chapter I explained how nagauta grew out of shorter pieces in order to provide a more suitable accompaniment for the dancing of the kabuki stage. While in later years it became further enmeshed in the overall kabuki dramatic structure, nagauta's orientation has been and still is primarily based on the dance. Thus, a study of the major dance form of nagauta will reveal the basic compositional factors underlying all nagauta and, by inference, much of the other theatre music of Japan.

The kabuki dance form is organized classically into six sections: the okiuta, the michiyuki, the kudoki, the odoriji, the chirashi, and the dangire. By comparing these sections with those of jōruri form and noh form one can see immediately the close relation between the nomenclature and order of parts. Further musical analysis will reveal their differences.

The oki, as in jōruri, is introductory in nature. This holds true for the text as well as the music. The dramatic function of the oki is to prepare the audience for the entrance of the main actor as in the early parts of noh and jōruri forms. In the kabuki this is done either by describing the character who is about to appear or by the setting of the scene. For example, the opening words of *Gorō* (see Part IV, page 298) call out his name and tell that he is out to revenge the death of his father. By contrast, the opening of another piece dealing with the same story, *Sukeroku* (Yoshizumi, III–4, p. 1), describes the setting, which is the Yoshiwara pleasure district of Tokyo. Before the singing begins in *Sukeroku* there is an instrumental introduction. As in kumiuta this is called the maebiki. The maebiki of *Sukeroku* is somewhat unusual in that it was added to the piece some years after its composition without any special dramatic purpose.[10] Usually, however, these introductions are related to the mood of the composition. For example, the dramatic shamisen introduction to *Kibun Daijin* (Yoshizumi, VIII–6), like the opening of Verdi's *Otello,* represents a storm through which the hero's boat is sailing on its way to port.

The okiuta or maebiki may also reflect the style of music from which a nagauta piece is derived. The maebiki of *Sukeroku* mentioned above is such a case. It is actually a katō-bushi melody, as the story originally appeared in the katō repertoire. The most frequent stylistic imitation in nagauta is of noh music because of the many kabuki stories adopted from the noh. The opening of *Tsuru-kame* (see Part IV, page 245) illustrates such a case. The imitation often lasts for only one or two lines of poetry after which the shamisen enters with a normal nagauta accompaniment as it does in *Tsuru-kame.* In some cases such as *Adachi ga Hara* (Yoshizumi, VI–4), however, the noh imitation goes on for some time. This serves two purposes. First, it firmly establishes the mood of a noh play and, second, it disposes quickly of a large section of text which the composer feels is necessary to the drama but not important enough to dwell on for a long time. In short, it is a type of recitative.

The function of the next section, the michiyuki, has already been explained in the discussion of noh and jōruri forms. The actor in kabuki makes his entrance via a ramp (the *hanamichi*) leading from the back of the auditorium to the stage. Theoretically, the entire michiyuki is performed on this ramp. Usually the actor stops two-thirds of the way down the ramp where he performs most of the michiyuki dancing or posturing *(shosa).* In some plays the entrance is made through a trap door *(seri)* after which the actor begins his dance or moves directly to the stage. The moment of stepping from the ramp to the stage is called the *inaori* and is often marked in the music. In kabuki, as in noh and jōruri, the music of the michiyuki section will depend on the character and the choreography. This music may be purely instrumental with drums and flutes as well as shamisen or it may be vocal. Off-stage (geza) music is often added to delineate the person or situation.

In kabuki dance form the next section is the soft, feminine kudoki. In keeping with its character drums are not used during this section. The shamisen line tends to become more simple. Between the quiet kudoki and the livelier odoriji there is often

[10] Atsumi, *Hōgaku Buyō Jiten,* p. 360.

a transitional section. This is sometimes called the *tsunagi,* a term already found in kumiuta form. The tempo increases in such cases and the *ō-tsuzumi* and *ko-tsuzumi,* hip and shoulder drums, may be added. The *taiko* stick drum, as will be seen, is saved for later.

The odoriji is the center of kabuki dance form, comparable to the kuse or mai of noh or the odori of jōruri. This section contains the main dance of the piece. Often it is called the *taikoji* because the taiko stick drum enters at this point. This is a tradition derived from the noh, for the taiko drum is seldom used before the mai in the last part of noh plays. In keeping with the change in mood the tuning of the shamisen usually is changed at this point. Also, the bamboo flute enters to provide a new timbre to the piece. The odoriji is usually sung, though it may have an extensive instrumental interlude *(ai* or *aikata)* within it.

After the odoriji there is sometimes another slower section which leads into the more brilliant chirashi. The other two drums often re-enter to liven up the rhythm. Instrumental interludes also contribute to the excitement. This section seems to be the freest. It could be compared (in this respect only) to the development section of a sonata-allegro piece of Western music. In the same way that the tegoto of kumiuta form were expanded into many subsections, the chirashi of nagauta are found to contain small kudoki, interludes, or dances. The general function of the chirashi, however, remains the same in that it rushes the music away from the main dance toward the finale.

The finale is known as the dangire. Actually, from the Western point of view one could consider many of the shorter chirashi sections as finales and call the dangire final cadences. This is more appropriate because the dangire sections are seldom more than a few bars long. Since nagauta pieces average some five hundred measures in length the chirashi does not seem to be a balanced section within the overall form. It is best to think of the chirashi and dangire as basically one unit. Under the jo-ha-kyū concept they could be considered the kyū, with the oki and michiyuki as the jo and the kudoki and odoriji as the ha.[11] Actually, there is no agreement among nagauta experts as to the placement of kabuki dance form within the jo-ha-kyū system. This is due, perhaps, to the freedom with which nagauta composers have treated the form. Nevertheless, even in these altered situations, kabuki dance form remains as the basic point of reference from which each composition is built.

[11] For a four-part division of nagauta see page 91.

It was intimated above that nagauta composers were prone to alter the basic dance form scheme and add sections based on other systems of organization. The most frequent of such mixtures appear in the many noh-style compositions written in the nineteenth century. A good example is *Tsuchigumo* (Yoshizumi, III–2), a famous noh and kabuki drama about a giant spider who comes disguised as a priest to the house of a prince made ill by one of his spells. His discovery, fight, flight, and final defeat in his cave make for an exciting and popular play. Let us look now at the music that contributes to this popularity.

The original nagauta version of this play was in three large sections of which only the first part is used today.[12] Comparing this version with the noh drama text[13] one finds that the first two pages of the nagauta words are taken directly from the noh, after which they tend to be quite different. A noh atmosphere for the opening is created by a short percussion introduction such as is often heard at the start of a noh-play shidai. If this is not used, the shamisen plays a maebiki which is marked shidai. This leads into a short noh-style singing section which is followed by a regular nagauta-style okiuta. At this point the text of the nagauta version and the noh piece separate.

The michiyuki begins instrumentally but uses both noh and nagauta-style passages. There follows a long section of noh-style recitative (sashi). The tuning changes to ni-agari (*op. cit.*, p. 8) as the maid enters the sick prince's room. As she is the only female character in the story her entrance is in the nature of a kudoki. The tuning returns to hon-chōshi for a rather long, sparse section in which the two principal actors exchange dialogue as in a noh mondō section. This leads into a dance section called *kagura,* using the taiko drum in the style of a kabuki form odoriji. It is followed by a fast instrumental interlude imitating the rhythm of horse hoofs as the pursuit of the giant spider begins. There is another exchange between the actors, mondō-style, and the chirashi section enters with a short, brilliant shamisen interlude which continues while the singers carry on in a kabuki heightened-speech style *(serifu)*. A standard ōza-tsuma-dangire (see Part IV, page 338) ends the composition.

Looking back over this analysis one finds a basic kabuki

---

[12] Atsumi, *Hōgaku Buyō Jiten*, p. 396.

[13] Each school of noh has a slightly different text. The one used here is the Kongō school version as found in Nōgami Toyoichirō, *Yōkyoku Zenshū* (Tokyo: Chūōkōron-sha, 1936), V, p. 529.

dance form extended by the insertion of certain noh conventions, such as a percussion prelude and the dialogue sections. This can be seen in the formal outline of *Tsuchigumo* shown below: (shidai), maebiki, michiyuki (sashi), kudoki, mondō, odoriji (kagura), mondō, chirashi, dangire.

In this case the noh influence has not disturbed greatly the basic formal outline, though the style of the music itself is different from that of a normal kabuki piece, particularly in its extensive use of heightened speech and ōzatsuma patterns.

Another popular noh story found in kabuki is *Funa Benkei*, Benkei on the boat. It tells of the separation of the hero Yoshitsune from his mistress Shizuka and the journey he and his retainer Benkei make across the sea despite a terrible storm thrown in their path by the ghost of a defeated general.

The nagauta version of this piece (Yoshizumi, VII–1) is extremely long and uses noh text throughout. This may be due to the fact that it was originally converted into nagauta in order that a well-known noh actor could perform it in the more popular theatre.[14] As presented in the noh version *Funa Benkei* consists of two acts which are in turn subdivided into jo, ha, and kyū sections.[15] By using the jo-ha-kyū outlines of the two acts along with certain kabuki conventions, the form of this piece becomes clear.

The first act is concerned with the separation of the lovers. In the nagauta version one finds a shidai sung as an accompanied solo, first in the lyric noh style and then in the simpler narrative style. The shamisen enters and continues the introductory (jo) section of Act I with a kabuki okiuta (*op. cit.*, pp. 2–5). It is interesting to note that in this part of the nagauta piece a noh lyric solo passage appears only in the section marked ageuta in the original noh text. The entire introductory section ends with a firm cadence, and the ha section begins with a noh narrative passage spoken by Benkei. This is his entrance and is the michiyuki, although he is technically the supporting actor. At this point a large portion of the noh text is deleted in the nagauta piece and an instrumental interlude is inserted to bring Benkei to the stage.

A mondō-like section of dialogue is now carried on between the three characters as they discuss the separation. This leads to a quiet kudoki (*op. cit.*, pp. 8–9) lamenting the departure.

---

[14] Atsumi, *Hōgaku Buyō Jiten*, p. 56.
[15] The text used for comparison is the Kita school version as found in Nōgami, *op. cit.*, V, pp. 435–56.

There is considerable argument as to whether the girl is to stay or go. It is carried on in alternating noh and nagauta styles. This leads to a dance which is listed in the noh text as a dance for the main actor, who in the noh play is the girl Shizuka.[16] This dance is accompanied by the ō-tsuzumi and ko-tsuzumi drums, as they are traditionally associated with girls of Shizuka's profession, court dancing girls (shirabyōshi). The dance is called the *iroe* rather than the main kuse dance of noh form because it is short and is basically a preparation for the longer dance that is to follow.[17] The nagauta iroe is set off by a change in tuning.

The next two pages of text (*op. cit.*, pp. 13–14) are used to build up to this main dance of the first act. The shamisen tuning changes, and the finale of Act I, the kyū section of the jo-ha-kyū, is a dance interlude. This is the kuse of the noh. The percussion accompaniment in the nagauta piece is derived from the original noh piece played at this time, "Chū no Mai." The last of the first-act text (*op. cit.*, p. 17) is begun with a short noh-style solo which becomes a rather active exchange between actors and chorus (like a noh rongi) culminating in the order from Benkei to cast off.

The nakairi consists of a shamisen interlude. It is followed by a short excerpt from a well-known kyōgen concerning the boatman which is used between the acts of the original noh play.

The introduction to Act II (the jo) consists of a furious shamisen overture depicting the rising storm. This goes quickly to the ha section of Act II which is a series of exchanges between Yoshitsune and Benkei, mondō style. Large parts of the original noh text are deleted. A shamisen interlude (*op. cit.*, p. 19) is substituted for some of it. The storm and the music mount to a climactic dance (*op. cit.*, p. 21), and the kyū section begins. The nagauta instrumental interlude and the original dance accompaniment in the noh drama are both called *hayabue*. The taiko drum enters at this time. It is here that Benkei does battle with the ghost by rubbing his Buddhist rosary in the face of the ghost at every attack. In the kabuki this scene is done in a series of posturings *(shosa)*. The text that follows is the same in both versions. The nagauta piece begins it with a noh singing solo (*op. cit.*, p. 22) and then changes to a normal accompanied

---

[16] The reason that she is the main character is because it enables the actor to come back in the second act as a ghost, since Shizuka is left behind in the first act.

[17] The iroe is a special short, feminine dance used in noh to set the atmosphere of the following kuse dance. See "Iroe," *Ongaku Jiten*, 1 (1955), p. 127.

nagauta style. This leads to a second dance (*op. cit.*, p. 24) done by the defeated ghost.[18] It is accompanied by instruments only. The remainder of the text (the kiri of the noh play) is treated in a mixture of noh and nagauta styles. The piece ends with a traditional chirashi and dangire.

In outline the form of *Funa Benkei* looks as shown in Table 3 (read left to right).

TABLE 3: *Formal outline of* Funa Benkei

NOH FORM	NOH TERMS	NAGAUTA SECTIONS	TUNING	ORCHESTRATION
		ACT I		
JO	shidai	shidai	hon-chōshi	vocal solo
		okiuta		accomp.
HA	ageuta	michiyuki		solo-instru. solo
	mondō			accomp.
		kudoki		accomp.
	iroe		ni-agari	solo-instru..
KYŪ			hon-chōshi	accomp.
	kuse	mai no ai		instru.
	rongi			solo-accomp.
	nakairi			instru.
		ACT II		
	kyōgen			accomp.
JO				instru.
HA	mondō			mixed
KYŪ	mai (hayabue)	odoriji (shosha)		instru. (taiko)
	mondō			solo-accomp.
	mai (hataraki)	ai		instru.
	kiri	chirashi		accomp.
				instru.
		dangire		accomp.

The opening section of this nagauta piece can be seen to follow along classic kabuki formal lines. Note that until the kyū section of Act I each new part is introduced by solo noh-style singing. This is not so true after the kudoki, where the music is

---

[18] The first dance of Act II can be considered to be the mai though it is done by two actors. This second, shorter dance is known as the *shite no hataraki* and is the solo dance for the main actor.

dependent on the original noh play for its formal organization, and the treatment becomes freer. All the dances (in the second column, the iroe, kuse, mai, and hataraki) are accompanied by instruments only. The taiko drum is withheld until the main dance of the second act in keeping with the noh tradition. This gives the dance (hayabue) the feeling of the kabuki form odoriji. The build-up to this dance uses a quickening pace of orchestration changes, and the transition between it and the next dance reverts to the noh solo followed by accompanied nagauta singing as found at the beginning of the piece. The second dance is derived from the original play and the finale returns to the kabuki style of ending.

The two pieces analyzed above illustrate the two basic approaches found in the mixture of noh and nagauta. The first shows a rather firm kabuki dance form extended by a few minor noh sections, the major parts being absorbed easily into the kabuki form. In the second case, the noh play is really the guiding formal factor. This nagauta piece makes as many major sections as possible fit into the standard kabuki form but must wander through a series of orchestration changes to compensate for the number of unfamiliar sections. In the noh, each of these sections has special musical characteristics but these are not always meaningful to nagauta musicians. Therefore, one gets the impression of a series of songs and interludes which move forward primarily through the story in the text rather than through musical means. When the piece arrives at a standard kabuki section such as the odoriji, familiar musical characteristics return and formal musical progress is felt once more. Such an example illustrates one of the main problems of nagauta development. In a music whose formal progress is dependent on traditional musical devices, it is very difficult to create a new device which will convey a similar meaning to new sections. As a rule in such new sections, the composers let the words carry the music on to its next formal goal.

The alternation of songs and instrumental interludes as found in kumiuta form is endemic in shamisen music. The deliberate use in nagauta of such an alternation as an outgrowth of kumiuta form appeared when concert (ozashiki) nagauta became popular. Since there was no longer any choreographic problem in this music, the composers felt freer to tamper with the traditional order of things. The best example of the use of kumiuta form in nagauta is the 1845 concert piece *Aki no Irogusa* (Yoshizumi, III–1). Its form is as follows: instrumental introduction, first song, interlude, second song, interlude, final song. Each of these sections is very long as in kumiuta. One very different element in this piece as compared with other nagauta is that the percussion is not used at all. Since kumiuta form is characteristic of koto music it is interesting to find that the second long shamisen interlude is an imitation of the koto piece "Midare."[19] In contrast with the noh-style nagauta just studied, *Aki no Irogusa* contains only one passage (*op. cit.*, p. 8) of ōzatsuma patterns. Despite all these "anti-dance" features, the composition was eventually taken over by various geisha dance schools. In keeping with the adventuresome spirit of this "new" nagauta, some performances include an obbligato koto part during the interludes.

TABLE 4: *Formal outline of* Azuma Hakkei

KUMIUTA SECTION	TUNING	NAGAUTA SECTION
instrumental introduction	hon-chōshi	maebiki
first song		okiuta
interlude		michiyuki
second song	ni-agari	kudoki
interlude		odoriji
third song	san-sagari	—
interlude		chirashi
final song		dangire

One of the earliest pieces of the concert nagauta type was the 1829 composition *Azuma Hakkei* (Yoshizumi, III–3). Its formal outline is shown in Table 4. One can see the possible similarity of the form of this piece to kabuki dance form. The introduction (maebiki) is only two lines long and the most lyric, kudoki-like song comes after the first extensive instrumental interlude and with a change of tuning to emphasize its change of mood. The first song, however, seems rather long for an okiuta and is not free enough rhythmically. The first interlude seems too long for a michiyuki. Also, no percussion is used. Most important, the song concerns the eight famous views of northeastern Japan and hence has no plot and no actors who might enter at this so-called michiyuki section. The moods of the music change with the scenes. Thus, the kabuki dance form shown in the outline does not represent a true picture of the form of the composition but rather illustrates how the transition was made from one formal principle to another. When nagauta ceased to be dance music it actually went back to an earlier form.

Unfortunately, in their reaction against the tyranny of the

[19] Atsumi, *Hōgaku Buyō Jiten*, p. 6.

dance style, the new composers also deleted the unique orchestral tradition of the nagauta hayashi group. They were left with a chamber ensemble playing compositions of orchestral length. While the lyricism is often striking, one misses the tighter structure and feeling of orchestration found in the traditional kabuki dance form pieces.

Jōruri form is so similar to that of nagauta that the two seldom need to be mixed. In the narrative-style (danmono) nagauta and in pieces classified as jōruri style there are, of course, many jōruri-like passages. For example, most of the piece *Sukeroku* imitates the style of the older katō-bushi jōruri composition on which it is based. This imitation appears in the shamisen. The vocal style of jōruri is generally too rough to be used by nagauta singers. Some of the dialogue sections of *Kibun Daijin* (Yoshizumi, VIII–6) and *Uki Daijin* (Yoshizumi, VIII–4) are quite close to the simpler style of jōruri narration. In addition to the indefinite contour of the vocal line, the soft plucking of the shamisen adds to this effect (see Example 1). Such accompaniments are characteristic of jōruri dialogues. One may find a monogatari section in nagauta, but in general the influence of jōruri is in the music style, not in the form. It should be mentioned, however, that in the kabuki theatre nagauta is mixed with various jōruri musics during one play. For example, players of nagauta, tokiwazu, and gidayū may be placed about the stage at the same time. They take turns in accompanying the play and occasionally play together. This so-called *kakeai* performance is not the same, however, as the combination of musics within one genre piece. Nevertheless, it does help to explain why so many jōruri borrowings are found in nagauta kabuki pieces when they are played by nagauta musicians alone.

Finally, we come to the question of new forms. The impact of the introduction of Western music was felt very strongly in all areas of Japanese traditional music. Some schools reacted by reinforcing their most classical traditions while others entered into competition with Western music by aping its superficial elements. Nagauta seems to have taken a middle position in the struggle. Some of the composers completely forsook the old ways and started writing shamisen concertos, but most of the writers since 1900 have augmented the old ideas, sped them up to match Western virtuosity, and retained the basic spirit of nagauta.

An excellent example of such a compromise is the 1911 piece *Kibun Daijin* (Yoshizumi, VIII–6). The composition concerns the life of a famous Edo period man who made a fortune shipping *mikan,* a type of tangerine, to Tokyo. The piece is marked as being in six sections (dan) in the manner of a jōruri composition. However, when one looks at the music the sixth dan is found to consist of many varied sections and is as long as all the other five sections combined. An outline of this piece is shown in Table 5.

TABLE 5: *Formal outline of* Kibun Daijin

PAGE	FORMAL UNIT	ORCHESTRATION	TUNING	COMMENT
1	introduction	hayashi		
1	first dan	shamisen	ichi-sagari hon-chōshi	maebiki type
2	second dan	voice & shamisen		boat song, sad
2	third dan			boat song, gay
3–4	fourth dan			narrative
5	fifth dan	folk hayashi	san-sagari	michiyuki type
8	sixth dan	shamisen & voice	hon-chōshi	kudoki
13	kouta		san-sagari	dialogue
14			hon-chōshi	tempo up
15		ō-tsuzumi & ko-tsuzumi		chirikara
16	odori uta	folk hayashi		
17				chirikara added
19	chirashi	taiko, noh flute, ō-tsuzumi & ko-tsuzumi		chirikara
20	dangire			

A violent noh hayashi dance piece is sometimes used to open this composition. Its purpose, however, is not to create the atmosphere of a noh drama as in the cases previously studied. Instead, it is used to set the mood for the shamisen introduction which depicts a storm buffeting Kibun's boat as he sails toward Tokyo. The shamisen introduction begins in an unusual tuning *(ichi-sagari)* and is replete with new and difficult passages which mark the influence of the Western virtuoso psychology. The tuning changes in the middle of this *tour de force* to add variety and also, perhaps, to return the players to more familiar ground. Another new element to be noticed in this opening is the frequent changes from solo to tutti passages.

The second dan is a melancholy boatman's song. The third section is another boat song of a gayer type. This song uses a stanza form with three repetitions of the same basic music in imitation of the folk style. Section four begins to tell the story of the trip to Tokyo as the tempo picks up. In section five the boat has arrived and all the excitement of dock activities and a festival in the colorful Kanda area of Tokyo are depicted with the sound of a folk ensemble playing the folk festival piece "Shichōme" while the shamisen, in a new tuning, plays its own bright melody.

The tuning changes once more, and after a sudden blast on the large off-stage ō-daiko drum signifying a change of scene, the shamisen plays sugagaki, a standard opening for jōruri pieces. A deep-toned bell is heard as section six begins in the romantic atmosphere of the geisha houses of the Yoshiwara district of Tokyo. The bell, the music, and the word "Yoshiwara" evoke in the minds of kabuki lovers a picture of the rows of teahouses and brothels that clustered around the famous Asakusa Kannon temple in old Edo much as they do today. In such a setting it is revealed that all the previous sections of this piece occurred in a dream of the second-generation Kibun. A nostalgic conversation is held between Kibun, the second, and his mistress, Kichō. Kibun's words are all sung while Kichō's are done in a kabuki conversational style with the quiet backing of the shamisen. Most of her comments are accompanied by the melody shown in Example 1. It is lengthened or shortened to fit the length of the conversation. This entire section is cast in the style of shinnai-bushi, a music well known in the geisha quarters of the Yoshiwara.[20]

EXAMPLE 1: *Background shamisen music for conversations*

The mixture of conversation and singing goes on about memories of Kibun's father and the problems of the lovers. This section culminates in an extremely lovely, sentimental kouta, a type of song often heard in geisha houses. The shamisen uses a common kouta tuning, san-sagari. The end of this song overlaps with a return of the conversation as often happens in actual party situations. The tuning changes, the mood brightens, and

[20] Asakawa Gyokuto, "Kibun Daijin," *Nihon Ongaku,* No. 75 (Aug., 1954), p. 12.

the ō-tsuzumi and ko-tsuzumi enter in kabuki (chirikara) style. The tuning changes once more and the festive mood of the fifth section returns, this time to accompany *daijin-mai,* a party dance popular in the Yoshiwara in the Edo period.[21] The folk hayashi ensemble contributes to this mood with the pattern "Kirin." Soon the ō-tsuzumi and ko-tsuzumi drums join in the dance music. The percussion ensemble drops out for a moment, only to return, this time, with a standard ensemble of ō-tsuzumi and ko-tsuzumi, taiko, and noh flute, which play in the exciting manner of a nagauta finale.

Among the many twentieth-century nagauta pieces *Kibun Daijin* is one of the few that has remained popular. It is to kabuki what an oratorio is to opera. It presents the mood of the story in both instrumental overtures and opening work songs. The plot is advanced by using nagauta-, jōruri-, and kabuki-style conversation techniques. The plot is contrived to allow for the inclusion of four extraneous songs, two boat songs, a party song, and a party dance. Popular moods are evoked; a storm, a street scene, a teahouse, and a geisha dance party. Finally, the full panoply of nagauta instrumental sounds is utilized in a constantly varied arrangement. Such a masterly handling of the myriad musical and dramatic elements inherent in nagauta is bound to cause a favorable reaction among theatre loving people.

From the formal standpoint this piece shows a compromise of traditional forms. The deliberate sectional designations are a direct imitation of the structure of jōruri dramas. At the same time, one can see a general outline of the kabuki dance form extended by the three extraneous songs (*op. cit.,* pp. 2, 13) and two narrative sections (*op. cit.,* pp. 3, 14). The old formal signals are not entirely missing, and the variety of sounds and pacing of the story produce in this music a good sense of formal progression. The continued success of this piece thus seems well warranted.

It was stated that Western forms such as concertos and sonatas have been used for shamisen music. Such music is outside the field of nagauta even though it may be played by nagauta musicians. Nagauta is basically an instrumental-vocal tradition more akin to the dance-drama or oratorio than to Western instrumental music. The development of themes is almost unknown in nagauta, since it has its own means of formal progression. The dynamism and logic of these formal processes will become clearer as the more specific techniques of musical organization are explained in the chapters ahead.

[21] Asakawa Gyokuto, "Kibun Daijin," *Nihon Ongaku,* No. 74 (July, 1954), p. 14.

PART TWO

Music and Instruments

CHAPTER FOUR

The Nagauta Voice

THE SINGER has been considered as the music star of the theatre since the earliest days of kabuki. Often the name of the shamisen composer of a certain nagauta piece has been forgotten while the name of the singer who first performed it is well known. Thus, it is evident that no discussion of nagauta would be complete without some attention given to the nagauta vocal tradition.

The professional nagauta singer combines a baritone and tenor range with an emphasis on tessitura singing.[1] The singer chooses a basic pitch for the accompanying shamisen from a twelve-note gamut extending from A, a minor tenth below middle C, to the G sharp, a diminished fourth below middle C. This pitch is usually the singer's lowest note as well, though he may occasionally go lower. From this pitch he can be expected to soar as high as the second octave with most of the piece hovering in the upper octave. While there is a wide range of basic pitches from which to choose, most pieces are tuned in the area of B flat to D below middle C.

The range of nagauta singing in itself is not unusual, but the manner of tone production creates a unique, non-Western sound. The tone is said to originate in the abdomen, and as it rises passes from a primarily chest tone to more of a head tone.[2] The throat remains very tense and the tone is forced into the upper register without resorting to falsetto.[3] In the twentieth century the Kenseikai school of nagauta under Kineya Kisa-

---

[1] Male and female vocal technique is considered to be the same and except for the octave difference their performances and training are identical. Though there are many respected female singers, however, only men are considered to be true professionals.

[2] Asakawa, *Nagauta no Kiso Kenkyū*, p. 152.

[3] It is not possible to assume that this was the case in the seventeenth and eighteenth centuries. However, this research is concerned primarily with contemporary practice.

burō began to use falsetto *(uragoe)* in the style of the softer kiyomoto and shinnai musics. This method nearly overwhelmed
the classical vocal style but of late there has been a tendency
to return to the traditional manner. One reason for the continued existence of this more difficult and, at times, painful
method is that it creates a much stronger more intense sound.
One of the most distressing sights in an amateur performance is
that of the contorted face and bulging neck muscles of a singer
attempting to perform tessitura sections in the classic manner.
By the same token, one of the genuine thrills of Japanese music
is a performance by a nagauta singing master. Such a man is
able to produce a tone of pristine clarity backed by a tremen-
dous pressure. The resultant sound produces an electric excitement similar to that felt when hearing an excellent tenor. The
acquisition of such a tone requires an extensive and intensive
training no less severe than that of a fine opera singer. The resultant voice in the Japanese example is no more natural or
unnatural than the Western one. Both are products of natural
endowment plus careful training.

The Japanese nagauta student acquires this tone in two ways.
First of all, he is exposed to the sound ideal by his culture in
the same way that a Westerner learns to recognize qualities
deemed desirable by his own culture or class. Knowing what he
is aiming for the Japanese student is then taken through a
standard repertoire with little direct reference to tone quality
except through imitation of his teacher's voice. There are no
warm-up exercises or vocal pedagogies. The entire technique
is learned through the singing of compositions. Pieces are
pitched low at first and then gradually raised. Sometimes the
pupil will be allowed to use falsetto, but he is encouraged to
switch to a natural voice as often as possible. Asakawa recom-
mends singing a song slightly higher than normal when first
learning a piece and then settling on a definite lower starting
pitch for concert use. In this way the singing will seem easier.
Though there are no set tonalities for nagauta pieces, each singer
tends to set his own tonality for the rendition of a particular
number.

Besides the high pitch of a majority of nagauta music, certain
other characteristics should be noted. One is a tendency for the
voice to sing "out of time" with the shamisen. This is not called
a syncopation but rather a form of "neutrality" *(fusoku-furi)*.
Perhaps the Japanese use this term to indicate that the vocal
line is sung without strong rhythmic accents. Actually, it would
be more correct in transcriptions to bar the vocal line in two-

four, starting on the second half of the shamisen's first beat or vice versa as shown in Example 2. One explanation for the development of this rhythmic device is that it allows the words to be heard clearly without being covered by the percussive sounds of the shamisen. Whatever its origins might be, the skillful use of this technique can add greatly to the artistry of a nagauta performance. One must add that the apparently innate tendency for singers all over the world to lag behind makes this technique very dangerous when employed by those who are less skillful.

EXAMPLE 2: *The voice and shamisen rhythmic relationship*

Because of the constant metric discrepancy between the shamisen and the voice, proper control of the tempo is very important. The responsibility for this control in dance performances lies primarily with the head shamisen player. Since his entire repertoire is memorized, he can watch the dancer from his position on the stage and co-ordinate the performance. In concert performances, however, there is a good deal more give and take between the singer and the shamisen. The tempos within one piece may change frequently and there must be a chamber-music-like feeling in the ensemble if the music is to flow smoothly. To assist the setting of tempos the shamisen player uses various short calls *(kakegoe)* which indicate the length of rests and cue in the singers. These calls, along with those of the drummers, have come to be considered as important parts of the overall sound of nagauta compositions.

Another important element in nagauta singing is the manner in which each line is closed, the so-called tail of the melody *(fushi-jiri)*. It is characteristic that each line ends with a short turn often terminating in pitchless sounds. These turns invariably finish below the original pitch, the direct drop of a whole step being the most common and simple mordent. Measure 6 of *Gorō* illustrates such an ending. To a certain extent these cadences provide the singer with opportunities to develop an individual style. There is no "correct" mordent in the sense of something intended by the composer. Instead, there are standard practices and individual idiosyncracies which the vocalist adds in keeping with a sense of nagauta style. The choice of an ending will depend on the surrounding musical phrases and the mood or meaning of the text.

Perhaps the most apparent characteristic of nagauta singing to the Westerner is the wide vibrato usually employed. This technique is also somewhat a matter of taste. In general, every tone of sufficient length is surrounded by a slow, wide, throaty vibrato. Such a convention is in danger of obscuring the subtler deliberate ornamentations of the line, and in the singing of less skillful performers the effect often seems to detract from the music. However, when singers attempt to reduce this vibrato they are found to be in disfavor with the *aficionados*.

Clarity in the delivery of the text is considered a *sine qua non* in contemporary nagauta singing. Asakawa feels that this was not the case in early lyric nagauta.[4] He states that it was only with the appearance of off-stage, solo nagauta of the meriyasu type (see page 21) that serious consideration was given to the clarity of the words. With the further development of jōruri-influenced nagauta the text became even more important.

The poetry of nagauta, even in the most narrative compositions, tends to be epigrammatic. Like most Japanese poetry, it leaves much to be implied by the listener. Its words are often fraught with double meanings, puns, and references which require a rather subtle literary background to appreciate. Because of this, professional singers are quite meticulous about diction, accent, and phrasing. The deliberate shifting of natural word accents á la Stravinsky is not common. Such a device would either change the meaning of the words or reduce the text to meaningless syllables.[5] It should be noted, however, that in certain slow, lyric passages, for example in measures 293–353 of *Tsuru-kame,* vocalises are sung on each syllable of the word so that it would be rather difficult to understand the word without previous knowledge of the text. This elongation of syllables is easily accomplished in Japanese because, like Italian, Japanese is a polysyllabic language with a vowel for almost every consonant. In present-day practice one finds that a majority of the audience is familiar with the text beforehand. Larger professional performances provide program notes which

[4] Asakawa, *Nagauta no Kiso Kenkyū,* p. 162.
[5] In Japanese one sound or sound complex can have many meanings depending on context. The use of long vowels can completely change the meaning as well. The meaning of any word is made clear by the written character, but in orally transmitted texts one must depend on the context.

explain the text and in the case of new pieces print the entire poem. Though the ideal of clarity is still emphasized in naga-uta teaching, one should note that, as in Western opera, the balance between lyricism and enunciation is never very stable.

In addition to the closing ornamentations, the wide vibrato, and the elongation of syllables there are also various shadings and subtleties of interpretation, known collectively as *fushi-mawashi,* which are characteristic of nagauta singing. The most common form of these changes occurs as a gentle undulation of tone on longer cadential notes, for example in measures 104–7 of *Goro.* Others consist of short guttural stops of the tone, slight upward or downward glissandi of the tone, or toneless mordents in preparation for a leap. Such vocal techniques are indicated in some modern notations,[6] but they are often altered by indi-vidual singers. In truth, the exact execution of all vocal music is open to individual interpretation as it is elsewhere in the world. As will be seen, the composition of nagauta is the product of several minds, and to some extent the creative process is con-tinued in performance through the skill of the nagauta vocalists.

A nagauta performance can use any number of singers, the normal number being three. In the music as printed today there are indications of sections to be sung by the main singer, by the secondary singers, or in tutti.[7] Contemporary performance practice tends to treat these indications in a rather cavalier fashion. In pieces derived from noh dramas in which the parts of the two principal actors are indicated and in narrative com-positions where actual dialogues are used, singers tend to assume more specific roles. Since a majority of nagauta texts, however, are commentaries upon a scene or action, reminders of past action, or descriptions of tableaux, the arrangment of solos and tuttis is not vital to the logic of the composition. Lyric, quiet sections, of course, tend to be solo while dramatic moments and finales are almost always tutti. It should be added that in com-positions which include percussion at these moments, the text is usually lost in the instrumental sound, the psychological im-pact of the gestalt being considered of greater significance than the understanding of the text. Unfortunately, modern Japanese recordings are made with the microphone in front of the main singer so that the true effect can only be heard in a live per-formance.

[6] See Yoshizumi Kosaburō, *Nagauta Shin-keikobon* (Tokyo: Hōgaku-sha. 1956), Vols. I–VIII.
[7] See Yoshizumi, *op. cit.* In this notation the first soloist's passages are indicated by the symbol ◯, the other soloists by ▢, and the tutti section by the symbol △.

Since nagauta is primarily theatre music the singer is sometimes required to provide dialogue. This is especially true in concert performances when the interjections of the actors and of the other kinds of musicians on stage are absent.[8] For example, the third line of page 249 of the *Gorō* transcription are performed in a kind of *sprechstimme* characteristic of kabuki declamation. This melodramatic tone is produced by keeping the tone in the throat and, with loose face muscles, by declaiming the line with an exaggerated, indefinite tonal contour.

Compositions closely related to noh pieces often contain passages in imitation of noh singing style. The opening of *Tsurukame* is an example of such an imitation. While the contour of the line looks very similar to that of noh singing, the delivery is only a rough approximation of the more introverted, chantlike style of the noh. In general, it can be said that whenever an element from the noh is taken over by the kabuki it is made more showy and usually is done at a faster tempo. It should be noted that these noh-style passages are either unaccompanied or backed by noh-style percussion parts or ōzatsuma shamisen patterns. The ōzatsuma patterns are also found frequently in the kabuki dialogues mentioned above.

Finally, two other styles of singing found in nagauta pieces should be mentioned, folk music and jōruri narrative styles. In many lighter compositions such as *Utsubozaru, Mitsumen,* and *Kanda Matsuri* there are sections which are meant to depict folk festivals or folk music. In such cases the singer is called upon to speak in a jaunty rhythmic patter song or imitate the highly ornamented style of the slower folk songs. The boat song mentioned earlier in the piece *Kibun Daijin* (Yoshizumi, VIII-6, pp. 2–3) is a good example of the latter technique. Though the melody is written and ornamented in such a folk manner, the singer seldom uses the harsher folk tone quality.

In some of the pieces derived from jōruri there are sections in which the dialogue is given in the style of a jōruri narrator. This style of declamation is similar to that of kabuki except that it is usually not so melodramatic, at least, not when it appears in nagauta music. Page 10 *(op. cit.)* of *Kibun Daijin* illustrates this style.[9] The shamisen accompaniment in such cases is played quietly in an off-stage manner (see Example 1).

Among Japanese vocal styles nagauta singing can be consid-

[8] As was mentioned earlier, nagauta is not the only music used in the kabuki. It is not uncommon to have three different sets of musicians on the stage alternating the style of music used during one play. For a description of such a situation see Malm, *op. cit.*, Chapter IX.

[9] For another discussion of this piece see page 43 ff.

ered as the standard classical technique along with the singing of koto songs. It stands in approximately the same relation to other vocal styles such as noh singing, gidayū, or shinnai as the Western lyric soprano stands to the Gregorian chanter, the romantic tenor, and the *bel canto* coloratura. Western singing style has not as yet seriously influenced nagauta singing except perhaps in regard to intonation. At the present time this vocal tradition is blessed with several excellent singers in both the kabuki and the concert stage.[10] The artistry of these men will do much to assure the continuance of the nagauta vocal tradition.

[10] Since the kabuki runs twelve months a year, twenty-eight days a month, the professional theatre artist seldom has an opportunity to appear in concert performances. Thus, these two traditions have built up rather independent organizations. The extensive vocal projection required in the kabuki makes the sound of a kabuki singer different from that of a concert artist. Because of this, a mixture of the two kinds of singers is sometimes difficult. It reminds one of a similar problem in the West which arose when Italian opera tenors began singing Palestrina or when Wagnerian sopranos performed Bach. Of course, the difference in Japan is that the two kinds of singers are both performing the same music.

CHAPTER FIVE

The Shamisen and Its Music

THE INSTRUMENT

The shamisen is a three-stringed plucked lute with a modified rectangular body and a long unfretted neck. It is the central instrumental component of the nagauta ensemble. Like the violin in the classical Western orchestra, the shamisen produces the basic line and color of the music. In conjunction with the voice it carries the main burden of the melody. Thus, an explanation of its technique and music is important to the full appreciation of nagauta.

The ancestor of the shamisen is the Chinese three-stringed lute, the *san-hsien*. The first known exportation of the san-hsien occurred in 1392[1] when it was included in the chattels of thirty-six families sent by the emperor of China to Okinawa to spread Chinese civilization and manners among the natives. In Okinawa the san-hsien became known as the *samisen*. This instrument was similar to the Chinese model except that it was smaller and had a more oval-shaped body.[2] As was mentioned earlier, this instrument found its way to the Japanese port of Sakai near Osaka around the year 1562. In Japan the instrument was first known as the samisen. Later, the Edo dialect changed the word to shamisen. This is the term used in modern Tokyo while the older pronunciation is found in Kyoto.

The Japanese changed more than just the name of this instrument. Physical innovations in the shamisen enabled it to surpass its ancestors in tone and technical possibilities. This, in turn, had an important effect on the future development of Japanese music. The first of these changes was that the snake-skin heads were replaced by cat or dog hide. These thinner,

---

[1] Tanabe, *Nihon no Ongaku,* p. 285.

[2] There are two types of *san-hsien* in China, one being much larger than the other. However, both are larger than the Ryukyu *samisen*.

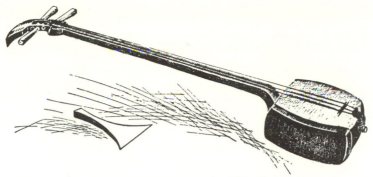

FIGURE 1: *The shamisen*

more sensitive surfaces were found to produce a more brilliant tone. They also reacted better to subtle strokes and slides upon the strings. In order to accommodate such skins the body shape was changed from an oval to a modified rectangle. Four slightly concave pieces of wood were used to construct the body instead of hollowing out one piece as is done for the Ryukyu samisen. The insides of these pieces were carved with special patterns called *ayasugi*, which further refined the tone of the instrument.

The traditional explanation for the change in skins is that the early Japanese shamisen players, being converted biwa-lute musicians, broke the snake skins with their heavy plectrums. Since large snakes were not plentiful in Japan other hides had to be tried. Eventually cat and dog were found to be the most satisfactory.

Another important innovation in the shamisen is also credited to the biwa background of its early players. This is the addition of a buzzing tone *(sawari)* characteristic of the biwa, particularly when played on the lowest string. The shamisen, with its long, thin neck and relatively small body, could not produce such a resonance naturally. Therefore, a special niche was cut into the neck just below the peg box as shown in Figure 2. In addition, a metal ridge was inserted part way along the edge of the peg box so that the upper strings were lifted above the carved out section of the neck, while the lowest string remained touching both sides of the hollow. This arrangement resulted in a biwa-like buzzing caused by the alternate touching of the two sides of this hollow by the lowest string as it vibrated.[3]

[3] Apparently the upper bridge was used alone at first and the niche was added in the eighteenth century. See Kikkawa Eishi, "An Introduction to the Research of the Shamisen," *Tōyō Ongaku Kenkyū* (Dec., 1958), Nos. 14–15, p. 60.

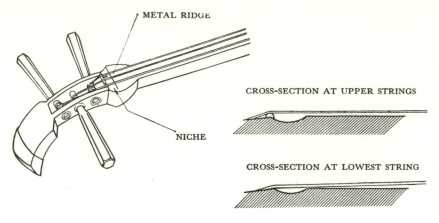

METAL RIDGE

NICHE

CROSS-SECTION AT UPPER STRINGS

CROSS-SECTION AT LOWEST STRING

FIGURE 2: *The peg-box niche of a shamieen*

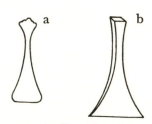

a   b

FIGURE 3: *Evolution of the shamisen plectrum*

A third innovation also reflects the influence of biwa music. This is the use of a large biwa type of plectrum. The sanhsien and Ryukyu samisen both used a finger pick made of bone or ivory. The shamisen, however, is first seen as being played with a flat wooden plectrum of the type associated with Heike- and court-biwa playing. The shape of this plectrum is shown in Figure 3 a. Later, more powerful plectrums *(bachi)* were developed by widening the playing edge and pointing the tips as shown in Figure 3 b. This arrangement allowed added force to the blow for volume while keeping a relatively thin and pointed section of the plectrum in actual contact with the string. This created a brilliant tone and at the same time allowed for greater virtuosity through alternate up and down strokes. Another important effect of this kind of plectrum is that its flat surface makes a percussive sound when it strikes against the skin immediately after plucking the string. This half-melodic, half-percussive sound is characteristic of the shamisen tone. The contemporary practice plectrum is made of three pieces of wood so joined that the rear has weight for balance while the edge has resiliency for tone. Concert plectrums are made of ivory.

As the different shamisen music styles developed, both the

plectrum and the shamisen were modified to produce the special tone qualities required. The earlier shamisen used for jōruri and popular music were generally larger in build than the present-day nagauta shamisen, with thicker skins and blunt plectrums. This type can best be seen today in gidayū music. The differences in shamisen are designated by the thickness of their necks, though other features are altered as well. The modern nagauta shamisen is a middle-sized *(chūzao)* instrument, the neck averaging 2.5 cm. in width and 75 cm. in length. The body is 18.5 cm. across at its widest point, and 9.5 cm. deep.

Other distinctions to be found in the various shamisen are the gauge of their strings and the size of their bridges. Nagauta strings come in three main gauges for use on the three positions. They are made of twisted silk or nylon. The nagauta bridge is rather light and made of ivory or plastic. There are varying sizes used according to individual taste.[4] However, nagauta bridges are never found to be as heavy as those used for gidayū and jiuta music.

EXAMPLE 3: *The three main shamisen tunings*

There are three normal tunings for the shamisen, shown in Example 3. They are a perfect fourth and a fifth (hon-chōshi, original tuning), a fifth and a fourth (ni-agari, raise the second), and two perfect fourths (san-sagari, lower the third). Other special tunings are found such as ichi-sagari, lower the first. These occur more often in modern pieces. In all such cases the meaning of the tuning can be ascertained by beginning with hon-chōshi and applying the instructions. One cannot speak of definite pitches for shamisen tunings, as the pitch of each performance, as was mentioned, is dependent upon the singer. The twelve basic pitches from which the basic note is chosen are known as *hon,* the numerator for long round things like strings or poles. These hon are heard as absolute pitches by professional nagauta musicians. Thus, if a singer wishes a piece to be in *nihon* or *sambon,* hon number two or three, the shamisen player can tune to the desired pitch (B flat or B natural). Before the twentieth century these pitches were not the same as those of

[4] A chart of string gauges and bridge weights preferred by leading performers can be found on page 130 of the *Tōyō Ongaku Kenkyū* (Dec., 1958), Nos. 14–15.

the Western tempered chromatic scale, but today they have been "adjusted" to the tempered system.[5] Tonal differences remain not in the basic tunings but in the playing of scales based on such pitches. However, the classic sense of scale intervals is likewise waning.

Shamisen music uses two basic scales, $yō$ and in,[6] as shown in Example 4. These scales use five basic tones of which two are variable and are in effect seven-toned scales from which pentatonic series are extracted. Modes are formed by beginning on the perfect fourth or fifth above the base tone as shown in Example 5. These are called plagal modes by Dr. Tanabe (see footnote 6). Modulation is also an important part of shamisen music, especially in the larger genres such as nagauta. These modulations are almost always to and from some form of the in scale, since in general it is the most prevalent in nagauta. Example 6 shows the basic modulatory scales found in nagauta with the note E being used as a hypothetical base tone. These scales and their uses will be discussed in greater detail during the analytic portions of this study. Before leaving this topic, however, it might be interesting to compare the concept of tunings mentioned above with the concept of scales as shown in Example 6. For the sake of this comparison we shall consider the opening tunings and the pitch centers of the first sections of the pieces only and E will be taken as the basic tonic.

Of the one hundred nagauta pieces studied fifty-eight began in hon-chōshi, twenty-one in ni-agari, eighteen in san-sagari, and three in ichi-sagari. Those pieces in hon-chōshi all began with the pitch center E, often modulated to B, and returned to E or ended on a half cadence in E at the end of the first section (the oki). The pieces beginning in ni-agari all began in either B or F sharp. Those starting in B often ended the first section in F sharp, thus following the same tonic to dominant pattern relationship found in hon-chōshi, except that the pitch is a fifth higher. The pieces in san-sagari were less consistent. All, however, used the pitch center A sometime during the opening section. Two of the three pieces in ichi-sagari begin in B, though one, *Kibun Daijin,* modulates greatly during the opening

[5] The author has observed the head shamisen player of the sacrosanct Tokyo kabuki theatre tune his ensemble with a chromatic pitch pipe.

[6] These two terms are the present-day Japanese nomenclature for the words *ritsu* and *zokugaku* scales found in Noel Peri's *Essai sur les gammes Japonaise,* Bibliotheque Musicale de Musée Guimet, . . . Series 2, No. 1. Paris: Geuthner, 1934. 70 pp. The author's concept of the Japanese modulation system is based primarily on his own analysis, although Japanese opinions were also considered. See Tanabe, *op. cit.,* pp. 50–65 and Shimofusa Kanichi. "Nihon Minyō to Onkai no Kenkyū," *Ongaku Bunka,* No. 75 (Tokyo: Ongaku no Tomo-sha, 1954), 105 pp.

EXAMPLE 4: *The yō and in scales*

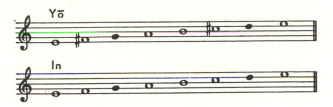

EXAMPLE 5: *Plagal modes in shamisen music*

EXAMPLE 6: *Basic modulatory scales in nagauta*

shamisen solo. The third piece, *Haru no Uta,* hovers around A.

It is evident from this study that, as far as the standard tunings are concerned, there are definite tonal reasons for the choice of tunings. Thus, in the analyses of entire compositions one can expect the change of tunings within each piece to indicate particular modulations. Also, the fact that a majority of pieces do change sunings (usually at the odoriji) shows that modulation is linked to form in a manner similar to that found in Western art music.

Before leaving the topic of tunings one should mention that

under the Japanese theory of ethos hon-chōshi is said to be best suited for solemn music, ni-agari for gay sections, and san-sagari for melancholy or serene music. While shamisen musicians say that they feel this theory to be true, a majority of changes in tuning seem to have little to do with their basic "mood," at least, if one can judge from the accompanying texts. One can cite the many sentimental meriyasu pieces that appear in san-sagari, gay dances such as the end of *Kanda Matsuri* (Yoshizumi, VIII-7), and solemn dances such as measures 519–75 of *Tsuru-kame*. In general, however, the Japanese theory of ethos, like the Western concept of happiness and sadness connected with major and minor scales, seems to be merely a rule of thumb which cannot be taken in too doctrinal a manner.

The playing technique of the shamisen consists basically of plucking the string with the plectrum held in the right hand and fingering along the neck with the middle three fingers of the left hand. Added refinements include the sliding of the left hand along the neck while holding down a finger on a string. This produces a glissando (see measure 44 of *Tsuru-kame*). Left-hand pizzicatos are common as are tones produced by striking a finger against the string immediately above a note already produced by a plectrum stroke. This effect makes a subtle grace note to the main pitch as seen in measures 86–87 of *Tsuru-kame*. Double and triple stops are used sparingly. Both up and down strokes with the plectrum are employed. The kouta style of playing is also heard on occasions. This softer sound is created by plucking the string with the right index finger only or with a small pick.

As indicated in the historical chapter, notation for the shamisen was rare until the twentieth century. Where it did exist it consisted of a solfège system which indicated rhythm but usually not specific pitches. Out of this system grew *kuchi-jamisen,* mouth shamisen, a method still in wide use today. It is an Edo version of the onomatopoetic syllables *(shōka)* used in ancient Japanese court music to help musicians in memorizing their parts.[7] Present-day kuchi-jamisen is organized as shown in Table 6. Nagauta musicians use these sounds as a frame of reference to specific passages both in conversation and in publications.[8]

---

[7] For a report on the development of *shōka* through Buddhist primary schools see Elizabeth May, *Japanese Children's Music Before and After Contact with the West* (Ph. D. dissertation, University of California, 1958), pp. 2–9.

[8] See, for example, the two volume study of nagauta pieces by Kineya Eizō, *Nagauta no Utaikata* (Tokyo: Sōgen-sha, 1932). In speaking with Japanese musicians concerning nagauta the author could never use "la, la, la" or "do, re, me." Only "ton, chiri, rin, tsu, ton" was understood.

In the twentieth century several attempts were made to notate shamisen music in a more accurate manner. Unadulterated Western-style notation was found to be unsatisfactory, not only because of the specific pitch connotations but also because of the difficulty in giving the proper rhythmic freedom to the vocal line. The two most successful and widespread systems used today are the so-called Kosaburōfu and bunkafu.[9] Kosaburōfu is written in Japanese style, starting from the right-hand corner and reading down, while bunkafu is written in the Western manner. Both use Arabic numerals, the first to indicate pitches, the second to indicate finger positions. Rhythm, fingering, and special effects all have specific signs. The voice part parallels that of the shamisen but is unmeasured to leave it rhythmically free. Both systems are admirably suited to the music for which they were designed.

TABLE 6: *The organization of kuchi-jamisen*

	downstroke open	fingered	upstroke open	upstroke fingered	left hand open	pizzicato fingered
1ST STRING	*ton* or *don*	*tsun*	*ren*	*ro*	*ren*	*rin*
2ND STRING	*ton*	*tsun*	*ren*	*run*	*ren*	*rin*
3RD STRING	*ten*	*chin* or *chi*	*ren*	*ri*	*ren*	*rin*

Double stops are *shan*

In nagauta notation one will frequently see what appears to be a divisi section in the shamisen part. The added line is the music of the uwajōshi shamisen, an obbligato instrument. It differs from the normal shamisen only in that an extra nut *(kase)* has been attached part way up the neck so that the instrument may be played an octave higher than the rest of the shamisen. Generally, the uwajōshi part is merely an elaboration of the basic melody though it may also be heard acting as a drone as, for example, in measures 40–70 of *Gorō*. In certain rare cases it plays an independent melody. For instance, it plays the theme from the koto piece "Rokudan" in the middle of the nagauta piece *Sukeroku* (Yoshizumi, III–4, p. 9). The reason for this novel bit of independence seems to be the fact that the titles of both pieces contain the number six *(roku)*. Despite these interesting exceptions the basic function of this shamisen is found to be heterophonic. The difficulty in playing uwajōshi parts lies in the fact that, while the melody is often closely re-

[9] A further explanation and examples can be seen in Malm, *op. cit.*, pp. 273–74.

lated to the piece as originally learned by the player, the tuning is usually different in order to make it easier to play an octave higher. Thus, playing the uwajōshi part involves totally new fingerings. Occasionally the shamisen part is further subdivided into three or more parts as in the latter part of *Echigojishi*.[10] The normal division, however, is two, and even this occurs only in instrumental interludes as a rule.

The nagauta shamisen could be called the violin of Japan. It is studied by many amateurs as a means of recreation and refinement. Until recently there was some resistance to its use among upper-class families who considered it too much of a geisha or theatre instrument. Despite the heavy inroads of Western music, shamisen-music publishers continue to flourish and all department stores have a row of factory built instruments for sale along with the ukuleles, trumpets, and saxophones. The maintenance of a tradition of fine instrument making still resides in the hands of private shamisen artisans. While not as numerous as in the Edo period, they are still kept busy with the demand for quality workmanship. It is hoped that their special skill will not fall victim to the further industrialization of Japan. At the present time, a good shamisen can be considered as equal to the finer products of instrument makers in other cultures.

SHAMISEN MUSIC

Shamisen music has been said to be not composition but merely an arrangement of stereotyped patterns.[11] While this view will be shown to be extreme, it does point up the fact that much of shamisen music involves the use of previously existing material.

The historical precedent for the use of melodic patterns is found in most pre-shamisen Japanese music styles. Perhaps the closest direct influence came from the biwa-lute tradition, particularly that of Heike-biwa music. This music consisted of short patterns and longer interludes, each with a special name which were used primarily between chanted lines of the text.[12] This means of musical organization is still found in the contemporary

[10] This can be seen in Western notation in number 3 of *Nagauta Gakufū*, Yoshizumi Kōjūrō, ed. (Tokyo: Yamada Shunhei, 1926).

[11] Kikkawa Eishi, "Samisen and Samisen Music," *KBS Bulletin*, No. 6 (June, 1952), pp. 5–6.

[12] An outline of Heike-biwa music can be found in the *Ongaku Jiten*, 9 (1956), p. 211. See also Kanetsune, *Nihon no Ongaku*, pp. 1–131. The names of many shamisen patterns are borrowed directly from the biwa tradition which in turn adopted titles from the nomenclature of earlier Buddhist and noh-drama music.

Chikuzen and Satsuma schools of biwa. As the tradition flourished special versions of certain patterns were created for particular pieces. When the same principles (and sometimes the same names and melodies) were applied to early jōruri music this proliferation of patterns became even more intense. To this day the puppet theatre music of gidayū is notated by pattern names even though the sophistication of the music has created extreme differences between the various versions of the same pattern.

The best study of the origin and growth of such standard melodies in shamisen music is the series of six lectures given by Machida Kashō before the 1955 meetings of the Society for Research in Asiatic Music of Japan.[13] Machida[14] shows in this series how a name could originate in some older form such as itchū, katō, or gidayū (he does not discuss pre-shamisen origins) and then be passed on through a series of other musics. Sometimes it maintained its musical outlines and sometimes it became greatly altered. For example, the pattern *reisei* as found in the katō-bushi piece *Matsu no Uchi* of 1718 is shown in Example 7 a. The nagauta piece *Tokiwa no Niwa* of 1852 uses the same named pattern as shown in Example 7 b. Over the intervening 134 years little change can be seen. However, in the earlier 1829 nagauta piece, *Azuma Hakkei,* shown in Example 7 c, one finds the opening phrase of reisei clearly stated but followed by different material. Machida does not make it clear whether the word reisei was actually used to notate this phrase in this example or in Example 7 d, but they obviously bear some relationship to the original melody. Example 7 d is taken from a shinnai-bushi composition *Kami-jiuchi* of the late eighteenth century.[15] Here one finds the first phrase less clearly indicated. The final example (7 e) is drawn from a reisei section of the tomimoto piece *Sono Omokage Asamagatake* of 1779. Though it is the closest in age to the first katō-bushi pattern, it is the most distant musically. The reason for the change in this case is that tomimoto music is characterized by an extreme simplicity. Because of this the original pattern had to be "toned down" to fit in the style.

In cases like Examples 7c and 7d it is common to find the word *kakari* or *gakari* attached to the pattern name. This means "based on the style of" and is found throughout the nagauta

[13] Machida Kashō, *Shamisen Seikyoku no Senritsukei no Kenkyū.* Mimeographed supplement to meetings 42–47 of the Tōyō Ongaku Gakkai (Tokyo, 1955), 6 vols.

[14] *Ibid.,* Vol. I, Examples 44, 45, 51, 58, and 54.

[15] See "Ten no Amijima," *Ongaku Jiten,* 7 (1956), p. 87.

EXAMPLE 7: *Examples of the pattern reisei*

repertoire whenever the style of another music or the contour of some standard melody is employed. For example, measures 13–20 of *Tsuru-kame* are known as Edo-gakari in the bungo, tomimoto, and nagauta traditions. The pattern seems to come from an earlier katō melody which was itself not titled, though it appeared in many katō pieces.[16] Melodically, it would seem to relate to one of the eighteen varieties of *yuri* patterns *(yuri, han-yuri, nanatsu-yuri, yuri-kaeshi,* etc.) listed in the *Edobushi Kongenki* of 1812.[17] However, for the purpose of understanding the compositional structure of nagauta shamisen music the historical origins of these shorter patterns is not essential. Indeed, as was hinted earlier, the cavalier manner in which the nomenclature of these patterns is applied to the music complicates the historical picture badly. On the other hand, the use of these patterns within the nagauta repertoire is of great importance.

The best-known and most-used set of borrowed patterns in nagauta are the so-called forty-eight ōzatsuma-te derived from the now defunct ōzatsuma-bushi tradition. These patterns are the basis of every recitative or extended transition section in nagauta; in fact, some pieces such as *Tsunayakata* (Yoshizumi, V–2 and *Mochizuki* (Yoshizumi, VII–7) are made up almost entirely of such patterns. Because of their frequent use they have been transcribed and are included in Part IV. These transcriptions are based on a list of Kineya Eizō[18] and personal inquiries among nagauta musicians. Since some of the patterns appear only in older, special pieces it was difficult to find informants who were able and willing to divulge the actual melody despite a rather possessive attitude toward the special pieces. As in the

---

[16] See Machida, *Shamisen Seikyoku no Senritsukei no Kenkyū,* Vol. III, items 4–13. Note that two of these items are derived from well-known nagauta pieces, namely *Yoshiwara Suzume* and *Ataka no Matsu.*

[17] *Ibid.,* II, quoted after item 3.

[18] Kineya Eizō, *op. cit.,* I, p. 257 ff. Kineya claims to have derived his list from that of Kineya Rokuzaemon the eleventh (1829–77), who was a famous composer of ōzatsuma-style pieces.

case of other patterns discussed so far, these melodies are open to variation as they are used in different pieces. Nevertheless, the hard core of ōzatsuma patterns remain standard[19] and characteristic of nagauta narrative and transitional sections.

Ōzatsuma patterns are divided into nine classifications as follows:

1. *jo,* 7 types
2. *kakari,* 5 types
3. *ji,* 12 types
4. *te,* 6 types
5. *tataki,* 2 types
6. *sanjū,* 4 types
7. *otoshi,* 6 types
8. *musubi,* 4 types
9. *dangire,* 2 types

The jo patterns are used for introductory music. For example, the opening of *Gorō* uses the best-known jo pattern. *Tobijo* can be found as the first shamisen notes of the piece *Kanjinchō* (Yoshizumi, V–3), and *nanorijo* appears as the first notes of the piece *Oimatsu* (Yoshizumi, II–2). The introduction of *Hashi Benkei* (Yoshizumi, III–8) consists of the pattern *daijo.* It is interesting to note that the patterns *tataki* and *tataki yaharigi-iroji* as transcribed seem to be outgrowths of this shorter jo pattern. Such close relations between patterns often makes it difficult to assign names to patterns unidentified in the original notation. For example, while the yawaragijo pattern is easy to recognize, one must be on guard not to confuse the pattern *hikiagejo* with *sanjū* shown later.

The kakari motives as used in ōzatsuma[20] appear more often at the beginning of a phrase within a composition. For example, measures 312–20 of *Gorō* are a variation of the *kimoigakari* pattern. The pure kakari pattern is used right after the vocal introduction to *Shakkyō* (Yoshizumi, V–5, p. 2).

The ji (base) patterns are those used most frequently to accompany recitative sections. An excellent example of this can be seen in measures 261–92 of *Tsuru-kame.* The accompaniment for this section consists of the following patterns, played in the order listed: *honji, kiriji, wariji, sekaji* (altered), *honji, kakeji, kiriji.*

These patterns, like the chords of eighteenth-century Western opera recitatives, support the words without hampering the

---

[19] In 1868 these patterns were so standard that a system of forty-eight symbols was devised which could be written along with the text as a kind of Japanese figured bass. See Iba, *op. cit.,* p. 502.

[20] Not to be confused with the *kakari* discussed earlier on pages 65–66.

rhythmic freedom of the narrator. Notice that there are "tonic" and "dominant" functions in these patterns. Honji states the tonic, in this transcription it is B, but immediately goes to the fifth, F sharp. Kiriji re-establishes the B tonic. The next two patterns take the music away from B for a longer time. Honji reappears, a more exotic form of the dominant is heard, and then a full cadence is achieved with another kiriji pattern. As will be pointed out in the study of the music of the other naga-uta instruments, this sense of progression from release to tension and back to release is well evolved in most areas of this sophisticated art music.

The te patterns are found most frequently in free-rhythm sections of introductions or extended cadences. Measures 7 and 9 of *Gorō* consist of the pattern *honte*, and measure 10 is *honte-oshigasane*. This is followed by a ji pattern and then *tobi-taki* is used, one of the two tataki patterns.[21] These tataki motives are always used to confirm the tonality of a cadence.

The four sanjū patterns are found at the opening of compositions, for example, at the beginning of *Mochizuki* (Yoshizumi, VII–7) or as free instrumental interludes in rather dramatic pieces, as is seen in *Kuramayama* (Yoshizumi, I–9, p. 11). In the kabuki the interludes used to consume time while the actor is changing costume are called *sanjū*. In such cases the shamisen player may begin with the ōzatsuma sanjū but will extend it in an improvisatory fashion. This is one of the few places where such liberty is allowed the nagauta musician. The term sanjū, by the way, has a long history in Japanese music dating back to early Buddhist music.[22]

The otoshi patterns, like the tataki group, are cadential though they usually are shorter than the former. Example 8 a shows the *chū-otoshi* pattern as used in *Kanjinchō* and Example 8 b shows the use of otoshi in the same piece. Measures 120–23 of *Tsuru-kame* are an example of a variation on the first pattern.

The musubi patterns lead to cadences as well. Example 8 c shows *ryo musubi-nagashi* used in such a manner in *Kanjinchō*. It is interesting to note that the first two musubi patterns use the words *ryo* and *ritsu*, old terms indicative of two scale systems. These two patterns cadence a fifth apart in the same relation as the scale ritsu is to ryo.[23]

The dangire patterns are reserved for final cadences. A

---

[21] Actually, one can say that there are two additional tataki patterns in numbers 11 and 12 of the ji patterns, especially number 12 since its function is so strongly cadential.

[22] See *Ongaku Jiten*, 4 (1955), p. 192.

[23] See *Ongaku Jiten*, 11 (1957), pp. 125, 159.

majority of nagauta pieces use at least the last six measures of this pattern at the finale as, for example, in the ending of *Tsuru-kame,* measure 752. There are other cadences, however, which are part of the dangire section of a composition but they need not necessarily be derived from these *ōzatsuma* patterns. An example of this type can be seen in the ending of *Gorō,* measure 519. The tuning of the shamisen, as was mentioned, makes a difference in the final cadence. For example, the standard hon-chōshi ending pattern is given in Example 9 a. Notice its similarity to the ōzatsuma dangire. The standard ni-agari ending is shown in Example 9 b. This pattern makes a cadence a fifth higher than Example 9 a.

The san-sagari cadence will vary depending on whether this tuning is preceded by hon-chōshi or ni-agari.[24] If it follows a ni-agari tuning the ending will be similar to Example 9 c, particularly in the fact that it will cadence on the fourth above the hon-chōshi tonic, in these transcriptions A above E. Example 9 c is of particular interest because it is played with exactly the same fingering as Example 9 b. The tuning alone creates the new pitches. Example 9 d shows a san-sagari ending after a hon-chōshi tuning. It can be noted in this case that the final is the same as that of a hon-chōshi cadence. Example 9 e gives another version of such a case more clearly related to the pattern as seen in Examples 9 a and 9 b.

As was pointed out concerning the opening tunings in relation to pitch center, it becomes evident that final tunings are

[24] Except for short meriyasu pieces, nagauta compositions are seldom completely in san-sagari. *Echigojishi* is the only noted exception the author has found so far.

EXAMPLE 9: *Standard shamisen endings and tunings*

a. SUEHIROGARI (Yoshizumi I–2, p. 6)

b. HANA NO TOMO (Yoshizumi 1–6, p. 4)

c. AKI NO IROGUSA (Yoshizumi III–1, p. 5)

d. SUKEROKU (Yoshizumi III–4, p. 12)

e. DANGIRE (Ongaku Jiten, 11, p. 193)

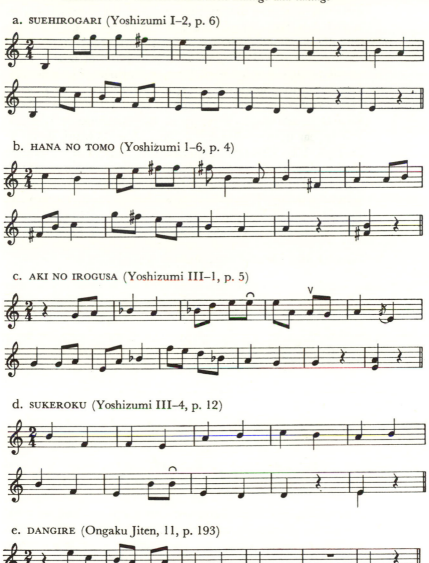

usually chosen in order to arrive at a specific final and that the patterns leading to the final cadence will be affected by this desired pitch center.

What has been said concerning beginning and ending patterns will be found to be generally true in other parts of the composition—patterns will be chosen not only to indicate a particular section of the form but also because they lead to certain pitches. For example, there is a pattern called tataki (apparently unrelated to the ōzatsuma pattern of the same name) which appears at the beginning of a majority of slower, more lyrical phrases. Its standard form is shown in Example 10a. This pattern is found, for example, at measure 57 of *Hana no Tomo* (Yoshizumi, I–6, p. 3) and at measures 292 and 244 of *Sukeroku* (Yoshizumi, III–4, pp. 6, 7). Variations on this pattern appear in many forms, the most common being shown in Example 10b. This form is found at measure 160 in *Hana no Tomo* and at measure 123 of *Aki no Irogusa* (Yoshizumi, III–1, p. 2) to mention but a few instances. Another version can be found at measure 120 of *Gorō*. Moreover, the same pattern can appear at a different pitch level as at measure 270 of *Wakanatsumi* (Yoshizumi, I–8, p. 4) and measure 390 of *Tsuru-kame*.

EXAMPLE 10: *The slow tataki patterns*

From the few examples given above one can see how the accusation of pattern arranging instead of composition was leveled at nagauta musicians. One can also see that these patterns give the composer a set of signals with which he can guide the enlightened listener through the different formal sections and moods desired. Such an approach to composition was common to Western music from the baroque through much of the romantic period, the difference being that the West relied primarily on harmonic techniques. The tremolo diminished chord became as indispensable to dramatic moments in romantic operas as the tonic six-four chord was a necessary herald of the cadenza in concertos. The perception of fugue, dance, and sonata-allegro forms was dependent on certain presumed harmonic sequences which signalled the beginning or ending of specific sections. To be sure, thematic material and its handling entered very greatly into the perception of form as well. Indeed, melody types were the essence of the baroque *Affectenlehre* and Wagner's leitmotiv technique.

Given a music without significant harmonies and without thematic development one can see that the use of stereotyped melodies became a very important and logical method of establishing the mood and formal progress of nagauta music. Taking an even broader view, one could say that as Western music evolved harmonic and thematic traditions of ever increasing complexity, so Japanese music from the early days of Buddhist chant to the flowering of the eighteenth-century theatre music developed the power of melodic reference, not within a single piece, but within an entire repertoire.

When one analyzes a nagauta piece, as will be done in Part III of this study, one finds that between the main formal patterns there appears original music or lesser patterns chosen for their consistency with the mood and formal location. If the structure of nagauta music were merely this it would be an interesting but not a particularly sophisticated form. However, so we have considered only the main shamisen music in isolation. It is time now to turn to the rest of the nagauta ensemble and see in what way it contributes to the structure of the music.

CHAPTER SIX

Drums of the Hayashi Ensemble

SOME OF the most exciting and spectacular music of the kabuki emanates from a group of three drummers and a flutist who form the lower tier of musicians on the stage. The variety of tones produced on the drums, the unworldly melodies of the flute, and the attentuated calls of the drummers form an exotic and, at first, mystifying element in the overall sound of kabuki music. This is the music of the hayashi, a vital undercurrent of rhythm and color which helps to speed kabuki music along its course.

The term hayashi is used in Japanese to indicate all kinds of small music ensembles usually made up of various flutes, drums, and gongs. In the kabuki, it refers primarily to the stage ensemble of one flute and three drums mentioned above. This ensemble was borrowed directly from the noh-drama instrumental group of the same name. As will be seen, some of the music was borrowed as well and was mixed with original kabuki hayashi patterns. The kabuki added the folk bamboo flute *(takebue)* to the group as an alternate instrument for the noh flutist. One could include the drummers' voices as part of the ensemble, since the calls (kakegoe) of the drummers are essential to both the aesthetic and the structure of the music.

THE Ō-TSUZUMI AND KO-TSUZUMI

The primary drum of the hayashi is the ko-tsuzumi, the small drum. It has an hourglass-shaped body and two horsehide heads. These are lashed to the body by means of a rope that passes back and forth between them. A second rope encircles the drum. It is used to apply tension to the skins so that the drum tones may be varied. The tones are further altered by directing blows to the center or edge of the drum with one to three fingers

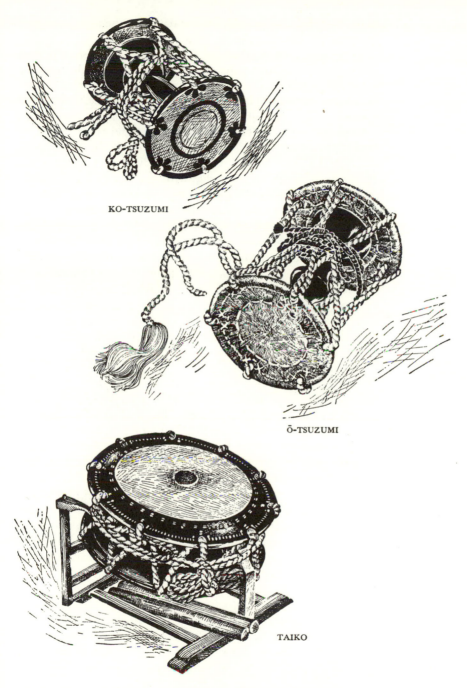

KO-TSUZUMI

Ō-TSUZUMI

TAIKO

FIGURE 4: *The drums of the hayashi ensemble*

of the right hand while holding the drum on the right shoulder, gripping the encircling ropes with the left hand.

There are four basic tones used in ko-tsuzumi music. The first is *pon,* played by hitting the center of the drum while applying a sudden, slight pressure on the encircling ropes which is immediately released. This produces a waver to the tone which is considered to be the *pièce de resistance* of ko-tsuzumi music. The second tone on the ko-tsuzumi is *pu* and is produced by hitting the center of the drum lightly with the index finger of the right hand with little rope tension. The next sound is *chi.* It is played lightly on the edge with one finger and stronger rope tension. The final sound is *ta* which is played strongly on the edge with two fingers and maximum rope tension.

The production of these tones requires a very subtle coordination of movements in addition to a skillful adjustment of the instrument itself. All the ropes must be tied at just the right tension for stage and weather conditions. A good illustration of the sensitivity of this drum is the fact that it must be tuned at every performance by the addition to the rear head of a small piece of paper *(chōshigami)* which has been moistened in the mouth. The addition or subtraction of one layer of this paper will have a significant effect upon the drum's tone.

The companion to this drum is the ō-tsuzumi, the large drum. It also has an hourglass-shaped body and two heads lashed to the body by ropes. However, the body is larger and the skins, usually cowhide, are much thicker. They are lashed very tightly against the body and are further tightened by a smaller rope which pulls together five strands of the lashing rope. In addition, the skins are usually heated before the performance so that they will best produce the sharp, dry, metallic sound so characteristic of this drum. The drum is held on the left hip with the left hand and struck with with one or two fingers of the right hand. Papier mâché thimbles are often worn by the players to increase the dryness of the drum's tone. There are two basic tones for the ō-tsuzumi, *tsu* which is played lightly and *chon* which is very strong.

THE TAIKO

The taiko stick drum is a barrel drum with two cowhide skins lashed to the body by an interlacing rope. Like the ō-tsuzumi, further tension is exerted on the skins by a second encircling rope which pulls the lashing rope closer to the body.[1] The re-

---

[1] Details concerning the tying of this drum can be found in Komparu Sōichi, *op. cit.,* pp. 9–17.

sultant high, crisp sound is softened slightly by a patch of deer-skin in the center of the playing head to which all the blows are directed. The classic noh taiko is played with two sticks (bachi) approximately 32 cm. in length and 2.5 cm. in diameter. In kabuki two thinner sticks are sometimes used instead to imitate the sound of folk or festival music.

There are three basic levels of strokes used on the taiko, small *(shō)*, medium *(chū)*, and large *(dai)*. Theoretically, these produce a corresponding amount of volume. In actual practice the small and medium tend to overlap. However, the physical movement involved in playing these different strokes is carefully regulated and the proper execution of taiko music by a professional is as pleasing to the eye as to the ear.

One distinctive characteristic of the smaller strokes is that the stick is allowed to remain on the head after the blow. This creates a very slight one-stick roll as the stick bounces. Such playing is called *osaeru,* pressing down. When a series of such strokes are played there is a tendency to accent the left hand (the right hand begins on the beat). Another common stroke is *kesu* in which both sticks are placed on the head lightly to deaden the tone. This stroke usually precedes the most spectacular movement, *kashira,* the taiko form of cadence. Kashira begins with both sticks rising from the drum. When they reach chest level the right stick returns to the drumhead while the left stick is placed behind the right shoulder. When the left stick reaches the shoulder the right stick suddenly rises over the head, poised for a large stroke. However, the left stick shoots away from the shoulder and gives the drum a strong glancing blow which is then followed by a large stroke with the right stick. This movement combined with the drum shouts (see measure 22 of *Tsuru-kame*) is always an exciting moment in nagauta or noh performances.

Though the taiko strokes are known by the names mentioned above, nagauta musicians tend to refer to stick-drum music in the mnemonic terms used to teach it. Thus, the small strokes are *tsu* (right hand) and *ku* (left), the middle-sized strokes are *te* (right) and *re* (left), and the large strokes are *ten* (see measures 39–52 of *Gorō*).

PERCUSSION MUSIC

The music for the three drums of the nagauta ensemble provides some of the most interesting material for analysis in all Japanese music and illustrates several unique Japanese approaches to music structure.

The drum music of nagauta is classified as serving one of two functions. The first is to accompany entrances and exits and help to delineate the character of the person on stage. Such music is called *deiri-bayashi*. The other function is to accompany dances. This music is called *maigoto-bayashi*. Both these functions are derivative of the uses of hayashi in the noh drama. This derivation is reflected, for example, in the deiri-bayashi nomenclature which uses such terms as shidai and issei, both names of entrance sections in the noh drama. The dance-music tradition is derived most closely from the dance (mai) sections of noh plays as well as from the intervals *(ma)* between verses of a noh play during which the hayashi plays short interludes.

Though this music may have originated in the noh tradition, it has added much in the way of its own style. Actually, the nagauta (kabuki) hayashi distinguishes between music that is derivative of the noh, called *hongyō,* and music which originated in the kabuki, called *honrai*. With these distinctions in mind it is best now to look at the music itself in more detail. For this purpose the music of the two tsuzumi will be studied first, followed by that of the taiko, and, finally, the music of all three will be viewed in relation to the overall structure of the music.

The two tsuzumi can be considered as one rhythmic unit, because, although they do perform independently sometimes, their basic use in nagauta is as a team and the organization of their music is the same.

Tsuzumi music derived from the noh consists of a number of stereotyped rhythmic patterns usually set in a frame of eight beats.[2] These patterns are found frequently in nagauta pieces derived from noh dramas, although their use is not restricted to such compositions. Neither are they kept separate from the other patterns, but they are mixed within one piece with patterns of purely kabuki origin.

Patterns derived from the noh have names as they do in noh music. These names usually, though not always, refer to the same rhythm patterns in both musics. However, each school of kabuki drumming[3] has developed minor variations in the performance of these various patterns, so that it is impossible to say which version is "correct" except in a sectarian manner. These differences are internal and do not alter the length of the phrase, so that two drummers from different schools can play

[2] For greater details see the author's, "The Rhythmic Orientation of Two Drums in the Japanese No Drama," *Ethnomusicology* (Sept., 1958), pp. 89–95.
[3] At present there are three main schools of kabuki drumming, the Tanaka, Mochizuki, and Tosa of which the first two are most active in Tokyo. The author studied under the Tanaka school.

together. Primarily these variations serve to assert the guild identity of the performer without interfering with the overall performance.

EXAMPLE 11: *Two versions of the pattern uchioroshi-tsune*

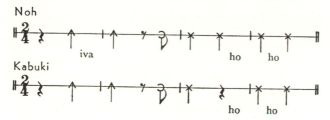

The variations between noh and kabuki versions of the same pattern appear to be slight when seen in notation. For instance, Example 11 shows the noh version (Kō school) and the kabuki version (Tanaka school) of the ko-tsuzumi pattern called *uchi-oroshi-tsune*.[4] In addition to the variation of beat six and the omission of one drum call, these versions vary in certain manners of performance not evident in the notation. For example, the voice quality of the drum calls is different, the noh style usually being more elaborate and attenuated. Also, the tempo of the noh version will tend to be slower. As was said earlier, in general, noh elements borrowed by the kabuki are speeded up and made more appealing to the general populace.

Example 11, it will be noted, is in the classical eight-beat frame of noh music. Other characteristic noh phenomena are the placement of the drum calls (kakegoe) and the degrees of activity on each beat. Classically, drum calls appear before the third, fifth, and seventh beats. In keeping with the introduction-scattering-finale theory (jo-ha-kyū) the first two beats are considered to be the introduction, the next two are the scattering, and the last four are the finale. This is the explanation for the characteristic silence on beat one and the drum calls on three, five, and seven. Drum calls need not appear in all these places though they are the most frequent locations. In Example 11 there is no call before beat five, perhaps because of the greater rhythmic activity (pu to pon) at that point. The additional drum call before beat eight in Example 11 is often found as a further incentive to the rushing mood of the finale. While the first function of these drum calls is to orient performers and listeners to the rhythmic location of every moment, they also serve to control the tempo and sometimes to enhance the mood

---

[4] The notation symbols used are explained at the beginning of Part IV.

of the music. They have become as much a part of the music as the rhythm itself.

In Japanese noh-music theory[5] the simplest tsuzumi rhythmic setting of a normal seven-five syllable line would be a series of patterns called *tsuzuke* followed by a cadential kashira pattern. In order to break up the monotony of such an accompaniment other patterns were substituted for some of the tsuzuke ones. The most common substitution is *mitsuji* (measures 494–501 of *Tsuru-kame*). As the order of substitutions was further codified there arose among noh musicians and devotees a conditioned reaction to the "pull" of certain patterns toward other patterns; in other words, there was a sense of rhythmic progression analogous to the feeling for chord sequence found in Western music. Since there are no chords as such in nagauta this principle becomes very important to the compositional logic and drive of the music. When one becomes sensitive to the tension- and release-producing qualities of rhythmic instead of harmonic sequences one feels that using tsuzuke, mitsuji, and kashira patterns is like harmonizing melodies with only primary triads.[6] As the use of secondary triads and modulations adds sophistication to the rendition of Western melodies, so the use of other more subtle rhythmic patterns provides a richer setting for nagauta music.

The special qualities of these drum patterns are further underlined by the fact that most are used only under special conditions. For example, in noh there are three rhythmic styles called *nori* which referred originally to the number of syllables to be sung within each eight beat phrase. The first is *ōnori* in which syllables occur on each beat. When two syllables occur in one beat it is called *chūnori*. The normal distribution of seven and five syllable poetic lines within eight beats is known as *hiranori*. The significance of these terms to drum music is that different patterns are used in each of these nori. For example, the tsuzumi pattern preference mentioned above is used in hiranori, while in ōnori the preference is for the patterns nagaji, takuji, and kashira. Thus, a piece can in effect "modulate" by a change in nori, which produces a new set of rhythmic patterns interrelated in a manner similar to the patterns of the previous nori but fresh in sound like the chords of a new key in a Western modulation. It should also be mentioned that these nori relate to the mood

[5] Kō Yoshimitsu, *Kō-ryū Ko-tsuzumi Seifu* (Tokyo: Nōgaku Shorin, 1955), p. 160.
[6] It is interesting that in *Tsuru-kame* a pure tsuzuke pattern is never used. An extended version *(tsuzuke-nobe)* is found in measures 559–68. A pure tsuzuke would be the equivalent of measures 559 through 566.

of a composition and are affected in noh music by the singing, whether it is in the strong *(tsuyōgin)* or soft *(yowagin)* style.

The instrumental interlude gaku at measure 519 of *Tsuru-kame* is a good example of a noh section transferred to a nagauta composition. It illustrates both how the rhythmic pattern sequences are used in such music and how they differ from the classic norm. While the ō-tsuzumi and ko-tsuzumi play different-named patterns the study of the ko-tsuzumi line alone will illustrate the principle at work in both.

The ko-tsuzumi music for this interlude is set in the hiranori style and consists of the following patterns, in sequence kan-mitsuji, uke-mitsuji, kan-mitsuji, jo-nagaji, tsuzuke-nobe, tsuzuke-hikae, uke-mitsuji, (kashira in taiko). Even without knowing the specific rhythmic connotations of these names it is evident that the choice of patterns has been in keeping with the overall hiranori rhythmic rules of sequence, as shown by the fact that tsuzuke and mitsuji are the most prevalent patterns for this section.

TABLE 7: *Two versions of ōnori ko-tsuzumi sequences*

I: TSURU-KAME	II: TEXTBOOK
1. (kashira, taiko)	1. kashira
2. kan-mitsuji	2. noru-uchioroshi
3. uchihanashi	
4. musubi-ashirai	
5. uke-mitsuji	
6. uchihanashi	3. uchihanashi
7. nagaji	4. nagaji
8. nagaji-chūyoru	5. nagaji
9. musubi-ashirai	6. musubi
10. ai-gashira	7. kashira

A more involved section in the ōnori style is seen at measures 634–79 in *Tsuru-kame*. Beginning with the taiko kashira pattern, the sequence for the ko-tsuzumi is as shown in column 1 of Table 7. As was mentioned the principal patterns in ōnori are kashira and ji, particularly nagaji and takuji. In the noh-drum textbook[7] the sequence for long passages in ōnori is given as shown in column II of Table 7. Comparing these two lists a sense of relationship and prescribed progression emerges. First, note that column II begins and ends with kashira. It leads through two different uchi patterns to the characteristic nagaji patterns. The cadence is formed by a musubi pattern and a

[7] Kō, *op. cit.*, p. 162.

kashira.[8] According to noh textbooks[9] an uke pattern can be substituted for noru-uchioroshi. It is this place in the sequence which is open to the most variation. It is similar to the freedom of movement found immediately after the tonic chord in Western traditional harmony. Looking at the list of patterns used in *Tsuru-kame* this place is indeed shown to be the most freely handled. Since the section is longer than the noh example given, the drum-part composer has added in a sufficient number of patterns to cover the length of time needed. The opening kashira appears in the taiko part only and is followed by a unit of four patterns (column I, Nos. 2–5) which expand the area normally using the noru-uchioroshi pattern. Notice that these four patterns form a unit with the very common mitsuji (2 and 5) at both ends, an uchihanashi (3), which is often found after a mitsuji pattern, and a cadence-implying musubi (4) preceding the second mitsuji. The musubi does not go to kashira as is normal because this is not a final cadence but rather a temporary digression from the main flow of the rhythmic line. Notice that pattern 5 is an uke, the kind of pattern mentioned above as a substitute for number 2 of the classical order.

After this digression has consumed sufficient time the patterns fall into the prescribed order as can be seen by comparing patterns 3, 4, 5, 6, and 7 of column II with patterns 6, 7, 8, 9, and 10 of column I. It will be noted that there are slight internal variations of patterns (musubi-ashirai for musubi, etc.). These families of patterns, the various kinds of ji, uchi, musubi, and tsuzuke patterns, might be compared with nearly related chords in Western harmony, which can be substituted for the basic unit. In both cases, such substitutions add variety and interest to the music.

At measure 313 of *Tsuru-kame* one finds the ō-tsuzumi playing a kabuki version of the noh pattern mitsuji while the ko-tsuzumi plays the same-named pattern (note, not the same rhythm). However, at measure 321 the two drums begin a pattern quite different from anything seen in the noh-derived (hongyō) music. This is an example of original kabuki (honrai) drum music. It differs from noh drumming in several ways. First of all, the noh patterns were conceived in relation to a vocal line set in eight-beat lines and divided at specific places. When this music was transferred to kabuki it was usually imposed upon a basically

---

[8] The cadence in hiranori and chūnori by contrast is formed by an odori and a kashira pattern. See Malm, " The Rhythmic Orientation of Two Drums in the Japanese No Drama," *Ethnomusicology* (Sept., 1958), p. 93.

[9] Kō, *op. cit.*, p. 161.

unrelated shamisen line so that its logic and structure were horizontally correct in terms of cadential goals at the end of musical lines but vertically chaotic. The kabuki patterns, on the other hand, were created expressly for the shamisen line and, as a rule, were conceived of vertically as supports for the rhythm of the shamisen melody. This becomes quite apparent if one compares the gaku interlude of *Tsuru-kame* (measures 519–75) with the michiyuki section (measures 39–75) of *Gorō*. While the noh patterns of the former are relatively long and begin and end independently of the shamisen phrasing, the drum music of the latter consists of shorter patterns that begin and end with the shamisen phrase. Notice also that the drum calls of the noh example tend to appear before the third, fifth, and seventh beats while the kabuki patterns use drum calls more often at the beginnings or endings of phrases. The first reflects the original orientation toward the standard seven-five syllable noh poetic line, while the second is based on the need for marking the length of rests between melodic phrases.

The normal term for kabuki style drumming is *chirikara*. This is derived from the mnemonics by which the music is taught. These mnemonic terms have been included in part of the transcription of the michiyuki section of *Gorō* mentioned above. It will be noticed that they are onomatopoetic renditions of the sounds produced by the drums.

While the usual length of chirikara patterns is from one to four beats, they can be joined into longer combinations. For example in measure 59 of *Gorō* one can see the chirikara pattern from which this style derives its name. It is followed in measure 60 by a similar pattern *(chiripopo)*, a slightly longer pattern (measures 61 and 62), and finally a cadential pattern in measure 63. These patterns do not have specific names nor do they always occur in the same order. However, their use in this way is frequent enough that professional part books need indicate them only by shorthand symbols.[10] For example, measure 59 by itself would be written # while the combination of measures 59 and 60 would be written ##.

Though these nameless patterns are freely mixed, it should be noted that certain ones seem to have cadential functions. Example 12 shows two such cadential patterns. Through the use of a restricted number of patterns at cadences by several generations of composers a feeling of sequence from one pattern to the next has been established. This is not dissimilar to the sensation of chord progression felt by the Westerner. We shall have oc-

[10] See Iba, *op. cit.*, p. 320.

EXAMPLE 12: *Two tsuzumi cadential patterns*

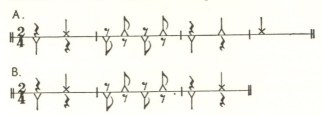

casion to refer to this similarity again when further relations of the hayashi to the melody are discussed.

Not all kabuki patterns are nameless. As the kabuki repertoire grew many special musical effects were required for specific choreographic or dramatic situations. Some of these special patterns have been retained and used in other plays for similar situations though their titles have nothing to do with the new use. Good examples of such patterns are *abare,* rushing about (measures 409–16 of *Goro*), and *iwato,*[11] stone door (measures 47–54). In some cases the reason for the title is known. For example, *higehiki,* pulling the beard (measure 401 of *Goro*),[12] is derived from the gesture of running one's fist up alternate sides of the face. This is a typical manly movement used by warriors in kabuki, and the higehiki music is used today for manly situations not involving this specific gesture. It becomes evident, therefore, that the name of a pattern need not necessarily be significant in relation to its use in kabuki music.

As was previously pointed out at measure 313 of *Tsuru-kame,* kabuki and noh patterns are not always kept separate. A vast majority of the drum music of *Tsuru-kame* is derived from noh music because the composition itself is so closely related to the noh play. On the other hand, most of the music of *Goro* is in pure kabuki style, reflecting the lack of a close connection between this composition and any noh dramas dealing with the same topic. However, by judicious mixtures of the two styles the music of the two tsuzumi creates varied settings for the melodic line of nagauta which either support it by underlining its rhythm or place it in relief by creating a rhythmic contrast.

Taiko-drum music, like that of the two drums already discussed, is of two basic types; that derived from the noh and original kabuki music. The taiko, however, is considered as

[11] This term is found in noh but the music is different. It is also found in folk theatricals. See *Ongaku Jiten,* 1 (1955), p. 128.

[12] There is another more involved version of this pattern. It can be found in the piece *Kikuju Kusazuribiki* (Bunka, 346).

separate from the other drums in both the noh and kabuki. Therefore, its use in both musics can be expected to be different. In basic structural concepts it is the same—its noh-style music consists of named, stereotyped patterns while its kabuki music has both named and un-named patterns. Its relation to the shamisen music, however, will be shown to be unique.

In noh-style music the taiko line, as in the case of the tsuzumi parts, is free from the shamisen rhythm and set within primarily eight-beat units. Perhaps the main difference between this music and that of the tsuzumi is that there is more of it.[13] Many times the tsuzumi will lapse into kabuki rhythms in order to support the shamisen line while the taiko will continue with noh patterns.

It is interesting to note the degree of similarity there is between kabuki-style noh sections and the original noh version of certain passages. For example, the gaku interlude of *Tsuru-kame* (measures 519–75) is an imitation of a standard noh-drama dance piece of the same name. Comparing the noh taiko part with that of the nagauta version,[14] they are found to start similarly (in the noh the pattern is *hitotsu-oki chū-gashira*). The next three patterns *(tsuke-gashira, oroshi,* and *kizami)* are the same. After that, however, the noh version carries on through some seven additional patterns before the next cadence[15] while the nagauta version cuts this to only two.

This process of "arranged" noh music is characteristic of all noh-style kabuki taiko music. It is in keeping with the similar kind of lip service that the kabuki plays derived from noh play to their predecessors. They begin in the same style, the tempo is speeded up, the original script is cut, and additional license is taken until the drama becomes more characteristically kabuki.

Kabuki taiko music not only abbreviates the noh sequence but it also creates a standard progression of patterns all its own. This is illustrated in Table 8. The left-hand column gives a typical order, though not the only one, for the noh taiko music to one section of the dance piece *kami-mai.* The middle-and right-hand columns show the taiko part for the same dance as it appears in the nagauta pieces *Wakana-tsumi* (Yoshizumi, I–8)

[13] For details see Malm, "An Introduction to Taiko Drum Music in the Japanese No Drama," *Ethnomusicology* (May, 1960), pp. 75–78.

[14] The noh version is found in Komparu, *op. cit.,* pp. 254–57. The nagauta version was acquired through private lessons.

[15] The exact number of patterns cannot be stated since the number of repetitions of the basic pattern (kizami) depends on the school of the dancer. This is another example of the confusion engendered by the intransigent guild system in the Japanese theatre arts.

and *Oimatsu* (Yoshizumi, II–2).[16] One can see at a glance the similarities and differences between these versions. Kizami (see *Tsuru-kame,* measures 544–51) is the basic pattern in all cases, and the preparation for the cadence is always made by a form of the uchi pattern. The main point of departure is the greater variety and number of patterns found within the entire unit of the purely noh-style drumming.

TABLE 8: *Three versions of the taiko part to kami-mai*

NOH	WAKANA-TSUMI	OIMATSU
—	kashira	kashira
tsuke-gashira	tsuke-gashira	tsuke-gashira
oroshi	oroshi	oroshi
taka-kizami	taka-kizami	taka-kizami
hane	hane	hane
kizami (3 times)	kizami (3 times)	kizami (twice)
taka-kizami, hane	taku, nobe-tataki	taka-kizami, hane
nagaji	naga-nagaji	kizami (3 times)
taka-kizami, kiri	takakizami	—
kizami (3 to 7)	kizami (once)	—
uchikiri	age-uchikake	age-uchikiri
—	uchikomi	—
kashira	kashira	kashira

The kabuki versions of these taiko parts follow a very similar order as can be seen in Table 8. The first part of this stereotyped order is the same as in the noh. The section begins with a tsuke-gashira (normally preceded by an introductory kashira) and proceeds to an oroshi, followed by some form of kizami.[17] The final cadences are also similar with either age-uchikiri or uchi-komi preceding the final kashira. The middle section, however, is open to the greatest variation as it is in the Western musical tradition. In all music structures the establishment of a secure beginning and an equally recognizable destination makes a sense of musical progress possible. In the construction of noh-style taiko music one can see these principles very much at work.

Purely kabuki taiko patterns tend to be named more often than the kabuki tsuzumi patterns. In fact, the titles of several common tsuzumi patterns such as abare and iwato mentioned

[16] Noh dances are divided into sections (dan). The noh version in Table 8 is the second dan as shown in Komparu, *op. cit.,* p. 256. The nagauta columns were learned privately.
[17] Kizami and taka-kizami differ only in that the strokes are small in the former and large in the latter.

earlier are said to have originated in the taiko tradition.[18] A typical example of a kabuki taiko section is the michiyuki of *Gorō* (measures 39–75). Beginning on the second beat of measure 39 the patterns used are as shown in Table 9. At first sight the only words which look familiar are ji and kashira. However, ji is rather a universal word in Japanese music and neither of the

TABLE 9: *Taiko patterns for the michiyuki of* Gorō

MEASURES	NAME
1. 39–43	wataribyōshi
2. 43–46	ji-norikomi
3. 47–54	kuse
4. 54–58	ji-nobi
5. 59–66	kuse
6. 67–70	unnamed
7. 71–72	unnamed
8. 73–75	motsu-kashira

ji patterns listed above bear any significant relation to the miji-kaji or nagaji of noh-style taiko music. Kashira has already been shown to be a generic term for drum cadences in noh and kabuki music, so its use here does not necessarily indicate any noh influence. The name *wataribyōshi* does appear in the standard list of noh taiko patterns,[19] but the kabuki pattern of the same name is different rhythmically as shown in Example 13 (in mnemonic syllables).

EXAMPLE 13: *Noh and kabuki versions of the pattern wataribyōshi*

NOH	1	2	3	4	5	6	7	8	1
						tere	ten	ten	ten
KABUKI	1	2	3	4	5	6	7	8	1
		ten	ten	ten	tere	tsuku	tsu	ten	ten

The term kuse in Table 9 is not found in the noh-drum tradition though it is the name of part of the play, and unnamed patterns are practically non-existent in noh. Thus, this interlude reveals a concept of taiko music quite different from that of noh. The patterns in Table 9 still tend toward an eight-beat-unit orientation though their use in this passage might lead one to think otherwise. The first pattern is eight beats long, but the next is only seven. Number three (kuse) is fifteen

[18] See Mochizuki Taiinosuke, "Nagauta Hayashi Hayawakari," *Shamisengaku* (July, 1935), p. 54.
[19] See Komparu, *op. cit.*, p. 110, item 62.

beats long, four (ji-nobi) is eight, and there is a two-beat caesura. The next kuse (number five) is sixteen beats long, and the unnamed patterns are eight and four beats. The final kashira is five or six beats long depending on one's point of view. These irregular lengths seem to belie the earlier statement concerning the retention of the eight-beat orientation in kabuki taiko music. However, when each of these patterns is played separately it is found to fit into an eight-beat frame. This is, in fact, the way these patterns are taught. When they are combined in a particular piece some of their unsounded beats are usurped by other patterns creating the sensation of uneven pattern lengths. Why is this done? One answer is suggested by comparing the phrasing of the shamisen line with that of the drum during this same passage—measures 39–75 of *Gorō*. Starting with the first beat of measure 39 the shamisen phrases are divided as shown in Table 10.

TABLE 10: *Shamisen phrases for the michiyuki of* Gorō

NO.	MEASURES	NO. OF BEATS
1	39–42	8
2	43–46	8
3	47–50	8
4	51–54	8
5	55–57	6
	two-beat rest	
6	59–62	8
7	63–66	8
8	67–70	8
9	71–73	6
10	74–76	6

Comparing this list with the sequence and placement of the drum pattern in Table 9 several interesting points emerge. First of all, the two instruments seem to start on a different beat one. The shamisen begins on the downbeat of measure 39 while the taiko enters on the upbeat. However, if one looks at the manner in which wataribyōshi, the first pattern, is taught as shown in Example 13 it will be seen that the first beat of the pattern is silent as is often the case in noh patterns. This puts the first beat one of wataribyōshi on the first beat of the second phrase of the shamisen (measure 43). Continuing to count in this manner, the next taiko pattern *(ji-norikomi)* begins on two and ends on eight as shown in Example 14. It is eight beats long, the silent first beat having been used by the final beat one of the previous pattern.

EXAMPLE 14: *The taiko pattern ji-norikomi*

1	2	3	4	5	6	7	8	1
	tsu	ku	tsu	tere	tsuku	tsu	ten	

This special manner of conceiving of the beat in terms of a silent one[20] produces a very important result. Though the musicians are thinking the first beat together, one instrument (the shamisen) makes it felt while the other (the taiko) does its best to distract from this beat one. The aural result is that of two lines out of phase with each other by one beat. This creates a special tension which tends to push the music forward in the same way that dissonant harmony gives impetus to Western music. Further ramifications of this technique will be shown in the explanation of the noh-flute music and its relation to the taiko part.

Looking once more at the taiko part for the michiyuki of *Goro* (measures 39–75) one finds that the system of drum calls is quite different from those found in noh-style music. Instead of appearing before beats three, five, and seven, they are found primarily between phrases as in the case of kabuki tsuzumi music. One might add that another difference between kabuki and noh taiko drum calls is their general scarcity in the kabuki and frequency in noh.

All kabuki taiko patterns are not as short as the ones studied in *Goro* so far. Sometimes a set of patterns are combined into a unit known by a special name. The individual patterns of which it is constructed may be combined in a different manner to form some other longer unit. However, not all the longer kabuki taiko patterns are so divisible. The finale of *Goro* (measures 466–505) consists of two renditions of the pattern *sarashi,* each requiring twenty-two measures. This pattern is not further subdivided into shorter named patterns but is learned as a unit. Its name refers to a popular kabuki dance technique in which the actor flaps two long streamers of gauze called sarashi in imitation of a folk method of bleaching and drying cloth. The exact same drum music is found in the sarashi dance section of the piece *Echigojishi* (Yoshizumi, III–5, p. 11). In *Goro,* however, no such movement occurs, and the use of this music is meant to engender a similar degree of excitement and not support a specific choreographic idea. This is a good example of how these patterns are used either for specific choreographic purposes or for general moods.

[20] A similar concept is found elsewhere in the Orient, for example, in Javanese gamelan music. See Mantle Hood, *The Nuclear Theme as a Determinant of Patet in Javanese Music* (Groningen: Wolters, 1954), p. 21.

The mood of folk festivals and of general proletarian activity is frequently the responsibility of the taiko along with the bamboo flute, because these instruments are closely related to folk instruments of the same names. Generally, this folk effect is enhanced by the use of two thinner sticks. Some of the patterns used for folk music are derived from the folk hayashi music. The terms *shaden, shishi, shichōme,* and *kamakura* are taken directly from the folk festival-music tradition. Patterns like *miyakagura* (temple sacred dance) reflect a similar origin. The opening of *Echigojishi* (Yoshizumi, III–5) uses one of the most popular kabuki folk taiko patterns, *shibai-shōten.*

Looking back over all the drum music discussed so far one finds that the noh-style music for all the drums consists of named patterns, set in an eight-beat orientation and internally divided by drum calls appearing before the third, fifth, and seventh or eighth beats. It was suggested that the beginning and endings of these eight-beat patterns were placed so as not to coincide with many of the shamisen phrases. Prescribed sequences of patterns were shown to be important elements in the logical progression of the music.

In kabuki-style drum patterns the tsuzumi were found to rely for the most part on combinations of the so-called chirikara rhythms while the taiko favored named, eight-beat patterns albeit these were rhythms and names usually different from those of the noh taiko. Kabuki drum calls were found between patterns rather than within them as in the noh. Finally, tsuzumi music seemed to support directly the rhythm of the shamisen line, while the taiko music formed a second line of rhythm seemingly independent of the rest of the ensemble. The full explanation of this interesting phenomena will be withheld until the entire hayashi ensemble including the flute has been discussed.

DRUM MUSIC IN RELATION TO FORM

Nagauta drum music has been explained according to its origins and its general use. It is now time to consider it in relation to the overall form of the music.

Fortunately for the research worker, there is an exception to the usually secret tradition of the hayashi guilds. In two series of articles[21] written for the now defunct *Shamisen-gaku* magazine

[21] Mochizuki Taiinosuke, "Nagauta Hayashi Hayawakari," *Shamisen-gaku* (Jan.. 1935–July, 1936), and "Nagauta Hayashi no Taii," *ibid.,* (Feb.–Apr., 1937).

Mochizuki Taiinosuke provided a fund of information about hayashi music which could normally be acquired only through years of apprenticeship in one of the hayashi guilds. The second set of articles is a revision of the first and the following information is abstracted from both versions.

In addition to the jo-ha-kyū division of the formal units of nagauta, Mochizuki uses a four-part division represented by the characters ki, shō, ten, ketsu.[22] The first character means to appear. In terms of the normal formal nomenclature of nagauta this area would include the okiuta and sometimes the michiyuki. For the drums it is the section using the greatest number of entrance-exit patterns (deiri-bayashi). The second symbol means to hear or acknowledge. This is said to be the dramaturgical center of the piece. Kudoki and monogatari sections belong here. The third character *(ten)* means the turning or change. This is the place where the odoriji is located. The final character *(ketsu)* means to tie up and refers to the closing sections of the piece—the chirashi and dangire.

On the basis of this concept Mochizuki analyses four compositions showing their psychological, melodic, and hayashi divisions. Tables 11 and 12 are derived from this analysis plus personal investigations of the pieces.

Table 11 shows the outline of two noh-style nagauta pieces. *Kanjinchō* (Yoshizumi, V–3) is taken from a famous noh play and *Tsunayakata* (Yoshizumi, V–2) is an ōzatsuma style of nagauta written at a time (1869) when noh influence was strong in nagauta. Looking at the hayashi parts of both pieces one finds many noh terms such as shidai, issei, ashirai, notto, and yose. In the third section of both pieces there is a dance derived from the noh (otoko-mai no sandanme and hayabue). The musical divisions of *Kanjinchō* contain standard kabuki and noh formal terms like oki, michiyuki, and kudoki. The instrumental interludes (notto-aikata, and mai-aikata) are likewise named after or accompanied in the drums by patterns reminiscent of the noh. *Tsunayakata* consists of a great many patterns borrowed from ōzatsuma music, but *Kanjinchō* shows the influence of several other narrative shamisen traditions in the sections marked geiki-gakari (from geiki-bushi), itchū-gakari (from itchū-bushi), handayū-gakari, and sekkyō-gakari (from handayū-bushi and sekkyō-jōruri).

Echigojishi (Yoshizumi, III–5) and *Tomoyakko* (Bunka, 3334) are both hengemono (see page 25) and more kabuki in spirit.

[22] 起承転結 Mochizuki, "Nagauta Hayashi Hayawakari," *ibid.*, (April, 1935), p. 48.

KANJINCHŌ			TSUNAYAKATA		
MUSIC	PAGE	HAYASHI	MUSIC	PAGE	HAYASHI
			PART I		
okiuta	1	shidai	okiuta	1	—
geiki-gakari	1	—	—	2	notto
			deru	3	issei
deru	2	yose	michiyuki	4	ashirai
michiyuki	3	ashirai	inaori	5	—
inaori	4	—			
			PART II		
notto ai	5	notto	shi	6	—
		(norito)	shodan	7	—
aikata	10	kogyoku	kudoki	8	—
kudoki	11	—			
itchū-gakari	11	—			
tagari	12	—			
			PART III		
sekkyō-gakari	14	—	ji	16	—
			ironori	16	—
handayū-gakari	15	—	hayabue aikata	17	hayabue
mai-aikata	16	otoko-mai no sandanme			
			PART IV		
chirashi	17	katamosu-kiri	kioi	18	chirashi
			—	19	tsukukake-oroshi
dangire	19	dangire	dangire	19	dangire

This is reflected in both the formal and drum-music terms.
The entrance in both dances is made with a rush so that the oki
and michiyuki are very close. The first section in each piece is
called the *deru*, the going out. The drum music for the entire
first section is replete with kabuki patterns (shibai-shōten, sarashi, etc.). The subsequent sections show an equal degree of
concentration on strictly kabuki patterns. It is interesting to

TABLE 12: *A comparative list of formal units in two kabuki-style nagauta*

ECHIGOJISHI			TOMOYAKKO		
MUSIC	PAGE	HAYASHI	MUSIC	PAGE	HAYASHI
PART I					
deru	1	oroshi	deru	1	oroshi
michiyuki	2	shibai-shōten	michiyuki	1	sarashi
—	2	itsutsudo	—	1	kyōgen-gakko
inaori	3	—			iwato
					abashi
					katamosukiri
					haya-watari
			inaori	3	—
PART II					
—	4	shibai-shōten	odoriji (yaroshi)	3	taikoji
nage	5	—	—	3	hōgo-sagariha
hamauta (kudoki)	6	—	tanzen-ai	4	kuse
odoriji	8	taikoji	kudoki	5	—
			tsunagi	6	daishō tsuzumi
PART III					
aikata	11	hyōshi	aikata	7	hyōshi
—	12	rokubyōshi			
ai	12	daishō tsuzumi			
—	13	rokubyōshi			
ai	13	daishō tsuzumi			
PART IV					
chirashi	14	sarashi	chirashi	8	hayawatari
dangire	14	dangire	dangire	9	dangire

note that there are two major dance sections in *Tomoyakko,* one at the beginning of Part II and another at the start of Part III. In hengemono pieces such mixtures of the regular order are not uncommon. The first dance (odoriji) uses the traditional taikoji accompaniment, while the second dance (aikata) employs what amounts to a chirikara drum part. This second dance illustrates another feature unique to kabuki-style nagauta. The score at this point (Bunka, 3334, p. 7) is marked *ashibyōshi,* foot rhythm, which means that the music plays a duet with the foot beats of the dancer.[23] Obviously this would be impossible if the drums were committed to playing predetermined rhythmic patterns exclusively.

What do these four examples show? First, one can observe an obvious difference in the handling of noh- and kabuki-style dance pieces. The choice and location of the various patterns in the noh-style pieces almost can be predicted once one is thoroughly acquainted with the style. The kabuki pieces, on the other hand, seem to be free in their treatment of the drum. However, the distinction between entrance-exit music and dance music is generally maintained. Theoretically, the use of patterns is more controlled than it would appear. For example, some patterns are placed according to their location in the beginning, middle, or last part of the piece. Table 13 gives a partial list of patterns organized in such a manner. It also indicates whether they are of kabuki (k) or noh (n) origin and whether they are deiri-bayashi (d) or dance music (maigoto-bayashi, m).[24]

Comparing this list with Tables 11 and 12 one finds a high degree of correlation between the theoretical placement of patterns into the beginning, middle, or end of a piece and the actual use of these patterns in the compositions studied. Note that fourteen of the seventeen patterns listed in the beginning sections are entrance music (deiri). It was mentioned earlier that the noh patterns appear most often in the noh-derived pieces and the kabuki patterns in the kabuki dance pieces. These lists bear this out.

Of the eleven middle patterns seven are dance music, which is logical since the all-important odoriji dance is normally in the middle of a piece. The last section has nine patterns listed of which five are dance music. Actors usually posture on stage at the finale, but some pieces end in a dramatic exit down the ramp, so there are exit patterns here as well. Of course, this list does not contain all the pattern names. There are many patterns of either noh or kabuki origin which are used in special situations whenever they may be needed. For example, the

---

[23] Though kabuki actors seldom wear shoes during dance sections, they can produce resonant foot beats due to the fact that the boards of the stage are laid loosely over a hollow area.

[24] Based on a chart in Mochizuki, "Nagauta Hayashi no Taii," *Shamisen-gaku* (March, 1937), p. 12, plus other lists in the series. The tripartite division is apparently meant to follow the jo-ha-kyū system and fit loosely over the four-part division of ki-shō-ten-ketsu used in Tables 11 and 12.

TABLE 13: *Classification, uses, and origins of selected hayashi patterns*

BEGINNING SECTION (MAEDAN)

shidai (N-D).	sagariha (N-D)
issei (N-D)	raijo (N-D)
yose (K-D)	wataribyōshi (K-D)
oroshi (K-D)	kyōgen-gakko (K-D)
tsujiuchi (K-D)	shibai-shōten (K-M)
seri (K-D)	chū no mai (N-M)
kakari (N-D)	nanori (N-D)
okidadaiko (K-M)	deha (N-D)
jo no mai (N-D)	

MIDDLE SECTION (NAKADAN)

hayabue (N-D)	tenjo no mai (N-M)
hayadaiko (N-D)	taikoji (K-M)
ha no mai (N-M)	hyōshi (K-special)
kagura (N-M)	dadaikoji (K-M)
kami-mai (N-M)	hayaraijo (N-special)
gaku (N-M)	

FINAL SECTION (ATODAN)

kakko (N-M)	hayawatari (K-D)
tsukukake-oroshi (K-D)	sarashi (K-M)
katamosukiri (K-M)	chirashi (K-M)
ranjo (N-D)	dangire (K-D)
inoru (N-M)	

abare and iwato seen in the first part of *Tomoyakko* are usually found when the actor is doing a type of gesture known as the *genroku-mie*.[25] Both patterns are found in the middle part of *Gorō* (measures 410 and 426) indicating that they move with the choreography rather than with the music, though usually both of these elements are closely linked.

The kabuki pattern chirashi is another example of a special pattern in that it is used only at the end of pieces. The noh-derived pattern hayaraijo is reserved for animal-like posturings. For example, it appears in the monkey dance *Geikizaru* (Yoshizumi, II-9). Mention was made earlier of various special patterns used to create a folk atmosphere. *Kasei-nembutsu* as found in the piece *Kanjo* (Yoshizumi, II-5) should be added to this list as one of the few direct references to Buddhist rather than

[25] Mochizuki, "Nagauta Hayashi Hayawakari," *Shamisen-gaku* (July, 1935), p. 52.

Shinto folk ceremonies. A nembutsu-odori, it may be recalled, was said to be the first dance done by Okuni in creating the kabuki. Finally, mention should be made of the special patterns reserved for the propitiatory dance *Sambasō* (Yoshizumi, II–1) and for the many lion dances *(shishimono)*. Such pieces tend to follow the choreography closely.

Looking once more at the analysis in Table 11 one can see that such patterns as appear both in these pieces and in Table 13 are consistently placed according to the beginning, middle, and end classifications. Ashirai, while not on the list, appears in exactly the same place in both pieces, making it at least a possible candidate for inclusion in the beginning patterns. Notto seems to be a freer pattern, appearing in the beginning of *Tsunayakata* and the early middle part of *Kanjinchō*. It can be found also in the later middle section of the piece *Kurumayama* (Yoshizumi, I–9, p. 6).

Turning to the two kabuki pieces in Table 12 one finds a general agreement between the formal units of the drum parts and the list in Table 13 though there are more special patterns used. The oroshi that opens both pieces appears on the list as a beginning pattern. This pattern has no relation to the noh taiko pattern of the same name except that both are performed on the taiko. The use of all the other patterns listed in *Echigo-jishi* are consistent with the listings in Table 13. *Itsutsudō*, not on the list, is another genroku-mie pattern. The word *hyōshi*, appearing in Part III of both pieces, refers to the chirikara style of tsuzumi music, which is used commonly though not exclusively at such a location in nagauta pieces. The *rokubyōshi* seen in *Echigojishi* is a type of kabuki rhythm found commonly in dance or posturing sections.[26] The term *daishō-tsuzumi* is another way of saying ō-tsuzumi and ko-tsuzumi, the two instruments being called the *daishō* by professional musicians. Here the term indicates a continuance of the use of these drums without the taiko. The entire last part of *Echigojishi* is, in fact, a *tour de force* for these two drums, as they play continuously and furiously for 220 measures. The author can vouch on personal experience for the difficulty and discomfort of such a sustained performance.

Tomoyakko seems to be more inconsistent. Sarashi is listed as an ending pattern, yet it appears during the michiyuki section of this piece. It may be remembered, however, that the sarashi music was meant originally to be used for a specific showy dance movement. The same kind of theatrical brilliance is used in the opening of *Tomoyakko* though the choreography is differ-

[26] See "Rokubyōshi," *Ongaku Jiten*, 11 (1957), pp. 242–43.

ent. As in *Gorō,* its use here may be one of mood rather than form.

Kyōgen-gakko in *Tomoyakko* is in its proper place at the beginning of the piece. The use of this pattern in other pieces can be seen in the transcriptions of this book (Part IV, page 339). Abashi, like iwato immediately before it, is another genroku-mie pattern. Katamosukiri and hayawatari are listed as ending patterns, yet in *Tomoyakko* they appear before the actor has even left the ramp. There is no explanation for this except to remark that the existence of two large dance sections in the piece and the fact that it is one of the many changes (henge) compositions would suggest that more liberty is taken with the form in such cases.

The taikoji section offers no problem. Hōgo-sagariha is a pattern used to capture the spirit of the dandies of old Edo (see tanzenmono, page 23) and is added because of the tanzen interlude that follows. Kuse, as a special taiko pattern, appears in *Tomoyakko* to continue the taiko accompaniment begun in the previous section. The daishō-tsuzumi section is not out of place when one considers that the odoriji section has already appeared. Note that the second dance is not called an odoriji and that it is accompanied not by the taiko but by the tsuzumi in chirikara fashion. The final hayawatari and dangire are in their proper places.

The analysis of four pieces out of a large repertoire does not prove a point. The consistency of the results coupled with observations from other pieces, however, certainly indicates a tendency if not a rule. A professional drummer has said that drum patterns are used for specific sections and a random sampling has indicated that what he says is generally true. During the great flourishing of nagauta in the nineteenth century, noh and kabuki tradition, whether of dance or other origin, tended to become mixed. What is most significant and exciting is that despite this diverse activity so much of the theoretical basis has remained in force. The choice of drum patterns, the order in which they are played, and the instrumentation used are definitely controlled by one or both of two factors, the music and the choreography. These traditions have been maintained for so long that the present-day players are hardly aware of the existence of rules. They know by traditional training what sounds right for each situation. This makes it possible for a nagauta piece to be a co-operative composition. The words and music are written, the dance is choreographed, and then the piece is turned over to a drummer who will know instinctively what is the proper accompaniment for each section. Japanese composition is not as self-conscious as in the West. This causes it to be rather reactionary and inflexible. Within the limitations set, however, the more accomplished musicians display an excellent sensitivity to the particular needs of each piece. The problem of further growth of this tradition is highly controversial. Our immediate concern, however, is not with the future of nagauta but with the musical details of its past. The structure and use of nagauta drum music as shown above is certainly one of the major contributions to the brilliance and logic of this long tradition.

CHAPTER SEVEN
Flutes of the Hayashi Ensemble

TWO FLUTES are used in nagauta. They are played by one man and never used together. The noh flute seems to be the earlier addition since it was used at the very beginning of kabuki along with the other noh instruments. The simple bamboo flute of the folk, however, plays music more purely derived from the kabuki tradition. Therefore, the first discussion will be about this simpler instrument.

THE BAMBOO FLUTE AND ITS MUSIC

The bamboo flute is called the *takebue, yokobue,* or *shinobue.* It comes in various sizes and has six or seven holes, professional musicians usually using the seven-holed variety. These holes are covered by the middle joint of the fingers, and each fingering[1] is capable of producing at least two tones by changes in embochure or half-holing. This system, known as *meri-kari,* is used to produce any of the Japanese scales desired. The flute has a practical range of two octaves and a third. The choice of the proper-sized flute is dependent on the basic tuning of the shamisen in each performance. The lowest-built flute begins on D, but the practical selection of flutes is from E to C and the ones most used begin on E, F, G, and A flat.[2] When the shamisen is in hon-chōshi the flute matches the fifth hole with the lowest string. In ni-agari the sixth hole is tuned with the lowest string. In san-sagari the fifth hole is matched with the top string. When a piece changes tunings and requires a flute in several sections, it may be necessary for the player to change flutes in order to play the music easily.

Though there are names for the holes on the bamboo flute,

---

[1] A fingering chart can be seen in Iba, *op. cit.,* pp. 203–5.
[2] Mochizuki, "Nagauta Hayashi Hayawakari," *Shamisen-gaku* (March, 1937), p. 68.

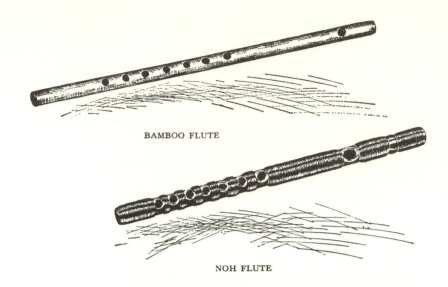

BAMBOO FLUTE

NOH FLUTE

FIGURE 5: *The flutes of the hayashi ensemble*

no notation is used for it in nagauta. The student must learn the music by reference to the shamisen line or simply memorize it by rote.

The most frequent use of the bamboo flute in nagauta is in the taikoji (odoriji) sections. These are almost always in the ni-agari or san-sagari tuning. *Gorō* and *Tsuru-kame* are examples of the former and *Echigojishi, Tokiwa no Niwa,* and *Yoshiwara Suzume* are examples of the latter, to mention but a few. The only standard pieces using bamboo flutes extensively in hon-chōshi are *Miyakodori* (Yoshizumi, III–7) and *Matsu no Midori* (Yoshizumi, II–12). In both cases the flute is used throughout the piece.

In all the pieces mentioned above, the flute is used to embroider the basic vocal or shamisen line. Measures 339–454 of *Gorō* illustrate this process very well. Notice how the flute adds a melisma to almost every turn in the melody. It skips freely between the voice and shamisen line because, once it has entered, it usually does not stop until the end of the odoriji section and thus has to find its parent melody wherever it can. Looking at this line one can understand why no independent notation system was developed for the bamboo flute. It has no need of one because it has no real musical independence. The melismas used are not always the same in every performance; but they are controlled by tradition, so that one learns to add them intuitively.

Not all bamboo-flute music is dependent on the basic shamisen line. The excerpt from *Utsubozaru* (Yoshizumi, VI–7, p. 3), transcribed in Part IV of this study (page 341), is an example of such a case. The flute melody here is almost entirely independent of the shamisen, agreeing only in general mode and in some cadences (measures 10, 13, and 35). Its independence is further emphasized by the exciting dissonances set up against the shamisen line such as seen in measures 18 and 66. Notice the delayed resolutions of such tones. This melody is known as *inakabue,* country flute. It is used in this case to add atmosphere to a section speaking of the autumn wind. This same melody appears in *Ataka no Matsu* (Yoshizumi, IV–3, p. 8) to imitate the wind in the fields. It can be seen that the long sustained quality of the melody makes it relatively easy to match it up with a different shamisen part in a different piece by judicious changes in the length of the holds. For example, compare the opening version of inakabue in the transcription (measure 6) with its repetition in measure 52. This also illustrates the fact that these tunes are really only types, not specific melodies. One must learn to apply them to each piece in a special way.

There are other similar tunes which are interpolated into the flute part in order to create specific atmospheres. For example, the melody *kusabue,* grass flute, is considered to be the same type as inakabue. It is found in the transcriptions (page 340) as played in the piece *Shigure* (Yoshizumi, V–4, p. 6). Comparing this melody with inakabue, one finds the same extended note values and descending line but no real thematic connection. Another such example is a flute melody called *ondo,* the name of a type of folk-dance music which is used, for instance, in *Tokiwa no Niwa* (Yoshizumi, IV–6, p. 10). Here the words speak of smoke rising from the chimney of a rustic thatched cottage.

In all three cases mentioned so far these special tunes appear fairly early in the compositions. In each piece the bamboo flute is used again during the odoriji section in its usual melismatic fashion. Thus, it is evident that the flute can be used in both ways within one composition.

Since the bamboo flute is as much a folk instrument as a part of the kabuki ensemble, it is employed whenever folk ensemble music is required. In such cases it plays tunes taken from the folk festival repertoire such as shichōme, yatai, kamakura, and others listed in the discussion of folk drum music (see page 90). This kind of flute playing can be heard in the piece *Kibun Daijin* discussed in Chapter III.

Finally, mention should be made of the melody *ryūjishi-haya-shi*, dragon music, which is used during the boat song of *Ura-shima* (Yoshizumi, I–11, p. 2). This piece is based on the Japanese legend of the boy who married the princess of the sea and upon returning to shore on a turtle turned into an old man. Apparently the use of this melody has Shinto religious overtones of a more formal nature than the folk-festival melodies mentioned above.

In summary, bamboo-flute music in nagauta is either completely controlled by the main melody or completely independent. In its dependent form it usually appears as part of the sound ideal of an odoriji section. When it is independent musically, it has some dramatic or textual reason for its presence. Such melodies can be used in various pieces with totally different shamisen lines. This illustrates once more the importance in nagauta of the horizontal and dramaturgical concepts of composition over the vertical and developmental principles favored in the West.

THE NOH FLUTE AND ITS MUSIC

The noh flute, sometimes called the *nōkan,* is very different from the bamboo flute both in its structure and in its use. It is approximately 39 cm. in length and is made of bamboo. Usually the bamboo is split into many strips and then turned inside out so that the bark is on the inside. The tube is then bound back together with cherry bark. This unique method of construction is said to be important to the tone. Another unique feature of the noh flute is a special cylinder inserted in the tube between the mouth hole and the first finger hole. This upsets the acoustical properties of the flute in such a way that the overblown octaves become progressively flat as one goes up the scale until the last few notes produce not an octave but a minor seventh. The reason for this addition is not known. Perhaps it has some connection with the noh tonal sytem, which is built around two conjunct fourths, thus outlining a minor seventh.[3] In any case, it contributes to the distinctive tone of the instrument.

The noh flute has seven finger holes. The pitch of the instrument varies depending on the length. If D is taken as the lowest pitch, the seven basic pitches would be approximately D, E,

[3] See Malm, *Japanese Music and Musical Instruments,* p. 128.

G, A, A♯, B, and C♯. There are, however, some twenty-two fingerings on the flute in addition to the use of half-holing and lipping which produce two or three different versions of each so-called basic pitch.[4] Its practical range is approximately two octaves and a fifth, though the lower range is seldom used. An important part of the noh flute technique is to start with a rush of air which gradually becomes a sound and rises to a rather indistinct pitch. Thus, intended pitches are often difficult to determine in noh-flute music.

The noh flute is said to use two of the ancient court-music modes, ōshiki-chō and banshiki-chō, shown in their classic form in Example 15.[5] Pieces like chū no mai, kami-mai, jo no mai, and otoko-mai are classed as ōshiki-chō pieces while haya-mai and banshiki-gaku are in the banshiki mode. However, the deliberate clouding of almost every pitch in performance makes it rather difficult and even pointless to try to determine the exact mode of the flute part. This is especially true in nagauta since the mode of the noh flute has nothing to do with the mode of the particular piece in which it is used.

EXAMPLE 15: *The two modes of the noh flute*

Ōshiki - chō

Banshiki - chō

Noh-flute notation is as vague as its pitches. It consists of a solmization *(shōka)* which vaguely indicates the contour of the line, the words used having no specific tonal meaning. This solmization is written out for the first part of measures 39–51 of *Gorō*. It is only through lessons and familiarity with the repertoire that one can learn to read the actual script.[6]

Noh-flute music consists of the arrangement of a large number of stereotyped patterns. These patterns are internally constructed of still shorter standard phrases which may be found in other melodies but arranged in a different order. In a classic

[4] A fingering chart can be seen in Iba, *op. cit.*, pp. 194–95.
[5] *Ibid.*, p. 196.
[6] An example of this notation can be seen in Appendix I of Malm, *Japanese Music and Musical Instruments*, p. 266.

noh-flute piece there is a short introduction followed by a basic melody, called the *ji,* repeated several times. The various sections (dan) that follow take this basic melody and continue to repeat it, adding very subtle melismas and pitch variations to it. New material is also interpolated, which may in turn be varied in the next section. The original melody returns at the end and the piece closes with a short coda, usually the first line of the basic melody. This kind of sectional variation form with added material is found in later Japanese genres such as koto music.

These long pieces are seldom used in their entirety in nagauta. Instead, they are shortened and simplified as in the case of other noh musics borrowed by the kabuki. An example of such a borrowed section is the flute part of the interlude *gaku* in *Tsuru-kame* (measures 519–75). The second repeat of the basic melody starts at measure 559 but it is greatly abbreviated because of the shortness of this interlude. Note that the repeat begins a microtone lower than the original version.

The flute line in this interlude, as in most noh-flute music, is phrased in eight-beat sections. Since the shamisen phrases in groups of four measures, the noh-flute phrases co-ordinate with them even though the particular melody used has nothing to do with the shamisen part. These co-ordinant first beats appear at measures 519, 527, 535, etc. Note that, as mentioned earlier, the taiko player also thinks of these beats as one, but to the ear they sound like beat eight. This gives the effect of cross phrasing which is characteristic of such noh-style nagauta passages. It is like two scales on a slide rule that remain internally rigid but when set in a new relation result in a new reading. In the case of this music the result is an effect of a music always a little out of phase with itself and hence always pushing forward toward some point of resolution. This phenomenon, as was said, is a very important factor in the dynamism of nagauta music.

Not all noh-flute music in nagauta is derived from old noh pieces. For instance, the flute part for the michiyuki of *Gorō* (measures 39–75) is an example of a kabuki-style noh-flute part.[7] Notice that in this case the flute music is phrased with the taiko while the shamisen and the other two drums appear to be together. In terms of the slide-rule analogy used above, the scales have been moved into a new relation. The flute melody from the last beat of measure 43 through the first beat of meas-

[7] This flute part is notated as taught to the author. Comparing it with recorded performances gives one some idea of the freedom with which pitch is treated in noh-flute music.

ure 54 consists of two melodies called *ji* and *kuse,* preceded by a short introduction. At measure 54 these two are repeated, the only difference being the insertion of an extra measure rest at 58. There are many such kabuki melodies for the noh flute which are used if needed. For example, the flute and taiko pattern called kyōgen-gakko is found often in nagauta. Page 335 of the transcriptions shows four different renditions of this pattern. The first version is the melody as taught to the author by Tanaka Denjirō, a well-known kabuki flutist. The second is from a tape of a performance of *Yōrō* (Yoshizumi, VIII–5) played by a Mochizuki school musician in Tokyo on December 1, 1956. The third and fourth versions are two lines from *Asazumabune* (Bunka, 3351) as performed by a Tanaka musician on the same concert. In both the lines of *Asazumabune* and in *Yōrō* the drum line remains the same, though in each case the shamisen melody is different. The lesson version and the second taiko version were learned as part of the beginners' piece *Suehirogari* (Yoshizumi, I–2, p. 1).

Comparing first the lesson version with the second *Asazumabune* version one can see that the student version is a greatly simplified outline of the melody as used in professional performances. In keeping with the apprentice system such a discrepancy excludes the beginner from professional activity until he has been in the guild long enough to be taught or discover for himself the particular way in which each tune is played in each piece. The two lines of *Asazumabune* illustrate further that an exact reproduction of the melodic line is not characteristic of nagauta flute music. More than any other instrument in the ensemble, the flute is free to alter its music within the general contour of the accepted norm. This is peculiar to the flute because its function is so often non-melodic in the sense that the notes it plays are not as important as the dramatic or formal significance of its entry.

Comparing the Mochizuki version from *Yōrō* with the other three, one sees a different playing style as well as a different concept of the melody. The constant upward glissando of the tone plus the grace notes help to cloud the basic line.[8] Notice that all four versions use basically a three-note scale with the tonic in the center. This tonic appears at the end of every phrase in all versions. Thus, one finds in kabuki flute music a more flexible treatment of standard melodies than is normally found

[8] Differences of equal magnitude in playing and performance style are found among the various noh theatre flutists. Nagauta flute schools usually trace their history back to one of these noh schools.

in other noh-derived musics in the kabuki. Even the two versions of the kabuki-style taiko pattern shown for kyōgen-gakko are more closely related than the flute melodies.

There are many other noh-flute melodies which are coupled with taiko patterns. For example, abare found at measure 410 in *Gorō* has an equivalent noh-flute melody. However, it is not used at this point because the bamboo flute is already in action, and it is the odoriji section in which the taiko and bamboo flute sounds are preferred to that of the noh flute.

From a formal standpoint the noh flute is heard most frequently at the opening and michiyuki sections and finales. Of course, in pieces derived from noh plays one can expect to find it more often than in pure kabuki pieces. The gaku interlude in *Tsuru-kame*, for example, is a clear case of noh influence. Nevertheless, the noh flute will be found in the finale of every piece using a hayashi group even if it plays only the last few notes. Typical noh-flute final cadence formulas are found at the end of both *Gorō* and *Tsuru-kame*.

In addition to the noh-derived melodies and the taiko-linked kabuki patterns, the noh flute uses certain special tunes for dramatic effect. For example, the sound of the flute in the court orchestra is imitated in *Gojōbashi* (Bunka, 3338), since the story deals with the imperial palace in Tokyo. The flute is also used for bird imitations and to create special atmospheres, usually in conjunction with the off-stage musicians.

In general the noh flute is used quite sparingly in nagauta. Like a cymbal or a snare drum in the Western orchestra, its tone color is so unique and bright that it can easily become disturbing if over-used. In pieces derived from noh it is an excellent device for retaining the noh flavor of the music without sacrificing the kabuki idiom. The almost total lack of any tonal connection between it and the rest of the ensemble places it in a very special functional category. One function, as mentioned, is to provide special moods. Its other purpose, however, is involved with its relation to the taiko drum and its general lack of relation to the shamisen as noted in the michiyuki of *Gorō*.

In this section the tsuzumi act as rhythmic supports for the shamisen line. This is the normal function of percussion parts in Western music—support of the melodic rhythm. It was noted that the taiko and flute parts seemed to be closely related, though they were in discord with the rest of the ensemble. Might it not be possible that these two instruments form a third unit of sound which serves to drive the other two (the melodic and rhythmic) forward until concord is reached? This, after all, is one basic function of the third unit in Western music, harmony, and it has been evident that harmony as such does not exist in nagauta. Nevertheless, the principle of jo-ha-kyū indicates that the Japanese have a concept of the seemingly universal law of tension and-release in art. In situations such as the one described above it seems quite possible that this third force has indeed been created out of these two instruments to function in the same way as harmony in the West. It sets up tensions against the melody which seek their resolution and show their logic in a horizontal-temporal plane. Viewed vertically such musical situations seem chaotic, just as certain harmonic moments in Western music can only be explained in relation to their resolutions. Such a view of kabuki-style taiko and noh-flute music explains not only their relation to the rest of the ensemble but also the logic of the indistinct melodic line of the flute and the discrepancy between the aural and mental image of the drum phrasing. Coupled with the laws of order discovered in the study of drum patterns, this idea of the third unit in nagauta speaks strongly for the claim that nagauta is a highly evolved, sophisticated, and logically constructed art form.

CHAPTER EIGHT

The Off-stage Ensemble
and Its Music

IN THE stage-right flat of every kabuki set there is a slatted window. A bamboo curtain hangs behind this window to keep the audience from seeing in. If one could venture behind this curtain one would see a small, dark room full of drums, gongs, bells, and busy musicians. This is the world of the *geza*, the off-stage music of the kabuki.

Geza originated in the early eighteenth century as an accompaniment for certain comic styles of kabuki dance.[1] At first various lyric shamisen musics were used, primarily of the nagauta meriyasu type. As kabuki productions became more elaborate the geza musicians were called upon to play a host of percussion and other instruments. Thus, geza became the special-effects department as well as an extension of the stage music ensemble.

The term geza originally meant the outside place (外座) though later it was written as the lower place (下座), because the room, known as the *kuromisu* (black curtain), was below a similar alcove used by the jōruri musicians. This alcove was and still is on the second floor at stage left, though the geza now is normally located at stage right. From this position the musicians can see the stage clearly as well as look down the ramp that leads from the back of the theatre. Geza music is traditionally under the control of nagauta musicians. Today certain players specialize in this off-stage music, though they usually begin as regular nagauta musicians. A resumé of the basic instruments of the geza and their use will give an idea of the variety of sounds emanating from this fascinating kabuki convention. It will also reveal the various functions they perform.

The three standard nagauta drums are found in geza music also. They take over some of the music normally assigned to the

[1] "Geza ongaku," *Ongaku Jiten,* 3 (1956), p. 271.

stage drummers as well as add special patterns of their own. For example, in plays set in the mountains one will often hear two ko-tsuzumi in opposite wings of the stage playing *kodama,* echo. First one will play a few beats and then the other will echo them.

The off-stage room normally has two taiko because they are combined with the flute to play the opening and closing music of a performance. For example, the ending pattern *uchidashi* is used after the curtain is closed to retain an air of excitement after the play is over. This pattern is heard at the end of many nagauta recordings.

The next most common drum of the geza is the *ō-daiko,* a large membranophone with two tacked heads. It is played on one head with two long tapered sticks. This drum has a long tradition as part of the kabuki. It was originally placed in a tower over the entrance of the old kabuki compound and used to signal the opening of the performance as well as sound the alarm if troops were needed to quell a rowdy audience. Today the old opening signal, *ichiban-daiko,* is still played at the beginning of a performance. From the standpoint of nagauta the most important use of the ō-daiko as well as the other geza instruments is to create special atmospheres. For example, the sound of wind or rain are common effects played on the ō-daiko. The sounds used, however, do not imitate real wind or rain directly. It is necessary to keep them stylized in order that the music may blend with the non-realistic acting tradition of classic kabuki plays. A pattern can be altered to indicate different intensities of rain, for once the convention has been established the audience becomes capable of recognizing several shadings of meaning.

Sometimes patterns are used when the element depicted does not figure in the scene at all. In such cases it is felt that the quality of that element is present rather than the thing itself. For example, one might hear the drum pattern for wind in a quiet, windless night scene when a robber is peering into a house. The chilling effect of the wind and the cold eye of the robber are enough similar in the kabuki musician's mind to warrant the use of the same music for both.

In addition to its many theatrical uses, the ō-daiko is found often as a coloristic addition to nagauta music. In *Gorō* the ō-daiko can be added to the taiko part itsutsu-kashira at measure 402 and abare at measure 410. Other more manly pieces such as *Tomoyakko* (Bunka, 3334) and *Tsuchigumo* (Yoshizumi, III–2) employ the ō-daiko to reinforce the regular taiko sound.

Another use of the ō-daiko is to imitate the large folk drum of the same name. The opening folk pattern of *Echigojishi* (Yoshizumi, III–5) is such a case. A similar use can be heard in the two folk-festival sections of *Kibun Daijin* discussed earlier (see pages 43–46).

The *hyōshigi,* two rectangular blocks of wood, are the next best known kabuki off-stage instruments. They are played by a special stagehand who warns the entire theatre of the number of minutes before curtain time by striking the two sticks together. The curtain opens and closes with an accelerating series of clacks from this instrument. It also is used on a flat board placed on the left corner of the stage apron during fight scenes to add noise to the battle. Its use in nagauta is limited to those mentioned above and hence it is really not part of the music proper.

Among the brass idiophones the most common is the *suri-gane,* a small gong held in the hand or suspended and played on the inside with a small bone mallet. It is used primarily in folk-music imitations such as the two festive scenes in *Kibun Daijin* mentioned earlier.[2] It may be added to the wataribyōshi drum pattern found at measure 39 of *Gorō* or the kyōgen-gakko pattern in *Asazumabune* shown in the transcriptions (page 339). As part of the regular folk ensemble, its uses are governed by the need for a folk sound.

Another common idiophone is the *hontsuri-gane,* a temple-style bell hit with a large padded hammer. In addition to its use in temple scenes, it appears as a signalling device like the ō-daiko. It can be heard in *Kibun Daijin* during the quiet section set in the Yoshiwara.

There are several other gongs and bells of which only a few need be mentioned. The *orugōru* is a set of small bells of Buddhist origin. They are used to indicate lightness as in the scene in *Renjishi* (Yoshizumi, IV–I) when the lion chases the butterflies. Other Buddhist instruments such as the hand bell *(rei),* bowl gong *(kin)* and pan drum *(uchiwa-daiko)* are sometimes used in kabuki, usually to produce a religious effect. A knobbed gong *(dora)* is also used for temple scenes. Sleigh bells *(ekiro)* are used when a peasant effect or the presence of horses is desired. Insect imitations are performed on a small gong set on three legs called the *matsu-mushi,* the pine insect. It is used in insect interludes such as are found in *Aki no Irogusa* (Yoshizumi, III–1) and *Azumabune* (Bunka, 3351).

[2] A clear sounding but arranged example of suri-gane playing can be heard in the piece "Omatsuribayashi" on the American Columbia LP record, The Azuma Kabuki Musicians (ML 4925).

Cymbals, castanets, and other kinds of drums are used in the geza, but their importance is more dramatic than musical. In closing one should mention the sixteen-keyed xylophone *(mokkin)* borrowed from Chinese music. This instrument is meant to support comic dances and is played in a desultory fashion, the rhythm being more important than the actual notes struck.

The mokkin is the first melodic off-stage instrument mentioned so far. However, it is not the only one. In modern kabuki the end-blown flute *(shakuhachi)*, the small three- or four-stringed *(kokyū)*, and the thirteen-stringed zither (koto) are sometimes used, but the main melodic instruments of the kabuki, on stage or off, are the shamisen and the two nagauta flutes.

The flutes are used off-stage much as they are when they are part of the stage ensemble and need not be discussed further. The only difference in their off-stage music is that they combine with the off-stage percussionists instead of the on-stage group. In kabuki plays they are used when the nagauta ensemble is silent and flute music is required. In concert performances their role is taken by the on-stage flute player.

The geza shamisen, while less colorful than its on-stage counterpart, is one of the most vital components of the off-stage ensemble. It is in geza shamisen music that the leitmotiv technique of kabuki music is developed to its greatest extent. For instance, Example 16 is a melody called *yuki,* snow. It is used in the kabuki whenever there is need of a cold, dark atmosphere, even though snow may not be falling. Combined with the muffled beats of the ōdaiko, it evokes just such an atmosphere, especially when experienced in the middle of a tense kabuki play. This tune is derived from a jiuta piece of the same name[3] and now by association produces a cold effect upon the enlightened listener.

The effect of deep darkness and mystery is evoked by a solo shamisen pattern related to the famous ōzatsuma melodies mentioned earlier. This pattern, called *shinobi-sanjū,* consists primarily of a series of repeated notes. These are meant to imitate the sound of the summer cicada. Normally a large bell is used with this melody in imitation of the night temple bells. This example is one of the few that tends to be naturalistic.

A more genuinely leitmotivic melody is *kangen,* which is used to create an atmosphere of the court. Measures 90–98 of *Tsurukame* make use of the opening of this melody. This is a good

[3] The complete melody can be seen in *Collection of Japanese Popular Music,* Nishino Torakichi, ed. (Osaka: Mike Gakki-ya, 1906), Vol. 6, p. 213.

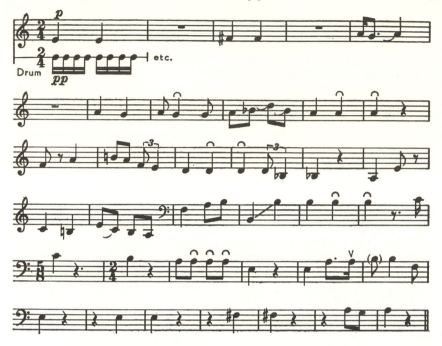

example of the actual use of a geza melody within the framework of a nagauta piece instead of its being simply another contribution to the overall effect of a kabuki play. It is in this way that the off-stage tradition became important to the study of nagauta.

It should be obvious by now that a large part of the appreciation of geza music depends on previous knowledge of the melodies and patterns used. As was said, it is similar in technique to the leitmotiv idea of Wagnerian opera. It is interesting to note how this similar device developed in kabuki some one hundred and fifty years before the time of Wagner.

From the standpoint of appreciating nagauta, the off-stage tradition should be recognized as serving two purposes. First, it intensifies the significance of specific moments by bringing into the music instruments or melodies associated with particular situations. Secondly, it adds a great number of new tone colors with which to vary the nagauta-ensemble sound. This is one reason why nagauta can be considered the most orchestrally oriented of all Japanese musics. An important distinction to be made in nagauta, however, is that tonal color is never used for its own sake. It is always related to the text or dancing in a rigid manner little known in the Western concept of orchestration. Geza music is exciting and colorful, but like all other aspects of nagauta it is always controlled by tradition to an extent often unsuspected by the casual listener. Once more law and order are found to reign in the world of nagauta music.

PART THREE

Analysis

CHAPTER NINE

Analysis of Tsuru-kame

THE PREVIOUS two sections of this study have presented the myriad historical, theoretical, and practical facts which form the nagauta tradition. With these as a background it is now possible to study a composition and, with the aid of the transcription (and ideally a recording), try to tie all these disparate facts into one musical unit.

The first full-length transcription to be studied will be *Tsuru-kame*. The reader is reminded once more that the actual pitch level chosen for the transcription is arbitrary, since the basic pitch varies with the range of the singer. The intervallic relations between the pitches, however, may be taken as basically those of the tempered scale unless otherwise indicated. In checking recordings against a Stroboconn it was found that variations from tempered pitches seldom exceeded ten cents. The greatest variations occur in the playing of half step upper neighbors (F and C), which tend to be smaller than a half step lower neighbors (A and D), which tend to be raised when sung in a cadence.

Tsuru-kame was written in 1851 by Kineya Rokuzaemon, the tenth. Originally it was intended to be a concert piece, but it has since become popular with dancers. It is considered to be the first genuine noh-derived (utamono) nagauta. The text is taken from the Kita school noh play *Gekkyūden*. This is basically the same text as is found in the play *Tsuru-kame* of the other schools of noh.

This play is rather short and is congratulatory in nature, the crane *(tsuru)* and the tortoise *(kame)* being good-luck symbols in Japan. In the noh drama the dances of these two creatures are performed by child actors, the main actor *(shite)* being the emperor and the supporting actor *(waki)* being a nobleman. The paraphrase of the text which begins each sectional discussion of the nagauta piece does not attempt to capture the heavy formality of the language. Even so great a translator as Arthur Waley has despaired of catching this flavor in English versions of noh dramas.[1] One can, however, at least indicate the grandiose nature of the scenes described and the ceremonial pomp the text seeks to convey.

Before beginning the analysis in detail one should be aware of the order of events in the play and the general formal divisions into which they fall. The jo-ha-kyū division given below is based on the organization of the original play,[2] while the specific sections of the music are taken from a study of the nagauta composition itself. The outline and synopsis are as follows:

JO (1–260)
1. OKI (1–129): the scene in the palace is set.
2. AGEUTA (130–260): the beauties of the palace garden are told.

HA (261–575)
3. MONDŌ (261–92): a nobleman and the emperor decide that the sacred creatures should dance.
4. CHŪ NO MAI (293–353): the tortoise and the crane dance.
5. ODORIJI (354–518): the longevity of the creatures is described.
6. GAKU (519–75): the emperor dances.

KYŪ (576–759)
7. KIRI (576–679): the beauty of the emperor's robes is described as the nobles raise their voices in praise.
8. CHIRASHI-DANGIRE (680–759): prosperity is wished for all the land and longevity is wished for the emperor.

Each of these sections will now be discussed in turn using the numbers given above.

1. THE OKI (1–129)

THE TEXT: The opening text describes an annual court banquet, which marks the awakening of spring. It is set in the court of the Chinese emperor though in actuality it refers to the Japanese court. The text says that the emperor himself observes the sun and moon shining through the gate of eternal youth.

THE SHAMISEN MUSIC: Since the shamisen part is the central core of any nagauta piece we shall turn our attention to its construction first. Table 14 outlines the phrase structures of the shamisen music for the entire oki. The meaning of each column is as follows:

[1] See Arthur Waley, *The No Plays of Japan* (New York: Grove Press, 1957; original edition 1920), p. 32.
[2] *Yōkyoku Zenshū*, Nogami Toyoichirō, ed. (Tokyo: 1935), Vol. I, p. 385.

I. The chronological phrase number within the section, listed for convenience in reference to specific passages.

II. The measure numbers of each phrase.

III. The total length of the phrase in bars.

IV. The length of motives within each phrase. The choice of phrases and motive lengths is based on a study of each case and a knowledge of the general nagauta style. One will note, for example, that rests have been included in some cases as part of a phrase; one becomes aware of this as a standard procedure after extensive exposure to the idiom.

V. The opening pitches of the phrase. The pitches from B a half step below middle C to A a major sixth above middle C are indicated by capital letters. The next octave higher is written in lower-case letters, and the octave above that is shown in lower case letters plus a prime sign. If there is a pitch below the lowest B it is shown in capital letters plus a prime sign. Letters joined together at the top indicate double stops.

VI. The ending pitches of the phrase.

VII. The basic pitch center progression from the start of a phrase to its end. Intermediate centers are not shown. In some cases centers are implied rather than played.

VIII. The basic direction of the phrase: up (U), down (D), static (S), or curved (C). In the latter case the motion is as much up as it is down despite the relative positions of the first and last pitch center.

TABLE 14: *Outline of the shamisen part for the oki of* Tsuru-kame

I	II	III	IV	V	VI	VII		VIII
1	7–8	—	free	E				S
2	9–12	4	4	Ab (fe)	Ab	e	b	D
3	13–20	8	4 4	afe	eb	e	b	D
4	21–28	8	4 4	B	FEE	B	E	C
5	29–36	8	3 5	b	DEB	b	B	D
6	37–44	8	2 6	b	dee	d	e	U
7	45–52	8	4 (3–1)	ab'f	Ab	e	b	D
8	53–60	8	1 4 2 1	dc♯	GF♯	c♯	F♯	D
9	61–68	8	4 4	GF♯	CB	F♯	B	D
10	69–72	4	4	B̂b	B̂b	b	b	S
11	73–82	10	3 4 3	B	Ab̂b	B	b	U
12	83–89	7	3 4	ecb	Ab	b	b	C
13	90–97	8	4 4	Âb	f♯cb	b	b	S
14	98–104	7	4 3	AbGF♯	deb A	b	A	C
15	105–111	7	3 4	A	Ab	A	b	U
16	112–119	8	4 4	cb	DE	b	E	D

I	II	III	IV	V	VI	VII	VIII
17	120–122	3	3	bb	bF♯	b F♯	D
18	123	—	free	F♯	Ab	F♯ b	U
19	124	—	free	Bb	Bb	b b	S
20	125	—	free	BF♯	F♯	B F♯	U
21	126–129	5	1 1 1 2	BF♯	BB	F♯ B	D

SUMMARY OF TABLE 14

I & II. There are a total of 21 phrases. The last four have been set apart because they consist exclusively of ōzatsuma patterns.

III. The frequency of each type of phrase length is as follows:

9   eight bars
2   four bars
3   seven bars
1   ten bars
1   five bars
1   three bars
4   free

IV. The motivic division is as follows:

4   free
3   undivided
6   symmetrical
8   asymmetrical

V. The opening movements are summarized below as to whether they (1) began with a movement from a lower neighbor to a pitch center, an upper neighbor to a pitch center, (2) remained stationary, or (3) used some other motion. In deciding which designation is correct each situation must be studied as a whole and the problems of rhythm and non-essential tones must be considered. Hereafter the following abbreviations will be used: LN, whole step lower neighbors resolving up; UN, whole or half step neighbors resolving down; S, a stationary; and PC, pitch center. Special situations will be indicated by the interval or direction involved.

4   LN
5   UN
10   S
2   5th

VI. The symbols used to summarize the cadences will be the same as those mentioned above concerning column V.

8   LN
5   UN
4   S

<pre>
                3   5th
                1   4th
</pre>

VII. A study of the basic pitch-center progressions reveals the
following observations:

<pre>
                E   leads to B
                B   leads to E, F♯, C♯, or A
                F♯ leads to B
                C♯ leads to F♯
                A   leads to B
</pre>

VIII. The summary of the general direction of each phrase
gives the following results:

<pre>
                5   U
                9   D
                4   S
                3   C
</pre>

From the above information certain tendencies can be noted.
Column III reveals a preference for eight- or four-bar phrases.
This is especially evident if one discounts the opening free phrase
and the traditionally free ōzatsuma phrases at the end of the
section. Among the relatively large number of asymmetrically
divided phrases shown in column IV a majority use combinations of three- and four-bar groups. An investigation of the
eight instances of three-bar motives in this section reveals a
common agogic organization of short-short-long. All end with
a half note, a quarter and a rest, or a bar of silence. Perhaps
these shorter phrases are necessary to overcome the loss in melodic dynamism caused by the break in rhythmic flow. Possible
support for this idea is the fact that all the three-bar phrases,
with the exception of the one found in phrase 12, end on a
principal tone or its fifth. This principal tone usually has been
established as a pitch center by the use of upper or lower
neighbors or its fifth. In some cases the principal tone appears
to be the fifth of yet another pitch center. For the sake of analysis
these principal tones and fifths will be called melodically consonant pitches—pitches which require no further resolution.
Notes other than pitch centers and their fifths are considered to
be melodically dissonant—they require further resolution.

The importance of this concept of consonant and dissonant
melodic tones is evident if one looks at pauses in the melody
which do not occur at the end of phrases. The first such pause,
that is, a half note or a quater plus a rest, occurs in measure 14
on an F which resolves to E. The next such situation occurs on
an F (30) which resolves to E and the next half note (33) is a
D which resolves to E. In measure 45 yet another half note F

is found which resolves to E, while the pause on C♯(53) is ambiguous. The next half note on G (56) resolves to F♯. The one dissonant ending of a three-bar motive (85) is an F which is resolved in the voice part. Note that this motive occurs within, not at the end of, the phrase. A glance at column VI in Table 14 will show that the ends of phrases, by contrast, consistently occur on consonant tones. Thus, one can see in this first analysis evidence in support of an important nagauta principle, that long, non-cadential notes tend to be tense, unresolved pitches in order that the melodic line can be kept "alive" until it reaches a suitable cadence. The use of the three-bar phrase may be yet another means of accomplishing this end.

The validity of thinking of naguta music as being organized around pitch centers which are created by cadence patterns of neighbor tones or fifths is well supported by the information found in columns V and VI. No other means of opening or closing a phrase is found except for the repetition of the pitch center itself. The latter technique seems more evident at the beginning of phrases, while the cadence formula of lower neighbor to the pitch center is used more frequently at the end of the phrase.

Column VII reveals that a majority of the root movements are between notes a fifth apart. The two exceptions are A, which is approached from and returns to B, and C♯, which is approached from B but resolves down a fifth to F♯. The overall pitch progression can be said to be from E with many half cadences to F♯ (phrase 8) and then to B (phrase 10). After a short phrase in A, B returns for the final cadence.

The particular types of melodic movement and contour used by the shamisen will be discussed later in relation to the entire piece. One can note from the summary of column VIII that there is a prevalence of phrases that move down, and looking at the music one can find occasional balancing of the contours of antecedent and consequent phrases as, for example, is seen in the descending line in measures 29–36 and the ascending phrase that follows in measures 37–43.

Finally, one should note the use of stereotyped melodic patterns. Measures 90–97 contain the melody called *kangen,* which is meant to represent the sound of court music. This pattern was mentioned earlier as serving the same function for the off-stage kabuki music. The enriched sound of the double stops may be a compensation for the elimination of the drums at measure 89. The use of this pattern in this piece is certainly appropriate. The text that follows speaks of the multitude of officials who have crowded to the imperial audience and raise their voices as one (in praise), the sound echoing enormously against the heavens.

The other named patterns used are those of the final four ōzatsuma phrases. They are as follows: phrase 18, honji; and phrases 19–21, tobi-tataki.

THE VOCAL MUSIC: Table 15 outlines the vocal music for this section. The meaning of each column is the same as in Table 14 (see the explanation on page 119). As was shown in Example 2, the vocal part is usually in syncopation with the shamisen. Because of this it has been necessary in many cases to ignore the exact placement of the first or last note of a vocal phrase in determining the measure numbers for that phrase since the numbers are based on the barring of the shamisen part. The letters in parentheses in column VI indicate closing ornaments and should not be considered as the true finalis. Finally, in column II one will find certain measure numbers missing. These measures contain shamisen interludes of only a few beats' duration. Longer passages are numbered as separate phrases even if the voice does not enter. This is done in order to coordinate as much as possible the phrase numbers of the two charts from the same section of the piece.

TABLE 15: *Outline of the vocal part for the oki of* Tsuru-kame

I	II	III	IV	V	VI	VII		VIII
1	7	–	free	Ab	DE	b	E	D
2	10–13	4	4	de	b(A)	e	b	D
3	14–23	10	2 8	fe	Ab(A)	e	b	D
4	24–27		tacet					
5	28–35	8	4 4	cb	DE(D)	b	E	D
6	36–44	9	6 3	cb	de(d)	b	e	U
7	45–52	8	4 4	efe	Ab(cb)	e	b	D
8	53–60	8	8	bc♯	EF♯	b	F♯	D
9	62–67	6	6	EGF♯	A'B(A')	E	B	D
10	68–74		tacet					
11	75–82	8	3 5	Ab	b(A)	b	b	S
12	84–91	8	3 5	Ab	AbA	b	b	S
13	92–93		tacet					
14	94–102	9	4 5	Ab	EF♯(E)	b	F♯	D
15	104–111	8	4 4	AGA	Ab(cb)	A	b	U
16	112–118	7	4 3	Acb	DE(D)	b	E	D
17	119–122	4	2 2	Ab	b(A)F♯	b	F♯	D
18	123–	–	free	Ab	Ab	b		S

I	II	III	IV	V	VI	VII	VIII
19	124–	–	free	Ab	c♯F♯	b F♯	D
20	125–	–	free	F♯	EF♯(E)	F♯	S
21	126–129	5	2 3	EF♯	A'B(A)	F♯B	D

SUMMARY OF TABLE 15

i & ii. There are 18 sung phrases.

iii. The frequency of each type of phrase length is as follows:

> 6 eight bars
> 2 four bars
> 2 nine bars
> 1 ten bars
> 1 seven bars
> 1 six bars
> 1 five bars
> 4 free

iv. The motivic divisions are as follows:

> 4 free
> 3 undivided
> 4 symmetrical
> 7 asymmetrical

v. The opening movement of phrases was arranged in the following manner:

> 10 LN
> 4 UN
> 3 S
> 1 PC to UN

vi. The cadence formulas are summarized as follows:

> 13 LN
> 3 S
> 1 5th
> 1 4th

vii. The basic pitch progressions move in the following order:

> E leads to B
> B leads to F♯ or E
> F♯ leads to B

viii. A summary of the general direction of each phrase gives the following results:

> 2 U
> 12 D
> 4 S

The vocal line concurs with the shamisen part in the prevalence of eight- and four-bar phrases during this section. It will be noted, however, that phrases of the same length do not always occur at the same time. The deliberate overlap of vocal entrances with shamisen cadences appears to be another device directed at maintaining the melodic flow. For example, in phrases 5, 6, and 17 the shamisen ends on a consonant note (E or B) while the voice enters on a dissonance (C or A). In phrase 10 the voice repeats the A sounded in the shamisen but goes immediately to the lower neighbor G. In such ways the voice line not only effects a smooth entrance but also creates new melodic tensions in the music.

The variety of motivic divisions in the vocal part does not differ greatly from that of the shamisen. The types of asymmetrical units used, however, are more varied. The text is a contributing factor in this case.

The most striking difference between the two parts is found in columns V and VI. The extensive use in the vocal part of lower neighbors resolving to pitch centers appears in both the opening and cadencing of phrases and appears to be quite idiomatic. The pitch progressions follow the same order as those shown in the shamisen part and both parts show a preference for descending lines. The idiomatic melodic movements of the vocal part will be discussed at the end of the analysis when the piece is viewed as a whole. One should note, however, that the opening vocal passage is a vague imitation of noh singing style. After this phrase the voice returns to nagauta singing.

THE HAYASHI MUSIC: The composition begins with a quiet hayashi introduction derived from the noh pattern *uchiage*. Actually, this replaces an introductory speech in the original text spoken by a kyōgen actor. After a vocal-shamisen introduction in a somewhat free tempo, the drums return (measure 21), preceded by the noh flute at 19. This full ensemble remains in use until measure 89. The music played by the hayashi at 21 is the noh-derived pattern *raijo*. This same pattern is used at this point in the original play.[3] The drum calls *(ho* and *iya* for the tsuzumi and *ho* and *yo* for the taiko) are alternated, with the result that the constant repetitions of the same pattern have the illusion of being different. The rhythmic line continues to move forward, since the strong accents in the tsuzumi and the taiko part never fall together. The taiko accents fall primarily on the beginning of shamisen phrases (29, 37, etc.). The other two drums mark

[3] *Yōkyoku Taikan,* Sanari Kentarō, ed. (Tokyo: Meiji Shoin, 1930–31), Vol. 3, p. 2097

the midway point in these phrases. Notice that the drums make an adjustment at measure 62 when the vocal line breaks away from its even phrasing.

The noh-flute music for this opening section is not so repetitious as the music of its percussive companions. The standard raijo melody is stretched over ten bars (19–29). The flute part usually begins later than the vocal-shamisen phrase and is played so that the final note ends with the main taiko accent. The noh flute often enters rather late in such noh hayashi accompanied nagauta beginnings, but in this case it enters with the other instruments because of the specific pattern (raijo) used. Nevertheless, the tendency for the flute to enter after the beginning of a shamisen phrase and its extensive use of long tones are idiomatic. Both techniques prevent the flute from distracting from the main melodic line as it easily might do since it is so unrelated to it.

The cadence that closes this hayashi section (88–89) uses the standard final sound for all four instruments. The flute always ends on a high pitch and the drums use the pattern kashira. Note that a sudden change of drum calls (to *yoi* at measure 81) signals the cadence.

SUMMARY OF THE OKI

Instrumentation: After a short noh-imitative section, the voice and shamisen are coupled with the noh hayashi. The last section uses voices and shamisen only.[4]

Vocal-shamisen lines: Eight- and four-bar phrases are most common. Descending lines are prevalent as are cadences from lower neighbors to pitch centers. The overlapping of cadences between the two parts helps to maintain a melodic flow as does the judicious placement of melodically dissonant tones and shortened phrase lengths.

Pitch centers: The shamisen is in the hon-chōshi tuning. The pitch center progression begins with an in scale built on E with many half cadences on B. F♯ appears which leads to B, followed by a short phrase in A which returns to B. After a cadence in E, B returns for the final section.

Tempo and rhythm: The tempo is free at the beginning and end. The middle section is moderate and steady, becoming slower after the percussion section (90). The drums use noh-style rhythms only.

General remarks: Special patterns to be noted are the melody kangen and the ōzatsuma patterns used for the final cadence.

[4] In the Mochizuki version of the drum part the tsuzumi continue during this section with noh patterns.

2. THE AGEUTA (130–260)

THE TEXT: The section marked ageuta is sung by the chorus in the original noh text. It describes the beauties of the imperial garden. The pebbles, it says, are like lines of gold and silver gravel. The portal is covered with brocade and lapis lazuli, while its beam is made of mother-of-pearl and agate. The edge of the garden pond reminds one of Mount Hōrai. Thanks are then given to the emperor for his many graces.

THE SHAMISEN MUSIC: Table 16 is an outline of the shamisen music for this section. An explanation of the meaning of each column and the symbols used in the summary will be found on page 119.

TABLE 16: *Outline of the shamisen part for the ageuta of* Tsuru-kame

I	II	III	IV	V	VI	VII		VIII
1	130–137	8	4 4	de	de	e	e	S
2	138–145	8	4 4	ab'	ab'	b'	b'	S
3	146–149	4	4	ab'	cb	b'	b	D
4	150–157	8	4 4	Ab	Ab	b	b	S
5	158–165	8	4 4	bGF♯	GF♯	b	F♯	D
6	166–173	8	4 2 2	AA	AB	A	b	U
7	174–177	4	4	fe	cb	e	b	D
8	178–185	8	2 2 4	b'af♯	cb	f♯	b	D
9	186–195	10	4 2 4	de	Ab	e	b	C
10	196–199	4	4	BG	BF♯	B	F♯	U
11	200–207	8	4 2 2	B	Ab	B	b	U
12	208–211	4	4	fe	ee	e	e	S
13	212–219	8	4 4	cb	GF♯	b	F♯	D
14	220–225	6	6	fe	de	e	e	C
15	226–233	8	4 4	Ab	FE	B	E	D
16	234–239	6	6	de	FE	e	E	D
17	240–247	8	4 4	f♯	cb	f♯	b	D
18	248–255	8	2 2 4	E	Ee	E	E	C
19	256–260	–	free	afe	Ab	e	b	D

SUMMARY OF TABLE 16

I & II. There are a total of 19 phrases.

III. The frequency of each type of phrase length is:

11	eight bars
4	four bars
2	six bars
1	ten bars

                              1   free
IV. The motivic divisions are:
                              1   free
                              6   undivided
                              7   symmetrical
                              5   asymmetrical
V. The opening movement of phrases is arranged in the following manner:
                              7   LN
                              6   UN
                              4   S
                              1   3rd
                              1   3rd and UN
VI. The cadence formulas are summarized as follows:
                              8   LN
                              8   UN
                              2   S
                              1   4th
VII. The basic pitch progressions move in the following order:
                         E leads to B or F♯
                         B leads to F♯ or E
                         F♯ leads to B
The overall progression of the sections is E to B to E to B.
VIII. A summary of the general direction of each phrase gives the following results:
                              3   U
                              9   D
                              4   S
                              3   C

The prevalence of eight-bar phrases is even more noticeable in this section than in the previous part. Even the five asymmetrical divisions are based on groups of two's and four's within an eight-bar frame with the exception of phrase 9.

The tempo has increased in this section and the music does not rely so much on dissonant tones to maintain the melodic flow. The pauses within the phrases are found to be on stronger tones. An increase in the use of anacruses may be seen. This may be a compensation for the dynamism lost by the absence of the tenser tones in the melody. It is interesting to note, for example, that in phrase 6 (measures 166–73) there is a return to dissonant tones (A and F) at the same time that there is a reduction in rhythmic activity and a greater spacing of notes.

In the jo section preference was given to stationary beginnings of phrases, perhaps to set the pitch relationships. In the more dramatic ageuta section one finds a greater variety of entrances. The cadence patterns, however, remain about the same, though it was mentioned that the caesuras within phrases tended to be more consonant. Pitch progressions and the general directions of phrases are the same as in the previous section. Lines directed downward are in the majority.

THE VOCAL MUSIC: The vocal part for the ageuta is outlined in Table 17. For the sake of ease in comparing shamisen and vocal outlines, phrases for shamisen alone have been counted in the numbering so as to make the phrase numbers of the two charts as similar as possible.

TABLE 17: *Outline of the vocal part to the ageuta of* Tsuru-kame

I	II	III	IV	V	VI	VII	VIII
1	130–141	12	4 8	de	de(d)	e	S
2	142–145		tacet				
3	146–149	4	4	ef♯	f♯b	f♯ b	D
4	150–157	8	8	Ab	Ab(A)	b b	S
5	158–165		tacet				
6	166–173	8	4 4	Ab	Ab	b b	S
7	174–179	6	6	dfe	Ab	e b	D
8	180–185		tacet				
9	186–193	8	4 4	d(e)	bA	e A(b)	D
10	196–200	4	4	GB	EF♯(E)	G(F♯) F♯	D
11	201		tacet				
12	208		tacet				
13	212–219	8	8	Ab	GF♯	b F♯	D
14	220–225	6	6	fe	de	e e	C
15	226–233	8	4 4	Ab	FE	b E	D
16	234–241	8	8	de	FE(B)	e E	D
17	242		tacet				
18	248		tacet				
19	256–260	–	free	dfe	Ab	e b	D

SUMMARY OF TABLE 17

I & II. There are 12 sung phrases.

III. The frequency of each type of phrase length is as follows:

   6 eight bars
   2 four bars
   1 twelve bars
   2 six bars
   1 free

iv. The motivic divisions are as follows:

1 free
7 undivided
3 symmetrical
1 asymmetrical

v. The opening movements of phrases are arranged as follows:

8 LN
3 UN
1 3rd

vi. The cadence formulas are summarized as follows:

8 LN
2 UN
0 S
1 4th
1 PC to LN

vii. The basic pitch progressions move in the following manners:

E leads to B or F♯
B leads to E or F♯
F♯ leads to B or E (see discussion below)

viii. A summary of the general direction of each phrase gives the following results:

0 U
8 D
3 S
1 C

Comparing this vocal line with its accompanying shamisen part as found in Table 16 one finds that the phrase lengths generally coincide. When the vocal part is longer, it is usually in the nature of an extended cadence which leads into an instrumental interlude. Likewise, with the exception of a beautifully tenuous twelve-bar line at the very beginning, the internal motivic structure is similar. The vocal part differs from the shamisen in the extensive use of lower neighbor cadences and openings, but it is the pitch-progression column which appears to be most unusual. Phrase 9 shows what appears to be a change to an A pitch center followed by another phrase opening with the lower neighbor of that pitch (G) which in turn resolves not to A but to F♯. Taking both the shamisen and vocal part together from measure 186 one finds that a long passage of repeated D's is followed by an E and then a B and A. This could be thought of as a phrase built on the yō scale, starting from A. The passage immediately before this phrase (180–85), however, firmly establishes a pitch center of B and the passage immediately after this phrase (192–95) pulls toward B though it is weakened by a series of F's. It is followed by a motive strongly in B (196–98). The deciding phrase is measures 192–95. If one thinks of this as being in A and using a yō scale (as it would have to be in order to have a B in it) then the normal note below A would be F♯ and not F. While the F does not belong to the normal B scale of either yō or in, it is found in the so-called plagal mode of the in scale (see Example 5). Therefore, it seems logical to suppose that this entire section from 180 to 198 is built around a B pitch center in which different scale structures are used, the apparent half cadence in the voice being resolved in the shamisen in the next two measures.

An apparent deviation from the movement in fifths appears in phrase 13 in which an F♯ seems to move directly to E. Looking at the music (measure 220), however, one finds that there is a rest and an F natural before the appearance of the E. This chromatic change is very important to the smooth resolution of the passage. The measures immediately before this lean strongly toward B so that this is not a case of a clearly established F♯ moving to an E as the chart might indicate.

Another observation on the vocal line is the concentration on downward moving lines. This is in keeping with the facts noted in the previous section of the piece (see Table 15). Finally, a study of the final ornaments of the vocal parts of both the oki (Table 15) and the ageuta (Table 17) reveals that a majority of these final notes are the lower neighbors of the true finalis. In one case (phrase 16 in Table 17) the drop is a fourth. Of the two cases which go above the final note and return to it (phrases 7 and 15 in Table 15), one returns to the pitch center because the shamisen enters immediately (see measure 53) and the other returns to the note at a moment when the shamisen is repeating the pitch center (see measure 111).

THE HAYASHI MUSIC: The opening passage for the ageuta (130–37) is unusual in its use of a solo ko-tsuzumi percussion accompaniment. The drum follows the rhythm of the shamisen and underlays the line with rich pon sounds. This may be a slight imitation of the noh-drum tradition, with its patterns which use consecutive pon sounds, or it may be more a matter of a very bright and different instrumentation for the opening of this new section.

The remainder of the ageuta is set in a rather standard chirikara procedure (see page 83). The two tsuzumi are used as a unit and show only very short moments of independence such as in measure 152. Even then, they relate to the shamisen line closely. The drum calls all occur between phrases in the kabuki fashion. At measure 226 there is a sudden change in style. The ō-tsuzumi plays the noh pattern uke and the ko-tsuzumi plays mitsuji. At this moment of change the shamisen melody becomes more restrained, perhaps to allow the vocal line more freedom to move in the manner of a noh singing part. The use of noh patterns continues until the sectional cadence at 256. The rhythmic relation between the drums and the vocal line in an eight-beat orientation certainly indicates a tendency toward noh style. Example 17 shows this relation for the vocal phrase beginning in measure 226.[5] At first, drum calls and beats fall before or on the expected beats (3 and 5). In actuality, however, the first drum beat in 226 is beat 3 of the pattern

EXAMPLE 17: *Relations between voice and drums in* Tsuru-kame

VOCAL BEATS	1	2	3	4	5	6	7	8
VOCAL LINE	hō—rai		san	mo		yoso na-ra-zu		
DRUMS			ho ↓		yo ∧	ho ↓		
	ho ⌐						yo ⌐	
DRUM BEAT	3	4	5	6	7	8	1	2

uke[6] so that the calls are before the fifth, seventh, and eighth beats of the drum line. This means that the eight-bar phrasing of the shamisen-vocal line is for the moment two beats ahead of the drum line. The tension created by this discrepancy is an important factor in the dynamism of the music. In the next phrase the voice once more uses eight beats, that is, eight measures. The shamisen phrase, however, is only six bars long. Thus, when the interlude begins the drums and shamisen are in a common rhythmic orientation. At this point, however, the counting is doubled, quarter notes being used as the basic orientation instead of halves. In the next to last phrase (248) the shamisen plays an eight-beat passage so that the final cadence of the drums overlaps into the beginning of the last vocal-shamisen phrase.

SUMMARY OF THE AGEUTA

Instrumentation: Voices, shamisen, and both tsuzumi are used.

[5] Compare this with examples in Malm, "The Rhythmic Orientation of Two Drums in the Japanese No Drama," *Ethnomusicology* (Sept., 1958), pp. 94–95.
[6] See Tazaki Nobujirō, *Kadono-ryū Ō-tsuzumi Kaitei* (Tokyo: Hinoki Shoten, 1925), p. 26.

The vocal-shamisen lines: Eight- and four-bar phrases are most common. Descending lines are prevalent, particularly in the vocal line. Lower neighbor cadences predominate. The internal structure of phrases is more even and makes greater use of consonant tones. This is partially offset by the extensive use of pickup notes in the shamisen part.

Pitch centers: The overall pitch progression for this section is E to B to E to B. The two apparent breaks in the movement via a cycle of fifths have been shown actually to involve a more subtle use of modulatory schemes than have hitherto been found in the music.

Tempo and rhythms: The tempo increase is accompanied by the use of strong kabuki-style drum music. When noh-drum patterns appear, the shamisen becomes more restrained, and the voice uses eight-beat phrase lengths.

General remarks: The change from kabuki to noh drumming is the point of greatest interest as well as the manner in which the drum phrases are matched or pitted against the vocal line.

3. THE MONDŌ (261–92)

THE TEXT: The mondō in the original play is a dialogue between a nobleman and the emperor. The nobleman says that he has something to communicate. The emperor asks what it is. He replies that almost every year on such happy occasions the sacred crane has danced after which court dances (bugaku) were performed in the palace. The emperor then commands that such a thing be done now also.

THE SHAMISEN MUSIC: An outline of the shamisen part is shown in Table 18. Since this section is almost entirely a recitative, a long measure of rest must be included in the determination of the length of various phrases.

TABLE 18: *Outline of the shamisen part for the mondō of* Tsuru-kame

I	II	III	IV	V	VI	VII		VIII
1	261–226	6	4 2	bF♯	Ab	b	b	S
2	267–270	4	4	c♯(d)	GF♯	c♯	F♯	D
3	271–277	7	4 3	bF♯	GF♯	b	F♯	D
4	278–281	4	4	bF♯	GF♯	b	F♯	D
5	282–285	4	4	b	Ab	b	b	S
6	286–292	–	free	Ab	FE	b	E	D

ɪ & ɪɪ. There are only 6 phrases.

ɪɪɪ. The frequency of each type of phrase length is as follows:

3 four bars
1 six bars
1 seven bars
1 free

ɪᴠ. The motivic divisions are as follows:

1 free
3 undivided
0 symmetrical
2 asymmetrical

ᴠ. The opening movements of phrases are arranged as follows:

1 LN
0 UN
1 S
3 4th
1 PC to UN

ᴠɪ. The cadence formulas are as follows:

2 LN
4 UN

ᴠɪɪ. The pitch progressions move in the following order:

B leads to C♯, F♯ or E (last time only)
C♯ leads to F♯
F♯ leads to B

ᴠɪɪɪ. The general direction of the phrases is as follows:

0 U
4 D
2 S

The reader may remember that the shamisen part of this section consists entirely of ōzatsuma patterns. These are listed on page 68. It was explained earlier how these patterns tend to begin with simple "tonic" patterns and become more remote only to return to the "tonic" pattern much in the manner of recitative harmonies in Western opera. The short phrases evident from the summation of Table 18 are also in keeping with the recitative-like function of this section.

One of the most interesting facts to be noted from the study of this brief section is the prevalence of B, F♯, and C♯ sounds. The overall pitch center progression is from B to F♯ to B and the E pitch center which so far has dominated this piece does not appear until the recitative is over. This will be shown to be very typical of nagauta recitatives. Another point of interest is the unusual opening pattern found in measure 267. At first it appears to be an exception to the normal movement of lines from neighbor tones to pitch centers. When viewed in its musical situation, however, it is found that the first two notes are an anacrusis to a measure that centers on F♯. Thus, the D may be considered as a passing tone between the C♯ and the F♯. A final point to be noted is the downward tendency of these patterns. This holds true for a majority of ōzatsuma passages.

THE VOCAL MUSIC: Much of the vocal part is done in a heightened speech manner so that specific speech determination is not possible.

TABLE 19: *Outline of the vocal part for the mondō of* Tsuru-kame

I	II	III	IV	V	VI	VII	VIII
1	261–266	6	4 2	Ab		b b	S
2	267–269	3	3	spoken			
3	270–276	7	4 3	spoken			
4	277–281	5	5	spoken			
5	282–285	4	4	Ab		b b	S
6	286–292	—	free	AFE	DE	E E	C

SUMMARY OF TABLE 19

I & II. Of the 6 phrases only the last one is completely sung in nagauta. Two others begin in singing and end in heightened speech.

III. The frequency of types of phrase lengths is as follows:

    1 four bars
    1 seven bars
    1 six bars
    1 five bars
    1 three bars
    1 free

IV. The motivic divisions are as follows:

    1 free
    3 undivided
    2 asymmetrical

V. Of the three sung phrases one uses an upper neighbor and two use a lower neighbor.

VI. The only sung cadence ends with a lower neighbor to pitch center progression.

VII & VIII. The only progression evident in the vocal part is from B to E and the line is basically static. One should note, however, that the contour of the spoken lines indicates that every line will rise and then return back down producing a final downward turn to each phrase.

The unusual phrase lengths and special manner of singing are part of a general effort on the part of the composer to evoke the atmosphere of noh singing. It is in this respect that the barring of the vocal line (which follows exactly that of the original nagauta notation) is most misleading. Actually, the line could be barred as shown in Example 18, if one followed the manner in which it is performed. Such a notation tradition, however, does not exist in Japan.

EXAMPLE 18: *A possible barring of the vocal part of the mondō of* Tsuru-kame

Viewing the one lyric phrase of this section (286–92) one finds that the languorous pace of the music is offset by an extensive and very lovely use of tense pitches—dissonant tones (A, F, and D) which wind their way slowly down from B to E.

THE HAYASHI MUSIC: Drums and flutes are not used in this section.

SUMMARY OF THE MONDŌ

Instrumentation: The music is set for one singer and one shamisen player except for the last phrase in which the other shamisen enter.

Vocal-shamisen parts: Both parts reveal a different approach to most of the elements of the music. The phrase lengths are more uneven and are shorter. The shamisen makes greater use of the F♯ and B areas. The overall effect is one of noh declamatory music, though the imitation is not direct. The prevalence of cadence patterns in the shamisen starting on upper neighbors is matched by the general movement of the lines downward.

Pitch progressions: The emphasis on B and F♯ is idiomatic of recitative sections. The basic progression is B to F♯ to B to E. B is treated as the central pitch for this section and therefore it is possible to jump from it to other pitches farther away than one fifth. Thus, one finds the use of C♯ in phrase 2 after a cadence in B. Part of the reason for this progression is that the dialogue section is set in the yō scale on B rather than the in scale which contains the note C natural.

General remarks: The use of ōzatsuma patterns and their concomitant changes in phrasing and pitch centers sets this section off very clearly from the rest of the piece. This section serves as an excellent musical buffer between the lively ageuta and the more lyric section that is to follow.

4. THE CHŪ NO MAI (293–347)

THE TEXT: The next section of the original play is the dance of the crane and the tortoise. The text says that both creatures have been living for many decades. The original music in the noh drama is derived from the standard dance piece "Chū no Mai," hence the use of that title for this section of the nagauta piece. It is very serene and rather like a kudoki except for the instrumentation which includes the tsuzumi as well as singers and shamisen.

THE SHAMISEN MUSIC

TABLE 20: *Outline of the shamisen part for the chū no mai in* Tsuru-kame

I	II	III	IV	V	VI	VII		VIII
1	293–299	7	7	F♯(G)	cb	F♯	b	U
2	300–306 ×	6	6	E	C	E		S
3	307–313	7	7	E	b	E	b	C
4	314–320 ×	6	6	E	C	E		S
5	321–324	4	4	E	cb	Eb		C
6	325–331	7	7	F♯(G)	cb	F♯	b	U
7	332–338 ×	6	6	E	C	E		S
8	339–345	7	7	E	b	E	b	C
9	346–353	8	4 4	E	Ab	E	b	U

SUMMARY OF TABLE 20

I & II. There are 9 phrases in all. The three phrases marked with an × contain a bar of one-four which has been counted as part of the previous two-four measure in the counting of phrase lengths.

III. The frequency of each type of phrase length is as follows:

1	(last one)	eight bars
4		seven bars
3		six bars
1	(middle one)	four bars

IV. There is one symmetrical phrase and the others are undivided.

v. The opening movements of phrases are arranged as follows:

    0 LN
    0 UN
    7 S
    2 PC to UN

vi. The cadence formulas close as follows:

    1 (last one)   LN
    3   UN
    5 (three on unstable tones) S

vii. The pitch progressions are as follows:

    E leads to B
    B leads to E and F♯
    F♯ leads to B

The basic progression is between E and B.

viii. The general direction of the phrases is as follows:

    3 U
    3 C
    3 S

The shamisen-vocal setting of this dance is done in the form of a strophic song. There are two major strophes (293–324 and 325–49) plus an ending cadence. Within each strophe, however, there are several repeated phrases. Therefore, the form could be outlined as follows: (1) Introduction, A, B, A, B, (2) Introduction, A, B, A, C. The entire dance is a beautiful study in restrained nagauta lyricism. It is set off from the rest of the piece in many ways. First of all, it uses a yō scale on E as its basic structure and does not deviate from it though it does move to the fifth B. For example, the opening passage (293–324) arrives on a half cadence (B). F♯ begins this phrase, but there is a persistent use of the note E throughout the passage which keeps the B from sounding as the tonic pitch of the scale system. Table 20 reveals an unusually repetitive situation. All but the opening passages of each strophe begin on E and end on B. In addition, rhythmic and intervallic tensions are removed from the shamisen when the vocalist enters in order to enhance the mood of quiet dignity requisite for this dance. This is perhaps the most relaxed phrase in the entire piece. Compare this passage, for example, with measures 390–400 in which the shamisen part is equally sparse but supports a much more intense lyricism by its emphasis on neighbor tones.

There are yet other factors which enhance the uniqueness of this section. The use of curved and rising rather than falling lines as shown in Table 20 could perhaps be explained as an attempt to buoy up the lyricism. In addition, it is interesting to note the complete lack of anacruses in the shamisen part. This helps to reduce its sense of activity and contrasts sharply with the deliberate use of anacruses in more forceful sections such as the ageuta (130–260). Finally, one should note the special use of uneven phrases (7 followed by 6) and the interesting shortening of the antecedent phrase by three beats.

THE VOCAL MUSIC: As the most lyrical section in the piece, one can expect to find the vocal part most carefully constructed.

TABLE 21 : *Outline for the vocal part of the chū no mai of* Tsuru-kame

I	II	III	IV	V	VI	VII		VIII
1	293–		tacet					
2	300–308 ×	8	8	de	Ab(A)	e	b	D
3	309–313	5	5	bf♯	Ab(A)	(b)	f♯♭	D
4	314–322 ×	8	3 5	DE	A'b(CB)	E	B	D
5	323		tacet					
6	325		tacet					
7	332–340 ×	8	8	ee	Ab(A)	e	b	D
8	341–345	5	5	cf♯	Ab(A)	f♯	b	D
9	346–353	8	3 5	DE	Ab(A)	E	b	U

SUMMARY OF TABLE 21

I & II. There are 6 sung phrases. As explained earlier, the phrases marked with an × contain a bar of one-four which has been counted as part of the previous two-four measure in the counting of phrase lengths.

III. The types of phrases are as follows:

    4 eight bars
    2 five bars

IV. The motivic division is as follows:

    4   undivided
    2 (both are 3 and 5) asymmetrical

V. Opening movements are as follows:

    3 LN
    0 UN
    1 S
    1 5th
    1 dim. 5th

VI. Cadence formulas end in the following manner:

    6 LN
    0 UN

vii. The pitch progressions are as follows:

          E leads to B

          B leads to F♯ or E

          F♯ leads to B

viii. The direction of phrases is as follows:

          1   U

          5   D

          0   S

The vocal line reveals several interesting points not found in the shamisen part. First of all, its phrase structure is a combination of eight's and five's rather than seven's and six's. Looking at the music one finds that the voice enters a fraction before the beginning of phrase 2 (300) and continues its cadence while the shamisen begins a new phrase (308). It is just before this moment that the extra beat is added to the normal duple orientation of nagauta. The early entrance, the elongation in the middle by an extra beat, and the vocal cadence all contribute to the creation of a truly long vocal line. Note that this line drifts slowly from neighbor tones to consonant notes while the shamisen plays quietly on these consonances. The next vocal phrase (309) rises a fifth only to fall back a seventh to the lower neighbor of its starting point. The final phrase of the first strophe (314) returns to the undulating diatonic line but on a lower pitch level. The direction of the entire strophe, then, is downward from a high E to its lower octave with a short pause on the intervening B. Thus, the three phrases of the strophe balance artistically with the two ends being stylistically related and the middle phrase an active contrast and connection between them. When the strophe is repeated (332–53) the same process is followed until the last phrase in which the line suddenly rises to a final cadence on the B between the two E's (compare the endings of phrase 4 and phrase 9).

THE HAYASHI MUSIC: In this section only the two tsuzumi are used. The drum music for the beginning of the dance is an interesting example of chirikara rhythms being applied to a slow section. One would expect to find noh patterns in such a situation as this, since the atmosphere seems so closely related to that of the original noh dance. Perhaps the tension usually created by the use of noh patterns in conjunction with shamisen melodies was felt to be inappropriate. Actually, this drum phrase is a compromise because it mixes kabuki-style rhythmic support with a noh-like placement of the drum calls, thus producing a pseudo-noh-drama effect. Of particular interest is the yo (299) which trails off into the vocal section. Such a device is common in noh but rare in pure kabuki music.

The drums enter again in the middle of the first vocal phrase after a one-beat extension of the melodic cadence (305–6), using kabuki-style music.

The next melodic phrase (314–23) is basically the same as 300–9, the vocal line being an octave lower. This time, however, it is accompanied on the drums by a variation of the noh pattern mitsuji. As before, the second phrase in the shamisen and the drums overlaps the vocal cadence, and the drums return to kabuki patterns.

The second strophe (325–53) begins with the same drum accompaniment as before. At the cadence of the B section (344) they shift to an altered version of the noh pattern *uchiage*.[7] This pattern begins with a drum call iya, which gives one the impression of a cadential kashira pattern. It serves a double role in this case, however, creating both a cadence and the beginning of a new pattern. In the performance from which the transcription was made, the final drum cadence (352) is played slightly after the first beat while in the original drum notation it is shown as falling on the beat. Since, however, cadences are rhythmically flexible the "correct" placement is difficult to determine. In such quiet sections, performance practice would seem to indicate that the staggered cadences in the transcription are stylistically correct.

SUMMARY OF CHŪ NO MAI

Instrumentation: Voices, shamisen, and two tsuzumi are used.

Vocal-shamisen part: The style of both the shamisen and the vocal line have been considerably altered in order to create a new, more lyrical music. Two internally balanced strophes are set with a widely-spaced, consonant shamisen part over which the voice is able to soar easily. The phrasing is so constructed that melodic tension between the two parts is created in the central part of each strophe while a relative calm is maintained at each end. Though the pitch centers remain relatively static, the directions of the two lines do not coincide until the last phrase. By a combination of such features, the composer has created an artistic balance between a mood of calm and the necessity of musical movement.

Pitch progression: The overall movement is from E to B and back to E with the yō scale on E being the basis of the entire

[7] See Tazaki, *op. cit.*, p. 25.

section. Progressions keep to the cycle of fifths and the major tendency is for each line to begin on E and end on B.

Tempo and rhythm: The tempo is moderate to slow. The drum parts illustrate a subtle alternation of kabuki and noh patterns in such a way that the effect of noh music is created without the restrictive rhythmic problems endemic to it.

General remarks: As the most lyrical section, ample opportunity is given to the singer to show his abilities. The change in many of the characteristics of the music only serves to enhance the special quality of this section.

5. THE ODORIJI (354-518)

THE TEXT: This section is marked in the original play as the final dan of the ha.[8] It is called the odoriji here because, as will be shown, it has the major characteristics of such a section of a nagauta piece. The text speaks further of the tortoise and the crane. Both creatures have lived for centuries like the *hime* pine tree. What other example can one find of such longevity? The sacred crane with its feathery, sleeve-like wings dances and plays as it has through the ages. On the edge of the pond there is a thick grove of bamboo which has lived for ages just as the tortoise in the water. The tortoise performs in honor of the peaceful reign of his majesty. The tortoise and the crane offer prayers for long life to the emperor, who looks on appreciatively and then joins in the dance.

The instrumentation at the very opening is typical of an odoriji section, the taiko and bamboo flute joining with the voices and shamisen. The delayed entrance of the tsuzumi found here is also common. The taiko and flute are omitted from the last of this section in order to create a contrast when they return in the next part of the piece.

THE SHAMISEN MUSIC: At the beginning of this section the shamisen change their tuning to ni-agari. This is a common tuning for odoriji sections.

TABLE 22: *Outline of the shamisen part for the odoriji of* Tsuru-kame

I	II	III	IV		V		VI	VII		VIII
1	354-361	8	5	3	F♯		Ab	F♯	b	U
2	362-371	10	3	3 4	b		Ab	b	b	S
3	372-377	6	1	5	e(f)	c-b	bF♯	b	F♯	D
4	378-385	8	8		ef♯		f♯	f♯	f♯	S

[8] *Yōkyoku Zenshū*, Vol. I, p. 361.

I	II	III	IV				V	VI	VII		VIII
5	386–389	4	4				gf♯	cb	f♯	b	D
6	390–404	15	7	8			ef♯g	bF♯	f♯	F♯	D
7	405–414	10	3	2	2	3	bAb	EF♯	b	F♯	D
8	415–423	9	2	7			ef♯g	cb	f♯	b	D
9	424–427	4	4				ef♯	ceb	f♯	b	D
10	428–435	8	4	4			gf♯	cb	f♯	b	D
11	436–443	8	4	4			CB	ef♯	B	f♯	U
12	444–447	4	4				f♯	GF♯	f♯	F♯	D
13	448–451	4	4				BF♯	AB	B	B	S
14	452–466	15	3	4	8		cef♯	Ab	f♯	b	D
15	467–477	11	4	7			de	bF♯	e	F♯	D
16	478–484	7	7				Ab	bb	b	b	C
17	485–493 ×	8	4	4			G(F♯)	bc	F♯	b	U
18	494–500	7	4	3			bAb	b	b	b	S
19	501–506	6	3	3			cb	cb	b	b	S
20	507–512	6	3	3			c-(b)	cb	b	b	S
21	513–517	5	5				(B)GF♯	c♯bc♯	B	c♯	U
22	517–518	–	free				f♯ef♯	GF♯	f♯	F♯	D

SUMMARY OF TABLE 22

I & II. There are 22 phrases in the shamisen part. Phrase 17 contains a three-beat measure.

III. The frequency of each type of phrase length is as follows:

5	eight bars
4	four bars
1	five bars
3	six bars
2	seven bars
1	nine bars
2	ten bars
1	eleven bars
2	fifteen bars
1	free

IV. The motivic divisions are as follows:

7	undivided
4	symmetrical
10	asymmetrical
1	free

V. The opening movements of phrases are as follows:

5	LN
8	UN
6	S
1	5th

TSURU-KAME   143

2   unresolved upper neighbors

VI. The cadence formulas are as follows:

       6   LN
       8   UN
       4   S
       3   4th
       1   PC to UN

VII. The pitch progressions are as follows:

       E leads to B or F♯
       B leads to F♯ or E or C♯
       F♯ leads to B
       C♯ leads to F♯

VIII. The general directions of phrases are as follows:

       4   U
    11   D
       6   S
       1   C

The statistics derived from this section do not differ greatly from those of the first part of the piece. Eight- and four-bar phrases are once more in the majority as are asymmetrical divisions of the remaining phrases. There is a notable increase in the variety of phrases, particularly among those of greater length. These are created by the persistent pausing on unresolved dissonances. The best examples of this are the two fifteen-bar phrases (phrases 6 and 14). Both involve the use of the stereotyped shamisen melody tataki.[9] In the first example (390) the suspense of waiting for the resolution of the G to F♯ is cleverly attenuated by passing reference to the F♯ in the voice. At 396 the voice passes to E only to go on to the dissonant tone G. The vocal resolution again is on E while the shamisen removes the pitch center feeling from that E by going on to C. This note combines with A in the vocal line to surround B which in turn descends to F♯. The sophistication of such a passage is typical of the best of the nagauta tradition.

The second fifteen-bar phrase (452) uses the tataki pattern on a new pitch level. In this case it appears in the middle of the phrase (456). In phrase 8 (415) the opening three notes of a tataki pattern are heard. This time, however, the G is quickly resolved as the line moves on in quarter notes. It is interesting to note that phrase 10 (428) pauses once in its descent from F♯ to B and this pause is on a C. Thus, the moment of rhythmic rest is offset by the use of unresolved tones.

[9] See *Ongaku Jiten*, 6 (1957), p. 158. This pattern has no relation to the ōzatsuma pattern called tataki.

This use of melodically tense tones is evident in the first phrase of the last part of the odoriji (478–519). Of the three points of emphasis in phrase 16 (478) the first two are dissonant (C in 479 and G in 481) and only the last one is consonant. Note that this last pitch B is repeated in the same bar (♩ ♩̆) rather than the usual manner (♩ ⅂ !♩̆ ⅂). This gives it a rhythmic life it would not have normally.

Phrase 15 (467) would seem to show an example of a break in the movement of pitch centers in a cycle of fifths. One finds in the music, however, that between the opening E and the closing F♯ there appears a passage which centers around B (471), thus maintaining the cyclic progression.

Finally, the prevalence of descending lines should be noted as another sign of a return to normal nagauta style in contrast with the special section just completed.

THE VOCAL MUSIC: The basic facts concerning the vocal part are shown in Table 23. Note that the number of phrases is different from that of the shamisen part. This is due to the difference in phrase lengths and also to the fact that the shamisen has several interludes of various lengths. Short tacet passages in the voice have sometimes been indicated only by missing measure numbers in column II.

TABLE 23: *Outline of the vocal part for the odoriji of* Tsuru-kame

I	II	III	IV	V	VI	VII	VIII
1	354		tacet				
2	360–371	12	7 5	bcb	Ab(A)	b b	S
3	372–377	6	6	cb	EF♯	b F♯	D
4	378–387	10	2 8	e(b′)	ef♯(e)	e f♯	U
5	392–399	8	5 3	eg(f♯)	(g)f♯(e)	e e	S
6	400–403	4	4	Ab	Ab	b b	S
7	404–410	7	3 4	F♯EF♯	Abcb	F♯ b	U
8	411–415	5	5	EF♯	EF♯(E)	F♯ F♯	S
9	416–427	12	3 3 6	g-f♯	Ab	f♯ b	D
10	428–439	12	3 4 5	ef♯	Ab(A)	f♯ b	D
11	440		tacet				
12	444		tacet				
13	448–451	4	4	EF♯	EF♯(GF♯)	F♯ F♯	S
14	452–456	5	5	bcb	Ab(A)	b b	C
15	457–465	9	6 3	c(b)	cb(A)	b b	S
16	466–472	7	3 4	bAb	cb(A)	b b	C
17	473–477	5	5	A-b	EF♯(E)	b F♯	D
18	478–484	7	3 4	Ab	eb	b b	C

I	II	III	IV	V	VI	VII	VIII
19	485–493 ×	8	4 4	Ab(G)F♯	Abc	F♯ b	C
20	494–500	7	7	Ab	bb	b b	S
21	501–506	6	6	Ab	cb	b b	S
22	507–512	6	6	Ab	cb	b b	S
23	513–516	4	4	bGF♯	bc♯(b)	b c♯	U
24	517–518	–	free	bf♯	EF♯	f♯ F♯	D

SUMMARY OF TABLE 23

I & II. The voice sings 21 phrases.

III. The frequency of each type of phrase length is as follows:

- 2 eight bars
- 3 four bars
- 4 seven bars
- 3 six bars
- 3 five bars
- 3 twelve bars
- 1 ten bars
- 1 nine bars
- 1 free

IV. The motivic divisions are:

- 1 free
- 10 undivided
- 1 symmetrical
- 9 asymmetrical

V. The opening movements are:

- 10 LN
- 4 UN
- 4 S
- 2 5th
- 1 3rd

VI. The cadence formulas are:

- 13 LN
- 5 UN
- 1 S
- 1 4th
- 1 PC to UN

VII. The pitch progressions are:

E leads to B and appears once between two F♯'s.

B leads to F♯ or C♯

C♯ leads to F♯

F♯ leads to B and once to E

VIII. The general direction of root movements is:

- 3 U

5 D
9 S
4 C

The vocal part, like the shamisen music, shows a greater variety of phrase lengths. There is more overlapping in the phrases of the two parts. The vocal phrases are less frequently divided and it is only toward the end of the section (phrase 18) that the two parts tend to phrase together.

Though the phrasing is more complex, one finds a significant reassertion of the importance of lower neighbors to the phrase structures of the vocal music. Movements from lower neighbors to pitch centers dominate both the openings and closings of phrases. Another interesting observation to be made is that the pitch center E, which previously has been very important, is here relegated to a transitional phrase between two F♯'s (phrase 4) plus an ambiguous situation (phrase 5). The change in tuning has apparently been accompanied by a new hierarchy of pitch-center relations. The shamisen part corroborates this fact as it also uses E only once (in phrase 15).

Perhaps the most unusual characteristic of the vocal line in the odoriji is the decrease in the number of descending lines in favor of static lines. This may be due in part to the increased number of words sung in each phrase, as, for example, in measures 494–500. Between the common pitch centers at the two ends of such phrases, however, one finds curved melodic lines, for example, measures 452–56 and 478–84. Note that six of the static lines center around B and two use F♯ and only one uses E. With the increase in tempo, rhythmic activity, and the number of words it would seem wise to refrain from complicated root movements, especially since the new tuning has necessitated the establishment of a new basic pitch relationship centered around B.

Before leaving the vocal part one should note the subtle transition which marks the beginning of the closing section of the odoriji (485–93). The line first encircles a low F♯ in a busy manner and then elongates the phrase (489) on the word "tsuru," beginning on the F♯ an octave higher. The drop to the dissonant C and the movement from A to C through their mutual resolution B on the word "kame" are performed in a rubato fashion. The C drops once more to A before the agitated finale begins and eventually finds its true resolution on B. Before that time, however, the composer has provided ample opportunity for the line to build up an air of expectancy through the exploitation of unresolved tones.

THE HAYASHI MUSIC: The entire hayashi ensemble is used for the section, with the bamboo flute being substituted for the noh flute. As was mentioned in earlier chapters, the traditional instrumentation of an odoriji will include this flute and the taiko.

The bamboo flute plays in all of the odoriji up to the transition (478). Its function remains the same throughout, that of embroidering and supporting the melodic line. The melismas notated here are typical but not the only possible ones. As mentioned in the earlier study of the flute music, the notation indicates only where the performer is to begin. Even in lessons only the basic melody is taught. The player must learn to add his own ornamentations by listening to his mentors.

TABLE 24: *Drum patterns for the odoriji of* Tsuru-kame

TAIKO	KO-TSUZUMI	Ō-TSUZUMI
1. uchidashi (361)	tsuke-hikae (364)	uchidashi (364)
2. tsuke-gashira (372)	uke-hashiri (372)	uke-gashira (372)
3. tsuke-gashira	uke-hashiri	uke-gashira
4. oroshi	uke-mitsuji	uke
5. kizami	uchihanashi	kashira
6. kizami	musubi-nagaji	ji
7. agete	↓	taka-kizami
8. uchikiri, kashira	ko	uchikiri
9. tsuke-gashira	uke-hashiri	uke-gashira
10. oroshi	uke-mitsuji	uke
11. taka-kizami	uchihanashi	nidanme
12. hiraki (hane)	musubi	uchikaeshi
13. uchikomi	uchikomi	uchikomi

The drum music for the odoriji is derived entirely from noh patterns. These are listed in Table 24 above. These thirteen patterns accompany the music from measures 361 through 475, at which point the transition begins. The arrow in line 7 and similar arrows in subsequent tables of drum music indicate that the previous pattern continues. The three parts are all based on the eight-beat orientation of the noh. Frequently the three drums will play noh patterns but begin on different counts. Comparing the music of this section, however, with the various patterns as taught out of context it is found that all the drums use the same beat "one." The drummers are counting one measure as one beat at this time so that the first drum beat number "one" falls on measure 356 and the next one is on 364, etc. The fact that these patterns do not sound as if they are beginning on that beat should not mislead the listener. The discrepancy between the overall drum beat and the sound was mentioned earlier as characteristic of the Japanese noh-music system (see page 88).

Though the drums move in equal phrases they do not seem merely to reinforce each other. For example, the only time all three drums play a commonly named pattern (which does not necessarily mean common rhythms) is at the final cadence. The taiko and ō-tsuzumi play kashira patterns at the other two cadences (lines 2 and 9). The entire taiko part, by the way, illustrates a standard progression of patterns as discussed in Chapter VI.

After line 8 (417–28) the progression in all three parts appears to begin again, lines 2 and 9 being identical. It is noteworthy that at the end of line 9 (436) the shamisen begins its interlude. In this way the new shamisen idea is matched by a repeat of the rhythmic pattern progressions.

The general relation between the drums and the shamisen phrases is another point of interest. The shamisen does not phrase as evenly as the drums though many of its phrases are eight beats long. For example, the shamisen phrase lengths for the opening of this section (354) are 8, 10, 6, 8, 4, 15, 10, 9, 4, and 8 measures (to measure 435). While the first phrase is eight beats long, it begins two beats before the first beat of the drum pattern (which is counted but not played). Therefore, the first drum sound actually heard (361) is beat "six" of the drum pattern but appears at the end of the first shamisen phrase. By such a system the drum part is seen once more to function as a foil for the exposition of the melody rather than just a rhythmic support.

During the beginning of the transition section (478) the drums drop out. When the tsuzumi return at 494 they begin with the noh pattern mitsuji and then play kabuki patterns. The change in style is quite logical and musical since the entire mood changes at this point and the tempo has quickened. The transition from the first pattern into the kabuki-style rhythms is an additional example of the skill of the men who arranged this composition. A further example of the subtlety of transitions in this piece is evident in the entrance of the taiko (518) which bridges the gap between the transition and the next section.

SUMMARY OF THE ODORIJI

Instrumentation: Singers, shamisen, bamboo flute, and taiko begin the music. This is the standard instrumentation for an odoriji. The tsuzumi join later and are the only percussion used during the transition section.

The vocal-shamisen lines: While eight- and four-bar phrases still prevail there is a greater variety of phrase structures in both parts, the shamisen particularly using longer phrases. These are often made possible by the use of unresolved tones at the end of the motive groups which delay the final cadence. The extensive use of lower neighbor cadences is noticeable in the vocal part along with a large number of static lines. Rhythmic activity in both parts in general has been increased.

Pitch center progressions: In the new tuning, ni-agari, the basic pitch center progression is from B with many half cadences to F♯ and back to B. There is little reference to the center E, and C♯ appears once, resolving to F♯.

Tempo and rhythm: The tempo begins moderately and increases toward the end. For the first part all three drums form a unit of noh-derived music while the flute joins the melodic group. The rhythmic phrases are deliberately out of phase with the melodic periods and follow standard orders of progression. The change to kabuki rhythms at the end is warranted by the increased activity and change in mood.

General remarks: The extensive use of noh patterns in this odoriji is in contrast with the normal kabuki orientation of such sections in most nagauta. The reason for the change is probably due to the origin of the text and the noh-dance quality found in the words of this particular section.

6. THE GAKU (519–75)

THE TEXT: The gaku section is the main dance (mai) of the principal actor in the original play.[10] It is accompanied by the hayashi without singing in the noh version, hence there is no text. The nagauta piece uses the hayashi with noh flute plus shamisen. An obbligato shamisen is added. This has been notated in the top line of the score and is marked uwajōshi.

THE SHAMISEN MUSIC: Table 25 outlines the principal shamisen line. This part is played in the hon-chōshi tuning.

TABLE 25: *Outline of the shamisen part for the gaku of* Tsuru-kame

I	II	III	IV	V	VI	VII		VIII
1	519–522	4	4	E	b	E	b	U
2	523–526	4	4	B	bc♯	B	c♯	U

[10] Takano, *op. cit.*, Vol. I, p. 361.

I	II	III	IV	V	VI	VII	VIII
3	327–530	4	4	f♯	B̂F♯	f♯ F♯	D
4	531–534	4	4	B̂F♯	B̂F♯	F♯ F♯	S
5	535–538	4	4	DC♯	BC♯	C♯ C♯	S
6	539–549	11	4 3 4	Bb(A)	b'(a)	b b'	U
7	550–557	8	4 4	b'gf♯	de	b' e	C
8	558–561	4	4	fae	e	e e	S
9	562–571	10	4 4 2	f♯e	Ab	f♯ b	C
10	572–575	4	4	b	b	b b	S

SUMMARY OF TABLE 25

ɪ & ɪɪ. There are 10 phrases.

ɪɪɪ. The frequency of each type of phrase length is:

    1   eight bars

    7   four bars

    1   eleven bars

    1   ten bars

ɪᴠ. The motivic divisions are:

    7   undivided

    1   symmetrical

    2   asymmetrical

ᴠ. The opening movement of phrases is as follows:

    0   LN

    2   UN

    5   S

    2   PC to LN

    1   3rd

ᴠɪ. The cadence formulas are as follows:

    4   LN

    0   UN

    5   S

    1   PC to LN

ᴠɪɪ. The pitch progressions are as follows:

    E leads to B or F♯

    B leads to C♯ or E

    F♯ leads to C♯ or B

    C♯ leads to B or F♯

ᴠɪɪɪ. The general direction of lines is:

    3   U

    1   D

    4   S

    2   C

The summary of this shamisen part reveals several unusual points. For the first time four-bar phrases take precedence over the eight-bar units. The two longer phrases (eleven and ten bars) are themselves subdivided into four-bar groups whenever possible, as is the eight-bar phrase. In addition, there is an unusual number of static progressions at both the beginnings and endings of phrases. It will be noted that few of the standard melodic types to be studied later (see Table 34) appear in this section. The music begins with two upward-directed phrases which in themselves are somewhat rare. Looking at the first five phrases one finds that the ending rhythm of the first two is identical, and the ending rhythm of the second group of three is also the same. These five phrases also end on very stable pitches, the weakest (C♯) appearing on the last phrase (537). The subsequent set of phrases follow groups of related rhythms as shown in Example 19. These phrases also illustrate the arsis and thesis principle in shamisen music. Phrase 6 (539) presents the question in B but ends on the tense tone A. The answer is given (543–49) in E ending on the note F and followed by a short motive exploiting an unresolved A. The next phrase returns to B, and its answer cadences in E. The two answering phrases (543–45 and 554–56) balance each other in contour, the first descending to a dissonance and the second ascending to a consonance. Such well-rounded phrases and periods might lead one to suspect Western influence if the date of the composition did not precede the entrance of Western music into Japan by some seventeen years.

EXAMPLE 19: *Rhythmic outlines of three phrases from* Tsuru-kame

In the last period the opening phrase (557) is in E and the answer (562) pulls to B. The use of the F natural (565) is a good example of the descending form of a scale being used in the midst of raised forms of the same scale degree. This note is particularly effective since it is the first quarter note after a long group of eights. Its resolution is coupled with a resurgence of rhythmic activity which speeds the music on to its concluding cadence.

The obbligato (uwajōshi) part illustrates a simple form of heterophony. Occasionally this line shows some melodic independence (see measures 535 and 556–59), but its general function is that of embroidering the main line. Perhaps the most striking moment to the Western ear is the sudden appearance of parallel thirds in measure 551. Note, however, that they are the result of a move to the lower neighbor of a drone on B in the obbligato part and are not a harmonization of the melody in the Western sense of the term.

THE VOCAL MUSIC: None present.

THE HAYASHI MUSIC: Since the original accompaniment of this dance was the hayashi alone, it is not surprising to find a strongly noh-oriented hayashi part in the nagauta piece. The noh flute plays the stereotyped melody gaku, one of the standard dance accompaniments. It is not played completely, as the nagauta interlude is not as long as the original noh dance. However, it phrases evenly in eight-bar groups starting from measure 519. In keeping with tradition, the countings of these phrases match exactly those of the taiko part.

TABLE 26: *Drum patterns for the gaku of* Tsuru-kame

TAIKO	KO-TSUZUMI	Ō-TSUZUMI
1. uchidashi (518)	kan-mitsuji (519)	uchidashi (521)
2. tsuke-gashira (527)	uke-mitsuji (527)	uke-gashira (527)
3. oroshi (535)	kan-mitsuji (535)	uke (537)
4. kizami (543)	jo-nagaji (543)	ji (543)
5. kizami (551)	↓	ji (551)
6. agete (559)	tsuzuke (559)	ji (559)
7. uchikiri (567)	nobe (567)	uchikiri (567)
8. kashira (572)	↓	↓
Patterns end 575	574	573

The drum parts are of particular interest. The patterns used are shown in Table 26 along with the measure number of beat "one" for each pattern. If one looks only at this chart, it would appear that all the parts are locked into a common rhythmic framework. When one looks at the transcription, however, the resultant rhythms seem to be surprisingly varied. As was mentioned before, the reason for this is that the various patterns have been arranged within the eight-beat phrase so that while the drums appear to phrase against each other, they actually are mentally using a common beat "one." This is the explanation of the apparently strange methods by which drum patterns are first learned. For example, the taiko pattern uchikiri (line 7) is listed as having a common beat "one" with the other drums.

This pattern, however, really begins on the beat "six" before this "one," so that on paper it looks as though the drums are phrasing together; but in practice the taiko begins three beats earlier (564). The pattern tsuke-gashira in line 2 is listed as having its first beat at measure 527, but in practice this pattern is learned as starting on beat "two" and continuing to the next beat "one." By such a method the player is able to play with ease the complicated cross phrasings by simply remembering each pattern in relation to its specific starting beat. Since teaching is entirely by rote, the drummer may never become aware of the exciting subtleties of rhythm that result from the combination of two or three such drum lines. For the listener, however, the effect is quite striking and also inexplicable until viewed from this special rhythmic orientation.

When this common rhythmic frame is combined with the shamisen yet another relationship is formed. Until measure 542 the shamisen cadences coincide with the eighth beat of the drums which, it must be remembered, does not *sound* as a final beat to the ear. A three-measure phrase (543–45) puts the shamisen one beat ahead of these eight-beat groups where it remains until 558. Here a four-bar phrase sets the shamisen further at odds with the drums until a final phrase (572–75), which ends on a drum count "one" for the first time.

Since the nagauta interlude is considerably shorter than the original noh dance, one cannot expect the drum music to coincide too closely with the original score. The taiko part offers the best example of the relationship that does remain. In the noh play this part of the piece is divided into five sections.[11] The number and type of patterns used in each section varies, but the general pattern is as follows: tsuke-gashira, oroshi, kizami, hane, kizami, uchikiri, kashira. Comparing this order with Table 26 one can see that the opening and closing patterns have been retained. If one looks at Table 24 and the lists in Chapter VI (pp. 85 and 86) as well, the adherence to standard rhythmic progressions also becomes most evident. To a lesser extent similar facts emerge from a comparison of the tsuzumi parts as listed in Tables 24 and 26.

An interesting change in standard procedure occurs at the end of the interlude. Instead of the usual final kashira patterns in all parts the tsuzumi progressions stop "unresolved" and only the taiko plays the cadence. The reasoning behind this unusual procedure may be that a full stop between the interlude and the

[11] See Komparu Sōichi, *Komparu-ryū Taiko Zensho* (Tokyo: Hinoki Shoten, 1955), pp. 255–58.

final section was felt to be undesirable. In waiting for the drum resolutions the ear makes the transition into the new section before it is aware of the change. A similar process can be accomplished with chords in Western music. In nagauta the power of rhythmic progression has been used with equal effectiveness.

SUMMARY OF THE GAKU

Instrumentation: Two shamisen parts plus a noh hayashi are used throughout.

The shamisen line: Four-bar, balanced phrasing is prevalent. Recurrent rhythm patterns, basically static phrase endings and beginnings, and the support of an obbligato part increase the cohesive strength of the melodic structure as compared with the generally through-composed shamisen parts found most frequently in vocal accompaniments.

Pitch progressions: Though the hon-chōshi tuning has returned, the pitch center E does not appear until halfway through the interlude (556). The basic progression is B to F♯ to B to E to B, so that the E is still not firmly established by the end of the interlude.

Rhythm and tempo: The tempo is moderate and the hayashi are organized as one unit set in a noh-style, eight-bar orientation. The shamisen does not always share this phrasing. The special relationship between the overall beats and the actual drum patterns creates rhythmic tensions of great importance to the character of the music. Standard pattern progressions are evident in the drum parts.

General remarks: The interlude uses many different devices to set the music off from the vocal sections of the piece. The balanced phrases and melodic and rhythmic tensions are combined with a colorful instrumentation to create a musically satisfying composition.

7. THE KIRI (576–679)

THE TEXT: The text of the kiri describes the emperor's robes. The sleeves are like the white angel robes of the palace.[12] They contain the beautiful colors of fall flowers like the edges of maple leaves in the rain. Long sleeves, white as a clean winter snow, flutter as the court nobles, dressed in light purple, raise their voices in song.

Shamisen, singers, and the three drums are used throughout this section except for the extended shamisen interlude. The

[12] Literally the moon temple, *gekkyūden,* hence the other name for the play.

noh flute appears only once at the cadence of the first phrase (584).

TABLE 27: *Outline of the shamisen part for the kiri of* Tsuru-kame

I	II	III	IV	V	VI	VII		VIII
1	576–583	8	4 2 2	B	b	B	b	C
2	584–591	8	8	GF♯	GF♯	F♯	F♯	S
3	592–599	8	4 2 2	B	b	B	b	C
4	600–603	4	4	fe	fe	e	e	S
5	604–611	8	8	fab'e	ee	e	e	C
6	612–619	8	4 4	f♯	b'	f♯	b'	U
7	628–627 × 7		2 (4 1)	b'	cb	b'	b	D
8	628–635	8	4 (3 1)	dc♯b	CB	b	B	D
9	636–639	4	4	bAb	FE	b	E	D
10	640–647	8	4 4	ab'	b'a	b'	b'	C
11	648–655	8	4 4	Ec'b'	fec	b'	e	D
12	656–663	8	4 2 2	ef♯	cb	f♯	b	D
13	664–667	4	4	BF♯	Ab	F♯	b	U
14	668–671	4	4	F-Ab	F(E)	F	(E)	C
15	672–679	8	4 4	Ede	bb	E	b	C

SUMMARY OF TABLE 27

I & II. There are 15 phrases in all. Phrase 7 contains a three-beat bar. Phrases 7 and 8 include bars of silence.

III. The frequency of each type of phrase length is as follows:

    10 eight bars
    4 four bars
    1 seven bars

IV. The motivic divisions are:

    6 undivided
    4 symmetrical
    5 asymmetrical

Three of the asymmetrical group are 4 2 2.

V. The opening movements are as follows:

    3 LN
    3 UN
    6 S
    2 5th
    1 tritone (phrase 14, unstable)

VI. Cadence formulas are as follows:

    1 LN
    8 UN

<pre>
              5   S
              1   PC to LN
</pre>
VII. Pitch progressions are:
<pre>
              E leads to B or F♯
              B leads to E or F♯
              F♯ leads to B
</pre>
VIII. The general direction of phrases is:
<pre>
              2   U
              5   D
              2   S
              6   C
</pre>

The most striking feature of this summary is the prevalence of eight-bar phrases. Perhaps this is related to the fact that the entire section is accompanied by noh-style drumming. The one seven-bar phrase occurs during an interlude in which the drums are not playing. Looking at the music one finds that this generally-even phrasing by no means results in static lines. The actual directions of the various lines are varied (see column VIII), and there is an unusual amount of rhythmic activity within each phrase. This is coupled with a careful choice of notes to create a dynamic line. For example, the opening line begins with a firm progression from B to E with a strong emphasis on the movement of F to E (579). This is followed by a sudden emphasis on F♯ and its neighbor G (584). This long passage on F♯ gives the impression of an extended half cadence which leads back to the repeat of the first phrase (phrase 1 and 3 are the same music). At measure 600 the line that previously went to F♯ now remains in the F-E area. The constant syncopation of phrase 5 (604) does not allow the E to come to rest until measure 610. No sooner has this happened than the F♯ reappears, leading back to B. By such a method a new mood of agitation is created. When combined with the quickening pace and the shorter distance between interludes a strong sense of musical excitement is felt.

THE VOCAL LINE: The vocal music is outlined in Table 28. Because of the overlap in phrasing between the shamisen and voice the tacet phrases for the voice are not marked by measure numbers.

TABLE 28: *Outline of the voice part for the kiri of* Tsuru-kame

I	II	III	IV	V	VI	VII	VIII
1	576–587	12	4 2 6	Ab	Ab	b b	C
2			tacet				

I	II	III	IV		V	VI	VII		VIII
3	592–599	8	4	4	FAb	Ab	b	b	C
4	600–603	4	4		EF-E	FE	E	E	S
5	604–615	12	4	8	ef-e	de(d)	e	e	S
6			tacet						
7			tacet						
8	636–643	8	4	4	bAb	DEDB	b	B	D
9	644–647	4	4		Ab	bA	b	b	S
10	648–651	4	4		Ac-b	AF	b	(E)	C
11	652–659	8	4	4	ce	f♯ed	(e)	e	S
12	660–663	4	4		f♯e	cb	(e)	b	D
13	664–667	4	4		bF♯	Ab	b	b	S
14	668–671	4	4		F	bF	(e)		S
15	672–679	8	5	3	de	Ab(A)	e	b	D

SUMMARY OF TABLE 28

ı & ıı. There are 12 sung phrases.

ııı. The frequency of each type of phrase length is as follows:

- 4 eight bars
- 6 four bars
- 2 twelve bars

ıv. The motivic divisions are:

- 6 undivided
- 3 symmetrical
- 3 asymmetrical

v. Opening movements are as follows:

- 4 LN
- 1 UN
- 4 S
- 1 4th
- 2 3rd

vı. Cadence formulas are as follows:

- 5 LN
- 3 UN
- 0 S
- 1 PC to LN
- 1 PC to dissonance
- 2 3rd

vıı. Pitch progressions are as follows:

E leads to B
B leads to E

vııı. The general direction of lines is:

- 0 U
- 3 D

6 S
3 C

The two twelve-bar phrases illustrate a typical nagauta vocal technique. Both of them consist of a normal phrase structure with the addition of a very long hold on the last syllable which trails over the beginning of a shamisen interlude. Except for these two places, there is generally more agreement between the voice and the shamisen as to phrase lengths than has been noted before. The faster tempo and the presence of the drums may have an influence on this.

Phrases 9, 10, and 14 are noteworthy for their use of dissonant endings. Note that at this new tempo there are fewer ending ornaments in the vocal line since there is less time for them and less chance of their being heard in the full sounds of the complete ensemble. Phrase 14 (668) is particularly interesting in its use of the note F and its tritone B which are resolved to E only in the shamisen. The prevalence of static lines in this section reflects the greater number of words sung in each phrase. A similar situation occurred in the odoriji (see Table 23). The concentration on the E and B areas for such static lines is also typical of both sections, though F♯ appears once in the former part.

THE HAYASHI MUSIC: The drum music for the kiri once more is derived solely from noh patterns. This presents a compositional problem. How can a new mood be set when the only changes in the ensemble are the entrance of the voices and absence of the flute? The problem is solved by playing the drums in cut time. The drum beats now are equal to quarter instead of half notes. The shamisen continues as before, so that the effect is quite brilliant. It gives the effect of kabuki-style drumming without sacrificing the important noh basis of the drum parts.

The patterns used from 576 through 612 are shown in Table 29. The measure numbers indicate the locations of beat "two" in the specific drum patterns (beat "one" in the new tempo is the upbeat).

TABLE 29: *Drum patterns for the kiri of* Tsuru-kame

TAIKO	KO-TSUZUMI	Ō-TSUZUMI
1. oroshi (576)	uke-mitsuji (576)	shodan (576)
2. uchikomi (580)	uchikomi (580)	uchikomi (580)
3. tsuke-gashira (588)[13]	uchikaeshi (585)	uchikaeshi (584)
4. oroshi (592)	uke-mitsuji (592)	shodan (592)

[13] This pattern is listed as the same as uchikaeshi in Komparu, *op. cit.*, p. 91.

TAIKO	KO-TSUZUMI	O-TSUZUMI
5. kizami (596)	uchihanashi (596)	(tacet)
6. kizami (600)	musubi-nagaji (600)	ji
7. age (604)	↓	taka-kizami (603)
8. uchikiri (606)	ko (609)	uchikiri (607)
9. kashira (610)	ai-gashira	ai-gashira
Patterns end 612	612	612

Once again the drums are seen to be strongly knit together by a common beat. It is not until longer patterns (musubi-nagaji) and shorter patterns (age) are mixed that these common beats are disturbed. The cadence brings the entire group back together. The patterns follow the same type of standard order discussed earlier. The ends of the drum patterns and the shamisen phrases coincide more often, perhaps because of the new tempo relationship. For example, the first beats of 583 and 591 are beat "eight" for the drums and a cadence for the shamisen. The first beats can never coincide since the drums are counting twice as fast as the shamisen and their "one" is on the upbeat of the shamisen's "one." Since the drum parts are traveling twice as fast as the shamisen the two can phrase together only on every other drum phrase. The reduction in tension resulting from these concurrences is more than compensated for by the increased rhythmic activity in all parts.

TABLE 30: *Drum patterns for the end of the kiri in* Tsuru-kame

TAIKO	KO-TSUZUMI	Ō-TSUZUMI
1. kashira (634)		
2. tsuke-gashira	uke-mitsuji (635)	uke (635)
3. oroshi	uchihanashi	ji
4. age, uchikiri	musubi	taka-kizami
5. kashira	ko	uchikiri
6. tsuke-gashira	uke-mitsuji	uke-mitsuji
7. oroshi	uchihanashi	↓
8. taka-kizami	nagaji	(tacet)
9. hane	↓	ji
10. kizami	musubi-nagaji	ji
11. age	↓	taka-kizami
12. uchikiri	ko	uchikiri
13. kashira	ai-gashira	ai-gashira

After the shamisen interlude the drums return with another set of drum patterns. These are listed in Table 30. After the transitional kashira pattern in the taiko the three drums enter in standard progressions. By comparing Table 29 and 30 one can see that the three lines use some of the same combinations of patterns in both instances. Compare, for example, lines 6, 7, 8, and 9 of Table 29 with lines 10, 11, 12, and 13 of Table 30. It is significant that these agreements occur at the final cadence. The mixture of patterns elsewhere varies (compare Table 29, line 5 with Table 30, line 3). Note, however, that at the first taiko cadence in Table 30 (line 5) the other drums play patterns that lead to cadences. They do not join in the actual cadence because this is only the midway point in the section.

The direct repeat of the first section of the text (576 and 592) is found in the original noh text. The breaking up of the music with instrumental interludes, however, is more in keeping with the shamisen tradition. This process will be discussed further after the final section has been analyzed.

SUMMARY OF THE KIRI

Instrumentation: Shamisen, voices, and the drums are used with one short flute entrance at the beginning. A shamisen obbligato part is used.

The vocal-shamisen lines: A return to eight-bar phrases in both parts is offset by an increased rhythmic activity in the shamisen and the voice. There is an alternation of vocal sections and instrumental interludes. The transitions between them are covered by extended vocal cadences.

Pitch progressions: The basic movement is from E to B to F♯ to B. The latter two appear very frequently as half cadence pitches so that the dynamism of the line is seldom lost.

Rhythm and tempo: The tempo increases only slightly but the sound is quite different as the drums continue to play noh-derived patterns but at twice their former speed. The interrelations of the drum parts vary except at the cadences. At this new speed the shamisen and drum phrases cadence together more frequently.

General remarks: In the alternation of vocal and instrumental sections it should be noted that the shamisen are given a completely solo section for the first time in the piece (616).

8. THE CHIRASHI AND DANGIRE (680–759)

THE TEXT: The final section of the text is still part of the kiri in the original play. It has been broken into two sections here because the music is so organized in the nagauta piece.

The text says that the emperor dances to bring prosperity to all the country for all eternity. The courtiers carry the shrine swiftly as the emperor returns to the place of longevity. The last line says that this is truly a felicitous occasion.

The instrumentation remains the same as before: singers, shamisen, and the drums with two shamisen parts being used in the interludes. The noh flute returns at the very end.

THE SHAMISEN MUSIC

TABLE 31: *Outline of the shamisen part for the finale of* Tsuru-kame

I	II	III	IV	V	VI	VII	VIII
1	680–687	8	8	gf♯	cb	f♯ b	D
2	688–695	8	4 4	de	bb	e b	D
3	696–699	4	4	b	GF♯	b F♯	D
4	700–705	6	6	eeb	eÊ	e e	C
5	706–713	8	8	BF♯	cb	B b	U
6	714–721	8	8	ef♯	cb	f♯ b	D
7	722–729	8	4 4	bF♯	Ab	b b	S
8	730–737	8	2 2 4	e-de	f♯	e f♯	U
9	738–745	8	4 4	gf♯	Ab	f♯ b	D
10	746–749	4	4	Bgf♯	cb	(B)f♯ b	D
11	750–759	–	(8) free	Ab	DE	b E	D

SUMMARY OF TABLE 31

I & II. There are 11 phrases. The last two form the dangire of the piece.

III. The frequency of each type of phrase length is:

- 7 eight bars
- 2 four bars
- 1 six bars
- 1 free

IV. The motivic divisions are as follows:

- 1 free
- 6 undivided
- 3 symmetrical
- 1 asymmetrical (2 2 4)

v. The opening movements of phrases are as follows:

- 3 LN
- 3 UN
- 3 S
- 2 5th

VI. The cadence formulas are:

- 3 LN

$$5 \quad UN$$
$$3 \quad S$$

vii. The pitch progressions are as follows:

E leads to B and F♯

B leads to F♯ and E

F♯ leads to B and E

The general progression is B-E-B-F♯-B-E.

viii. The general direction of lines is:

$$2 \quad U$$
$$7 \quad D$$
$$1 \quad S$$
$$1 \quad C$$

The basic eight- and four-bar phrase structure of the previous section is maintained in the finale. The only exception (700) occurs, as before, during a solo shamisen passage. The first of these shamisen interludes begins on an undivided eight-bar phrase of steady quarter notes which is accompanied by an eighth-note echo in the obbligato shamisen. This technique is very common during faster interludes in nagauta pieces. Note that the lack of anacruses (as compared with the ageuta section) adds emphasis to the strong rhythmic accents of this section.

The phrase movements offer no new situations but there is one unusual progression of pitch centers between phrases 3 and 4. This is the first time that F♯ has moved directly to E (see the previous discussion on page 145). It is important to note that between these two centers there is an entire measure of silence, which the composer may have felt provided a sufficient time span in which to make the change. Note should be made also of the return to the favoring of descending phrases. This has been missing since the odoriji.

THE VOCAL PART

TABLE 32: *Outline of the vocal part for the finale of* Tsuru-kame

I	II	III	IV	V	VI	VII	VIII
1	680–						
2	688–						
3	696–						
4	700–						
5	706–713	8	4 4	AF♯	cb	F♯ b	U
6	714–721	8	4 4	f♯e	cb	f♯ b	D
7	722–729	8	4 4	Ab-F♯	AbA	b b	S
8	730–737	8	4 4	de	f♯(e)	e f♯	U

I	II	III	IV	V	VI	VII	VIII
9	738–745	8	4 4	ef♯	Ab	f♯ b	D
10	746–752	7	7	ef♯	Ab(A)	f♯ b	D
11	753–756	4	4	Ab	DE(ED)	b E	D

SUMMARY OF TABLE 32

I & II. There are 7 sung phrases.

III. The frequency of each type of phrase length is as follows:

> 5 eight bars
> 1 four bars
> 1 seven bars

IV. The motivic divisions are:

> 2 undivided
> 5 symmetrical

V. The opening movements of phrases are:

> 5 LN
> 0 UN
> 0 S
> 1 PC to LN
> 1 down a minor third to PC

VI. The cadence formulas are as follows:

> 4 LN
> 2 UN
> 1 PC to LN

VII. The pitch progressions are:

> E leads to F♯
> B leads to E or F♯
> F♯ leads to B

VIII. The general direction of lines is:

> 2 U
> 4 D
> 1 S

The phrasing of the voice and shamisen agree until the very end, at which time the tempo becomes free and the shamisen must follow the retard of the singers. The one unusual vocal entrance is the first one, which drops a third (706). This note, however, is an anacrusis to the phrase. Note that the first phrase is divided into two chant-like sections and that the pitches emphasized are both dissonant (A and C). A similar situation is seen at measure 726. The following phrase concentrates on a stronger, higher pitch (e) followed by a still higher pitch (f♯). This line drops to the fifth below (b) and does not drop further until the final cadence on E. This contour produces a sense of climax shortly before the end of the piece in a manner not unfamiliar to Western ears. It should be noted also that the pitch-center E appears periodically throughout the last section but is used as a cadence pitch only once each in the shamisen and vocal parts. Even then it is not on the same phrase. It is only at the final cadence that both parts agree on the E and it is only then that the low E appears.

THE HAYASHI MUSIC: The percussion accompaniment for this section is derived from noh patterns as before. In this case, however, the particular group of patterns chosen has a special significance. The entire set of patterns from 706 to 746 is known collectively as *sandanme*. This large unit is used in the final sections of other pieces, for example, in *Suehirogari* (Yoshizumi, I–2, p. 6).

TABLE 33: *Drum patterns for the chirashi of* Tsuru-kame

	TAIKO	KO-TSUZUMI	Ō-TSUZUMI
1	tsuke-gashira (706)	uchisagari-ha	sandanme
2	oroshi	uchihanashi	↓
3	kizami	nagaji	↓
4	kizami	↓	ji
5	age	musubi	takakizami
6	uchikiri	dan-gashira	uchikiri
7	kashira	musubi-odorikaeshi	godanme
8	kashira	↓	↓
9	kashira	uchihanashi	↓
10	oroshi	ko	uchikomi
11	uchikomi	uchikomi	uchikaeshi
12	kashira	ai-gashira	ai-gashira

When this unit is broken down into its component patterns as shown in Table 33, it can be seen that certain standard progressions are still maintained. Lines 1–7 in the taiko part are a good example. At the same time, the tsuzumi use more unusual and complicated patterns, for example, lines 7–9. Note that at these moments the taiko uses simpler patterns in order not to cloud the perception of the tsuzumi lines. In general, the drum lines use the same eight-beat framework. When patterns of less than eight beats are used, such as age in the taiko (line 5), there appears another four-beat pattern later on to restore the concurrences (kashira in line 7). The rhythmic tension created in the meantime is important to the forward drive of the music. Notice that in the example cited the resolution of this discrepancy occurs at a cadence pattern in the taiko. As shown before, a cadence pattern simultaneously in all three drums does not occur until the end.

The relation of the drum lines to the shamisen is the same as in the previous section. In general, every other beat "two" of the drum phrases coincides with the beginning of a shamisen phrase (706, 714, 722, 730, etc.).

The entrance of the noh flute (742) is a standard signal for the dangire—the final cadence. The actual pitch it plays depends on the instrument used and does not necessarily have any significant pitch relationship to the shamisen or vocal line.

SUMMARY OF THE CHIRASHI AND DANGIRE

Instrumentation: Voices, shamisen, and three drums are used. The noh flute enters only at the final cadence.

The vocal-shamisen line: Eight- and four-bar phrases are prevalent in both parts. The large number of lower neighbor cadences in the vocal part and the lack of anacruses in the shamisen lines strengthen the structure of these final phrases. The general agreement between the two parts as to phrase lengths also contributes to this sense of clearly-defined phrases. The use of dissonant tones within these phrases keeps these lines from becoming too static.

Pitch progressions: Movement by fifths is used except for progressions from E to F♯. The overall progression is B-E-B-F♯-B-E. The final E is also the lowest E.

Rhythm and tempo: The tempo increases slightly during the shamisen interlude and returns to its previous tempo thereafter until a large retard at the end. The drums continue in noh-style at double time. In the final section a large unit, *sandanme,* is used which is traditionally indicative of the last part of the piece. The entry of the flute at the end confirms this indication. The drum parts are interlocked in a common eight-beat framework and, in general, agree with the shamisen as to the beginnings of phrases.

General remarks: The kiri and chirashi when taken as a unit (which they are in the original play) show an alternation of shamisen interludes and tutti sections. Such interludes have not appeared before in this piece. They are so written as to keep up the excitement while changing the tone color in order that the tutti sections may sound fresh as the music builds toward the finale.

MELODIC TYPES

Before summarizing the analysis of the entire composition, it is necessary to study the frequency of melodic types in both the shamisen and vocal parts. These types have been derived from a study of nagauta style in general and the music of the two pieces under analysis at present in particular. In determining what constitutes a melodic type and what is a variation of a type, two factors have been taken as essential. One is the general contour of the line and the other is the significant interval involved in the pattern. Rhythm has not been considered, though comments will be made concerning the rhythmic tendencies of certain types.

EXAMPLE 20: *Basic shamisen melodic types*

Example 20 shows the basic melodic types for the shamisen. These have been arranged arbitrarily by contour and the

Roman letters are not meant to indicate any hierarchy of types.

Type I is characterized by a descending line with the interval of a fourth or fifth between the basic pitches. Consonant pitches as defined earlier are considered as basic pitches. The first of these basic pitches is sometimes preceded by a half-step upper neighbor tone. Frequently this pattern is played with the rhythm ♪ ♪♪ or some closely related pattern. Note that the pattern beginning on F♯ often ends with an additional drop of a fourth at the end to the lower F♯.

Type II is an abbreviation of type I. It is descending and outlines the interval of a fourth. It is distinguished from type I by its lack of the upper neighbor and the use of only three notes. The rhythm of type I is also missing.

Type III rises before it drops. There is a fifth between its basic pitches but its distinguishing feature is the use of the downward skip on an augmented fourth. Possible ornamentations and additions to the line are shown in parentheses.

Type IV has the same contour as type III but has a fourth between its basic pitches and does not use the augmented fourth. This type often passes beyond the note of resolution to its lower neighbor, making a kind of half cadence.

Type V is the simplest type, consisting of a movement from a pitch center to its lower neighbor and back. It often involves the use of several repeated notes.

Type VI consists of two rising units separated by a downward skip. The basic pitches are a fourth or fifth apart and the downward skip, while usually a fifth, may be a seventh or sixth.

Type VII, the final type, is distinguished by its upward movement. There is usually a fourth between the basic pitches and the pattern is often preceded by a whole step lower neighbor to the first basic pitch. Because of its direction the rising pattern using the augmented fourth has also been included here.

These seven types do not account for all the melodic movement in shamisen music. They are meant to represent only the most typical and repetitive of the melodic patterns. Statistical abstractions from composed art musics can expect to be no more. The numbers in each column refer to the starting measure of the pattern, and the letter is the first note of the group.

Table 34 shows the frequency of use of the seven types of melodic movement listed above as found in *Tsuru-kame*. Measures 315–48 and 592–99 are repeats of preceding music and have not been included in compiling these figures.

The importance of the augmented fourth to shamisen melodic

TABLE 34: *Frequency of melodic types in the*
shamisen part of Tsuru-kame

I	II	III	IV	V	VI	VII
10–F	13–A	44–A	18–D	20–B		40–A
26–B	58–B	55–B	34–D	86–B		49–E
29–B	218–B	96–E	189–D	154–B		135–A
63–F#	255–A	98–A	401–A	194–B		273–F#
114–B	583–B	103–D	405–A	265–B		351–F
129–F#	696–B	226–A	690–D	284–B		359–F#
131–F	701–E	269–B		608–E		555–A
148–F#	720–E	276–B		730–E		571–F
163–C#		281–B				703–A
175–F		291–A				
184–F#		296–E				
220–F		303–E				
388–F#		308–E				
483–F#		340–E				
518–C#		356–E				
564–B		410–E				
578–B		420–E				
580–B		423–E				
605–F		432–E				
638–B		444–B				
641–F		452–E				
671–B		469–E				
674–F		474–E				
747–F#		566–E				
		604–A				
		624–E				
		632–E				
		640–A				
		686–E				
		740–E				
7–F#		1–D	4–D			2–F#
8–B	4–B	5–B	2–A	6–B		2–F
7–F	2–A	6–A		2–E		1–E
2–C#	2–E	18–E				4–A
24	8	30	6	8	0	9

movement becomes apparent immediately. Type III with its
very strong augmented fourth is the major pattern used. Note
that it is used most often to approach B (by starting on E). The
next most frequent pattern, type I, contains within it a tendency

toward the augmented fourth sound though it is somewhat reduced by the presence of another note between the two pitches involved. This type is used more often to cadence to E (by starting on B). The rising cadences (type VII) go most frequently to E (starting on A). They also show two uses of patterns exploiting the augmented fourth by beginning on F. Type VI is not important in this composition.

EXAMPLE 21: *Melodic types in nagauta vocal music*

The melodic types found in the vocal music have been reduced to seven types also as shown in Example 21. These do not correspond exactly with the seven shamisen types. One important difference is that there are no vocal types which are completely descending. Descending passages are prefaced with short ascending movements which are then followed by a drop.

In abstracting these types one must take into account the melismatic quality of the vocal line and look for what one considers to be the essentials of the line. Contour and the interval between basic pitches have again been used as a starting point. Where possible the patterns have been arranged to correspond in type number with their nearest related shamisen type. Some, it must be noted, cannot be so arranged.

Type I involves an upward movement to a note which then drops a fourth. This fourth is usually filled in by one additional note.

Type II resembles type I except that the interval drop is a fifth.

Type III follows the same general contour but involves the emphasis on the drop of an augmented fourth. The basic pitches are a fifth apart. Ornamentations may appear in several different locations as indicated in Example 21.

Type IV comprises two units of upward motion separated by a skip of a fifth. The interval between basic pitches is a fourth. One variation in the contour scheme has been included in this group.

Type V is similar to type IV in contour but the skip is a seventh or a sixth and the interval between the basic pitches is a fifth.

Type VI moves upward. The interval between the principal tones is a fourth and the first movement is a skip of a third. The augmented fourth example has also been included here.

Type VII is like type VI except that the interval between the principal tones is a fifth and the first movement is up a fourth.

Table 35 shows the frequency of these types in the vocal part of *Tsuru-kame*. The repeated section in measures 592–99 has been deleted.

TABLES 35: *Frequency of melodic types in the voice part of* Tsuru-kame

I	II	III	IV	V	VI	VII
18–D	7–A	55–B	10–D	309–F♯	135–B	
98–G	29–A	62–E	94–C	421–E	352–F	
121–A	83–A	113–A	132–D	453–E	607–B	
216–A	406–E	226–A	176–C		665–F♯	
379–G	432–E	236–A	260–D			
642–D	469–E	291–A	362–G			
674–F	475–G	304–E	376–G			
722–A	483–E	317–E				
	660–F♯	410–E				

I	II	III	IV	V	VI	VII
		518–B				
		576–A				
		638–A				
		738–E				
		746–E				
3–A	3–A	6–A	3–D	2–E	2–B	
2–D	4–E	6–E	2–C	1–F♯	1–F	
2–G	1–F♯	2–B	2–G		1–F♯	
1–F	I–G					
8	9	14	7	3	4	0

As in the shamisen part, the pattern using the drop of the augmented fourth is prevalent. More than half of the total patterns used fall into one of the first three types which have a common contour. Types IV and V are the next most frequent if they are taken as a unit because of their common contour. Their related shamisen melody type (VI) did not appear at all in this piece, though it does appear in other compositions. The pattern with a rising contour is the least frequent as one might guess from the study of general direction of vocal lines done in the earlier analysis of this chapter.

The smaller number of patterns found in the vocal part as compared with the shamisen line is explained in part by the greater length of the shamisen music. Another point worthy of note, however, is the fact that when one of these types is not being used the voice tends to undulate back and forth between consonant pitches and their upper and lower neighbors. This movement is, in a way, the true idiomatic melodic type of naga-uta vocal styling. It is the interpolation between these undulations of the seven more active melodic types listed above, however, that adds distinction to the individual composition. In closing, it should be noted that type VII is not used in this composition. It is listed because it is used in other pieces.

SUMMARY OF THE ANALYSIS

If all the summaries of the various charts are totaled, the results given below are obtained. The Roman numerals used refer to those found in the charts themselves.

I & II. There are a total of 113 phrases played by the shamisen, of which 82 are also sung. The discrepancies in the totals in the voice summaries in columns V, VI, and VIII are due to the incomplete phrases found in the mondō (see Table 19). The important information in all the columns, however, is not their totals but the comparative size of the numbers listed.

III. The frequency of each type of phrase length is as follows:

shamisen	voice	
44	27	eight bars
24	15	four bars
11	7	seven bars
10	7	six bars
5	2	ten bars
8	7	free
2	0	fifteen bars
2	0	eleven bars
2	7	five bars
1	3	nine bars
4	1	three bars
0	6	twelve bars
113	82	

IV. The motivic divisions are:

shamisen	voice	
8	7	free
46	35	undivided
26	16	symmetrical
33	24	asymmetrical
113	82	

V. The opening movements of phrases are as follows:

shamisen	voice	
23	42	LN
27	12	UN
42	8	S
7	3	5th
3	1	4th
2	2	PC to LN
3	1	PC to UN
6	6	others
113	75	

VI. Cadence formulas are as follows:

shamisen	voice	
33	50	LN
41	13	UN
28	4	S
2	2	5th
6	2	4th
1	1	PC to LN

2	1	PC to UN
0	3	others
113	77	

VII. Taking the eight divisions of the piece, root progressions are found as listed below. The numbers here represent the number of sections in which such a progression is found and not the frequency of its appearance within each section.

shamisen	voice	
7	5	E to B
5	2	E to F♯
8	5	B to E
7	4	B to F♯
3	1	B to C♯
8	5	F♯ to B
1	0	F♯ to C♯
1	2	F♯ to E
3	0	C♯ to F♯
1	0	C♯ to B

VIII. The general direction of lines is as follows:

shamisen	voice	
22	8	up
46	37	down
26	25	static
19	9	curved
113	79	

These numbers reveal what may be considered as being the characteristics of this composition. Eight- and four-bar phrases are decidedly the preferred units in this piece, and most phrases cannot be conveniently broken into smaller units. A review of the previous charts will show, however, that many of the eight-bar phrases have been subdivided into two groups of four bars each.

The majority of shamisen phrases begin with a stationary movement while the voice part uses the lower neighbor to pitch-center progressions most often. Movements from upper or lower neighbors to pitch centers and passages that remain on the same pitch account for a vast majority of phrase opening in both parts. The shamisen shows more freedom in the choice of less-used patterns.

Upper neighbor to pitch-center progressions are most frequent in the shamisen cadences, while the voice uses a clear majority of lower neighbor to pitch-center endings. The division between the three major types of endings is somewhat more evenly spread in the shamisen.

The most frequent pitch-center progressions are from F♯ to B and from B to E. The reverse progressions E to B and B to F♯ are next in frequency. Less common are the progressions C♯ to F♯, E to F♯, and B to C♯. Other movements appear infrequently. The disputed use of A was discussed on pages 130–31. Pitch progressions can then be summarized as generally going along a cycle of fifths between E and C♯ with the two most frequent exceptions being E to F♯, and B to C♯.

Both the shamisen and voice lines show a preference for descending lines, though there are a large number of ascending and static phrases appearing in the shamisen part. Finally, it must be remembered that studies in the individual phrases revealed a skillful use of unresolved tones and rhythmic patterns which served to create a flowing melodic line of balanced degrees of tension and release.

TABLE 36: *Double stops used in* Tsuru-kame

5THS	4THS	OCTAVES	UNISONS	7THS	9THS
7–E	532–E	91–B	76–82–B	90–B	92–D
529–B		92–B	285–B	93–B	
531–B		224–E	360–61–B		
532–B		254–E	759–E		
		266–B			

Since the emphasis in this analysis has been on the power of melodic writing there remains the task of accounting for the occasional harmonies produced in this music by the use of shamisen double stops. Table 36 lists all such situations. The columns indicate the kind of harmonic interval produced. The number tells in what measure it can be found, and the letter indicates the top pitch of the interval. Most of these, it will be seen, merely support cadences by the use of octaves or unisons. It is interesting to note that only four of the double stops occur when there is singing (90, 91, 76, and 360). In most cases this singing is an overlapping cadence. The seventh and ninth double stops are used during the kangen melody. They are created by strumming the open string while playing the melody. These are probably used to enrich the sound of the interlude. The same could be said for the double stops around measure 529.

Viewing the composition formally one finds that it is like the other noh-derived pieces studied earlier in that it shows a combination of noh and nagauta formal elements. Perhaps the most unique formal feature is the lack of a clear michiyuki section. This reflects the non-dance origin of the composition. It is significant, however, that the ageuta is treated instrumentally as if it were a michiyuki by using one of the few kabuki-derived drum patterns in the piece.

Another striking feature of this piece is the general lack of unaccompanied vocal-shamisen sections. Only at the end of the oki (90–129) and during the mondō do such sections occur. The shamisen is used alone only as interludes between the brilliant tuttis of the latter part of the piece. The heavy reliance upon hayashi support, however, does not mean that there is any lack of varied instrumentation. After the introduction of the entire group in the oki, only the voices, shamisen, and tsuzumi are used, the latter in kabuki style. The odoriji brings back the entire ensemble except that the bamboo flute has replaced the noh flute. The noh patterns used by the drums relate to each other by their special way of counting while aurally they produce rhythmic tensions against each other and the shamisen line. In addition, the regular order of rhythmic pattern progressions serves as a moving matrix in which the rest of the music is set. In this respect it is not unlike harmonic rhythm in Western music. The return of the noh flute during the second dance produces a new set of relationships and a new timbre. When it drops out, the double-time playing of the drums creates yet another instrumental effect. This, when altered with the shamisen interludes, leads to the finale.

The musicians who created *Tsuru-kame* as an orchestral piece have shown a sense of mastery of all the elements necessary for the creation of a musically logical, through-composed nagauta piece based on a noh-drama text. In the next analysis we shall see how an equally talented group of Japanese musicians treat a composition conceived wholly in terms of the kabuki dance-music tradition.

CHAPTER TEN
Analysis of Gorō Tokimune

GORŌ TOKIMUNE was composed in 1841 by the tenth Kineya Rokuzaemon.[1] It was written as one of the nine dances to be performed by the same actor (see the discussion on hengemono, page 25). From the beginning it has been very popular, both as a dance piece and in shamisen concerts. The author, in fact, made his Japanese singing debut with this composition in 1956.

As was explained earlier, the story of *Gorō* is part of a famous cycle known as the Soga saga. It deals with the attempts of the Soga brothers to avenge the death of their father. Though this tale has been dealt with in other genres, the nagauta version is entirely a product of the kabuki. Thus, it can be expected to illustrate the major characteristics of nagauta music in the kabuki dance form.

The words of this piece are replete with oblique references to people and places related to the story or symbolic of the situation. Because of this, a direct translation into English would make little sense without voluminous footnotes. I shall attempt in the sections that follow to give the general meaning and mood of the text rather than any literal translation.

Since *Gorō* is not based directly on any noh drama there is no stated tripartite division for it. It can, however, be divided into eight formal sections. These are listed below along with a synopsis of the action for each section. The presentation of the subsequent analysis will follow this outline.

1. OKI (1–38): The scene is set. Gorō's name is called.
2. MICHIYUKI (39–76): Gorō enters.
3. UTAGAKARI (77–120): The meetings of Gorō and his love, Shōshō, are mentioned. He reads a letter from her.
4. KUDOKI (121–223): A letter is written in rough reply. Wine is drunk.

[1] See Atsumi, *Hōgaku Buyō Jiten,* p. 72.

5. MAE (224–329): Gorō recalls his mission of vengeance.
6. ODORIJI (330–465): The love of Gorō and Shōshō is compared with the hopeless love of the nightingale for the plum tree.
7–8. CHIRASHI-DANGIRE (466–527): Gorō is praised for his filial loyalty.

1. THE OKI (1–38)

THE TEXT: The song opens by calling out the name, Gorō Toki-mune. Sworn enemy of his father's slayer, he perseveres in his efforts for revenge. With impatient heart he carries on even through the spring rains (Gorō enters with an umbrella). The last line is incomplete. It mentions his mistress, Shōshō of the brothel of Kehaizaki.

THE SHAMISEN MUSIC: The shamisen begin in the hon-chōshi tuning. Since the first twenty-four measures are for solo singer and shamisen they are played quite freely. The bar lines used in the transcription match the divisions shown in the native nota-tion. Because of this the phrasing of some of the passages is difficult to determine definitely. Such passages have been marked as free in column IV of Table 37. An explanation of the meaning of each column is found on page 119.

TABLE 37: *Outline of the shamisen part for the oki of* Gorō

I	II	III	IV	V	VI	VII		VIII
1.	1–5	5	2 3	bde	FE	b	E	D
2.	6– –	–	free	bF♯	b	b	b	S
3.	7–(8)	–	free	B	e	B	e	U
4.	9– –	–	free	B	e	B	e	U
5.	10– –	–	free	de	e	e	e	S
6.	11–(12)	–	free	bAb	b	b	b	S
7.	13–15	3	3	bF♯	GF♯	b	F♯	C
8.	16–18	3	free	Bb	BF♯	B	F♯	U
9.	19–21	3	3	F♯E	BF♯	F♯	F♯	C
10.	22–25	4	4	bAb	cbe	b	b	S
11.	26–35	10	6 4	cec(b)	FE	b	E	D
12.	36–38	–	free	afe	f♯Ab	e	b	D

SUMMARY OF TABLE 37

I & II.   There are 12 phrases.

III. The frequency of each type of phrase is as follows:

   1   four bars
   3   three bars

1 five bars
1 ten bars
6 free

iv. The motivic divisions are as follows:

3 undivided
0 symmetrical
2 asymmetrical
7 free

v. The opening movements are as follows:

1 LN
2 UN
5 S
2 4th
1 PC to LN
1 skip from PC

vi. The cadence formulas are:

1 LN
4 UN
5 S
2 5th

vii. The pitch progressions are as follows:

E leads to B
B leads to E or F♯
F♯ leads to B

viii. The general direction of lines is as follows:

3 U
3 D
4 S
2 C

The opening section, being in recitative style, shows a preference for free phrases. Only the basic pitch progressions between E, B, and F♯ are used, and static lines are in a slight majority. The usual variety in the opening movements is the result of the extensive use of ōzatsuma patterns in this section. Table 38 lists the names of these patterns in the order of their use.

TABLE 38: *The ōzatsuma patterns for the oki of* Gorō

MEASURE NO.	PATTERN NAME
1–5	jo[2]
6	chū-otoshi (alternate version)
7	honte
9	honte

[2] This pattern is also known as *geiki-gakari* because it originated in geiki-bushi, an early form of shamisen music.

MEASURE NO.	PATTERN NAME
10	honte-oshigasanu
11	nagashi
13–15	hajimiji (altered)
16–21	tataki yawarigi-iroiji (altered)
22	kiriji
23–24	suiji (altered)

In typical nagauta fashion, many of the patterns are altered to fit the requirements of the specific piece. Note that in this section the te and ji patterns are grouped together. Compare this with the order of patterns in the mondō of *Tsuru-kame* (page 68).

THE VOCAL MUSIC

TABLE 39: *Outline of the vocal part for the oki of* Gorō

I	II	III	IV	V	VI	VII		VIII
1			tacet					
2	5–6	–	free	Ab(F♯)	Ab	b	b	S
3	7		tacet					
4	8	–	free	Ab	bA	b	b	S
5	9–11	–	free	Ab-f♯	Ab	b	b	C
6	11	–	free	Ab	Ab	b	b	S
7	12–15	4	2 2	spoken				
8	16–17	2	free	Ab	F♯EF♯	b	F♯	D
9	18–20	3	3	EF♯	F♯E	F♯	F♯	S
10	21–24	4	2 2	spoken				
11	25–31	7	4 3	ec	bA	e	b	D
12	32–35	4	4	Ab	DE	b	E	D
13	36–38	3	free	fe	Ab	e	b	D

SUMMARY TABLE 39

I & II. There are 11 sung phrases.

III. The frequency of each type of phrase length is as follows:

3	four bars
2	three bars
1	seven bars
1	two bars
4	free

IV. The motivic divisions are:

6	free
2	undivided
2	symmetrical

                    1   asymmetrical

v. The opening movements are as follows:
                    7   LN
                    1   UN
                    1   skip down from PC
                    2   spoken

vi. The cadence formulas are:
                    6   LN
                    3   PC to LN
                    2   spoken

vii. The pitch progressions are as follows:
                    E leads to B
                    B leads to E or F♯
                    F♯ leads to B

viii. The general direction of lines is:
                    0   U
                    4   D
                    4   S
                    2   spoken
                    1   C

The vocal part with its long melismas on single syllables (phrase 5) follows a typical vocal style with the extensive use of movements from lower neighbor to pitch-centers at both the beginnings and endings of phrases. The three reversals of this procedure—from the pitch center to the lower neighbor—might be considered as slower versions of the standard closing ornaments which, it may be remembered, tend to drop a whole step at the end. Their use here helps to produce a feeling of incompleteness necessary to the continued movement of the musical line. The static pitch progressions of the first few phrases are in keeping with the introductory, chant-like nature of the music. This lack of upward moving lines is typical of nagauta vocal style. It should be noted, however, that between the two ends of the static lines there is a tendency for the line to rise, usually to the fifth, and then return to the original pitch.

At the chorus entrance (25) one can find an excellent example of the use of dissonant tones and their resolutions. C and A are emphasized in both the shamisen and vocal lines, and the three agogic accents of this passage (26–27, 31, and 34) pause either on the half step above or the whole step below the root or fifth of the in scale of E. Both the yō and in scales built on E or B are used during this opening section.

THE HAYASHI MUSIC: The drums and flute do not enter the oki

until the final cadence where they use the cadential kashira which overlap the beginning of the next section.

SUMMARY OF THE OKI

Instrumentation: Solo voice and shamisen are used until measure 25 at which point the chorus and other shamisen enter. The hayashi plays the final cadence only.

The vocal-shamisen line: An introductory mood is established by a prevalence of static phrases of relatively free length. Within these phrases, however, one finds extensive use of dissonant tones whose need for resolution is a driving force in the continuity of the lines.

Pitch progressions: The basic progressions between E, B, and F♯ are introduced. The overall movement is from E to B with many half cadences.

Rhythm and tempo: The tempo is free. At measure 25 it becomes more orderly, but the final cadence is free once more.

General remarks: The special characteristic of this section is the great use of ōzatsuma patterns in the shamisen.

2. THE MICHIYUKI (39–76)

THE TEXT: There is no singing in the michiyuki. It is scored for the full instrumental ensemble with noh flute. An obbligato shamisen plays a drone on E for much of the section. The words which appear below each part for the first two pages of the score are not text but mnemonics by which the various parts are learned.

THE SHAMISEN MUSIC

TABLE 40: *Outline of the shamisen part for the michiyuki of* Gorō

I	II	III	IV		V	VI	VII		VIII
1	39–46	8	4	4	ab′	ee	b′	e	D
2	47–50	4	4		Efe	cb	e	b	D
3	51–58	8	4	(3–1)	gf♯	bA	f♯	b	D
4	59–62	4	4		ecb	FE	b	E	D
5	63–70	8	4	4	DE	(A)bb	E	b	U
6	71–76	6	3	3	Ab	eE E͡e	b	e	U

SUMMARY OF TABLE 40

ɪ & ɪɪ. There are 6 phrases.
ɪɪɪ. The frequency of each type of phrase length is as follows:

3 eight bars

                    2   four bars
                    1   six bars
IV. The motivic divisions are:
                    2   undivided
                    4   symmetrical
V. The opening movements of phrases are as follows:
                    3   LN
                    3   UN
VI. Cadence formulas are as follows:
                    2   UN
                    3   S
                    1   PC to LN
VII. Pitch progressions are as follows:
                    E leads to B
                    B leads to E or F♯
                    F♯ leads to B
VIII. General directions of lines are:
                    2   U
                    4   D

This is the first instrumental interlude and also the first extended section in a steady tempo. It is marked by the appearance of eight- and four-bar phrases. In line 3 this quartal balance is maintained by inserting a measure rest at the end of the phrase, hence the indication 3–1 in Table 40. An explanation for the interesting fact that none of the lines remains static in this section might be that a sense of movement is important during the entrance of the main actor. This entrance is made at measure 63, the actor's wooden sandals clacking in time with the shamisen music as he marches down the ramp from the back of the theatre.

TABLE 41: *Melodic resolutions in the michiyuki of* Gorō

MEASURE NO.		1ST NOTE	RESOLUTION NOTE
1	39–42	A	B
2	43–46	D	E
3	47–48	(E) F	E
4	49–50	(E) C	B
5	51–54	G	F♯
6	55–58	E (F♯ G)	–
7	59–62	E	B
8	63–66	D	E
9	67–70	A	B
10	71–73	A	B
11	74–76	E	E

The importance of neighbor tones and their resolutions to a sense of movement in nagauta melodies is once more illustrated if one looks at the beginning notes of every motivic unit of the michiyuki. The eleven units are shown in Table 41.

The consistency in style is striking. In lines 3 and 4 the E occurs only as an eighth note before three repeats of the dissonant tones. In lines 7 and 11 the pitch-center E is firmly established. Line 6 begins on E but moves away immediately to a tense note (G). All the other units begin with a dissonance which either resolves down a half step or up a whole step. This kind of melodic construction is essential not only to nagauta but also seems to be characteristic of the majority of Japanese music composed since the sixteenth century.

THE VOCAL LINE: tacet.

THE HAYASHI MUSIC: The hayashi music of this section has already been discussed (see page 87). It was pointed out that a close connection exists between the music of the noh flute and the patterns of the taiko (listed also on page 87). These patterns were shown to be played in phrase lengths different from those of the shamisen part in order to create rhythmic tensions against the basic melody. The two tsuzumi, by contrast, were shown to be using chirikara patterns which directly support the shamisen line.

SUMMARY OF THE MICHIYUKI

Instrumentation: The full instrumental ensemble is used with noh flute and obbligato shamisen. There is no singing.

The shamisen line: Eight- and four-bar phrases predominate as do descending lines. Each melodic unit begins with a dissonant tone which resolves except for three examples which sound the basic pitch-center E.

Pitch-center progressions: The overall progression is E to B to E. F♯ is used as a fifth of B.

Tempo and rhythm: In the new steady tempo two levels of hayashi accompaniment are used. One unit, the two tsuzumi, support the shamisen line by underlining its rhythm. The other unit, the taiko and flute, enhance the dynamism of the music by working against the basic rhythm of the shamisen part.

General remarks: In keeping with its different function (entrance music), this section differs in almost every way from the previous section except in its choice of pitch centers.

3. THE UTAGAKARI (76–120)

THE TEXT: This section is a transition between the virile michi-yuki and the more romantic kudoki. The words continue the sentence begun just before the interlude. They say that Shōshō comes to Ōiso (their trysting place?) even as she has before on rainy days and snowy nights. The entire hayashi is silent during this section and only singers and shamisen are used as the stage dance and the lyric singing begin.

THE SHAMISEN LINE

TABLE 42: *Outline of the shamisen part for the utagakari of* Gorō

I	II	III	IV	V	VI	VII	VIII
1	77–85	9	3 3 3	BE	FE	B E	U
2	86–91	6	2 4	Bab	FE	B E	C
3	92–106	15	6 9	ce	de	e e	C
4	107–114	8	4 4	fe	F	e (E)	D
5	115–120	6	6	BF	fe	B e	U

SUMMARY OF TABLE 42

I & II. There are 5 phrases.
III. The types of phrases are as follows:

    1 eight bars
    2 six bars
    1 nine bars
    1 fifteen bars

IV. The motivic divisions are:

    1 undivided
    2 symmetrical
    2 asymmetrical

V. The opening movements are:

    1 LN
    1 UN
    1 4th
    1 skip up to PC
    1 skip up from PC (to tritone)

VI. The cadence formulas are:

    1 LN
    3 UN
    1 unresolved dissonance (UN)

VII. Pitch progressions are from B to E and E to B only.
VIII. The general direction of lines is:

```
2  U
1  D
2  C
```

Though the number of phrases in each section studied so far has been relatively small one can note a decided change in style in each section. The eight-bar orientation of the previous section has given way to a much more varied situation. This variety is evident in all phases of the melody from phrasing to melodic structure. The last two phrases (107) are noteworthy for their exploitation of the dissonance, F. The length of phrase 3 is the result of the use of such dissonant tones.

The lack of rhythmic drive in the shamisen part during the sung passages of this section is compensated for by the many stops in the line on dissonant tones, particularly the F mentioned above. During the interlude which closes this section the shamisen is more active.

THE VOCAL LINE

TABLE 43: *Outline of the vocal part of the utagakari of* Gorō

I	II	III	IV	V	VI	VII	VIII
1	76–87	12	4 8	e	db(A)	e b	D
2	88–92	5	5	Acb	DE	b E	D
3	93–99	7	3 4	ce	fe	e e	C
4	100–107	8	4 4	ece	b-de(d)	e e	S
5	108–		tacet				

SUMMARY OF TABLE 43

I & II. There are 4 sung phrases

III. There is one phrase each of twelve-, five-, seven-, and eight-bar lengths.

IV. The motivic divisions are:

    1 undivided

    1 symmetrical

    2 asymmetrical

V. Opening movements are:

    0 LN

    1 UN

    2 S

    1 skip up to PC

VI. Cadence formulas are:

    2 LN

    1 UN

    1 skip down to PC

VII. Only the progressions of B to E and E to B are used.

VIII. The general direction of lines is:

> 1   C
>
> 2   D
>
> 1   S

The long vocalises on the syllables that begin this section are typical of the nagauta lyrical style. The entire vocal line is made up of E and its neighbor tones F and D plus B and its neighbors A and C. The resolution of the C is sometimes delayed by an interpolation of E (93–95 and 100–2). The A and D are sometimes used as passing tones (86, 97, and 101). The fascination of the line, however, is found in the artistic placement of unresolved tones and the manner in which some of the resolutions are delayed. The summary of Table 43 reveals a vocal part equally as varied as that of the shamisen. The classification of the opening of phrase 2 (88) is problematic since both the upper and lower neighbors are used. The support of the shamisen on the C aided the decision in favor of the upper neighbor. In so short a section one cannot say that any pattern of procedure has been set but one can note the absence of any ascending lines.

THE HAYASHI MUSIC: tacet.

SUMMARY OF THE UTAGAKARI

Instrumentation: Voices and shamisen are used.

The vocal-shamisen lines: A variety of phrase lengths is found in both parts. Many of these are caused by extensive use of unresolved melodic tones which force the music on to some further delayed cadence. The shamisen plays more sparsely behind the voice part than when it is alone. Both parts tend to hover about E or B while stopping frequently on their neighbor tones.

Pitch progression: The overall pitch center is E. F$\sharp$ does not appear.

Tempo and rhythm: The tempo remains steady and moderate. No drums are used. Rhythmic activity in the shamisen is restricted to the interlude sections.

General remarks: This section functions as a transition between the michiyuki and the kudoki.

4. THE KUDOKI (121–223)

THE TEXT: The words of this section center around a letter that Gorō has received from Shōshō. It reveals some apparent fickle-

ness on her part to which he replies with rough words and then
proceeds to forget his troubles in drink. The choreography
pantomimes the letter reading, the writing of the reply, and,
finally, the drinking. There are puns and double entendres in
many of the words such as "yoi no tsuki" which can be trans-
lated as the evening moon or an evening of drunkenness.

The words metaphorically reveal a moment of hesitation in
Gorō's mind (191). They say that in spring it is likely to be
misty. Is it better to clear up or not to clear up? This could refer
to spring, drunkenness, or the business of revenge.

The kudoki, in keeping with the nagauta tradition noted
before, contains no percussion part, the entire section using only
singers and shamisen.

THE SHAMISEN MUSIC

TABLE 44: *Outline of the shamisen part for the kudoki of* Gorō

I	II	III	IV	V	VI	VII	VIII
1	121–128	8	8	fef	ef♯g	e f♯	U
2	129–134	6	3 3	f♯ec	cba	f♯ b	D
3	135–142	8	8	cb	EB	b B	D
4	143–151	9	6 3	b′	fe	b′ e	D
5	152–155	4	4	gf♯	bA	f♯ b	D
6	156–159	4	4	b A	FE	A E	D
7	160–169	10	2 8	e♭b	cb	e b	D
8	170–177	8	3 5	DE	EB	E B	D
9	178–181	4	4	Ab	GF♯	b F♯	D
10	182–186	5	2 1 2	Ab	CB	b B	C
11	187–191	5	5	Ab	ef♯	b f♯	U
12	192–198	7	5 2	f♯	de	f♯ e	D
13	199–207	9	4 5	f-e	FE	e E	D
14	208–211	4	4	ecb	FED	e E	D
15	212–219	8	4 (3–1)	EF	FA	E (b)	C
16	220–223	4	4	b	b	b b	S

SUMMARY OF TABLE 44

I & II. There are 16 shamisen phrases.
III. The frequency of each type of phrase length is as follows:

      4 eight bars
      5 four bars
      2 five bars
      1 six bars
      1 seven bars
      2 nine bars

<pre>
              1   ten bars
</pre>
iv. The motivic divisions are:
<pre>
              8   undivided
              1   symmetrical
              7   asymmetrical
</pre>
v. The opening melodic movements are:
<pre>
              4   LN
              5   UN
              3   S
              1   4th
              1   PC to LN
              1   PC to UN
              1   skip down from PC
</pre>
vi. Cadence formulas are as follows:
<pre>
              2   LN
              6   UN
              1   S
              2   4th
              3   PC to LN
              1   PC to UN
              1   unresolved dissonance
</pre>
vii. The pitch progressions are as follows:
<pre>
              E leads to B or F♯
              B leads to E or F♯ or A
              F♯ leads to B or E
              A leads to E
</pre>
viii. The general direction of lines is:
<pre>
              2   U
             11   D
              1   S
              2   C
</pre>

The return of eight- and four-bar phrases is notable in this section, though there is still considerable variety in the types used. Unlike previous situations studied, most of the quartal phrases are not subdivided or, if they are, the subdivision is asymmetric. Though there is a slight majority of progressions from upper neighbors to pitch centers, there is still a variety of methods for beginning a phrase. The cadence formulas seem even more usual. Note that five of these cadences end in dissonance. These may be explained in terms of the necessity of maintaining the flow of the music without the aid of a fast tempo or the percussion instruments. Once more the importance of melodic dissonance becomes evident.

The opening phrase (121) further illustrates this principle.

This phrase may be recognized as the same stereotyped melodic pattern called tataki that was found in *Tsuru-kame* (see page 144). It is commonly found in lyric sections, especially in kudoki, and hence is an important musical indication of the mood of the music that is to follow.

Pitch progressions in this section go further than any up to this point. Phrase 6 (156) contains one of the rare uses of the in scale built on A. The words at this moment mention the rough reply of Gorō's letter. Perhaps the sudden change of attitude may account for the unusual choice of pitch center. One can note in this same area the frequency with which rests in the shamisen part are preceded by unresolved tones (D, F, and C).

The sudden prevalence of descending phrases is new to this piece but typical to the style of this section as was seen in the previous analysis. Rhythmic activity is again generally restricted to sections in which the voice is silent. The one dotted rhythm in this section is used when Gorō pantomimes the drinking of wine. One wonders if this was intended to be a short bit of word painting.

THE VOCAL MUSIC

TABLE 45: *Outline of the vocal part for the kudoki of* Gorō

I	II	III	IV		V	VI	VII		VIII
1	121–128	8	4	4	efe	ef♯(e)	e	f♯	U
2	129–134	6	4	2	ef♯	cbA	f♯	b	D
3	135–142	8	4	4	bA(E)	EDB	b	B	D
4	143–148	6	6		b′	fe	b′	e	D
5	149–154	6	6		e	de(d)	e	e	S
6	156–159	4	4		db A	DE	A	E	D
7	160–163	4	4		ce	be	e	e	S
8	164–169	6	3	3	fe	Ab	e	b	D
9	170–177	8	5	3	ede	edb(A)	e	b	D
10	178–184	7	4	3	AbF♯	Ab	b	b	C
11	191–197	7	3	4	f♯ef♯	gf♯ge	f♯	f♯	S
12	198–204	7	5	2	bde	Ab(A)	b	b	C
13	207–210	4	4		Acb	FE	b	E	D
14	211–216	6	6		ede	eb(A)	e	b	D
15	218–223	6	6		Ab	Ab	b	b	S

SUMMARY OF TABLE 45

ɪ & ɪɪ. There are 15 sung phrases.

III. The frequency of each type of phrase length is:

    3   eight bars
    3   four bars
    6   six bars
    3   seven bars

IV. The motivic divisions are:

    7   undivided
    3   symmetrical
    5   asymmetrical

V. The opening movements are as follows:

    3   LN
    3   UN
    6   S
    1   PC to LN
    1   skip up to PC
    1   skip up away from PC

VI. The cadence formulas are:

    7   LN
    2   UN
    2   4th
    2   skip down to PC
    1   UN to LN
    1   PC to LN

VII. The pitch progressions are as follows:

    E leads to B or F♯ or A
    B leads to E or F♯
    F♯ leads to B
    A leads to E

VIII. The general directions of lines are:

    1   U
    8   D
    4   S
    2   C

The large number of six-bar phrases is caused by the lengthening of the final cadence of what in the shamisen part is a four-bar phrase. The three seven-bar phrases in a row occur at the point in the text in which the wine drinking is described. This is also the only spot in this section which uses kabuki-style speech in the midst of the singing. Perhaps truncated phrases are a form of musical drunkenness.

In this first lengthy vocal section one finds a continued variety of means for opening and closing cadences, though the static opening and the lower neighbor to pitch-center cadence have slight statistical majorities. In the light of previous analyses it is the skips to and from pitch centers which seem most novel.

Pitch progressions remain the same as those of the shamisen except for the movement from E to A. The large number of descending lines has been shown to be common.

THE HAYASHI MUSIC: tacet.

SUMMARY OF THE KUDOKI

Instrumentation: Voices and shamisen are used.

The vocal-shamisen line: Eight- and four-bar phrases are more prevalent in the shamisen than in the voice. Symmetrical divisions are the least used. Both parts use a variety of means to open and close phrases, though vocal cadences are somewhat less varied, progressions from lower neighbors to pitch centers being prevalent.

Pitch-center progressions: The overall movement is E-B-A-E-B-E with many half cadences. These may be engendered by the need for melodic continuity in such a long lyric section. A is a new pitch center to this piece.

Tempo and rhythm: The tempo is steady and moderate. Rhythmic activity is generally confined to the short instrumental interludes.

General remarks: The pattern tataki opens this section and indicates the general mood. Unusual pitch centers and rhythmic figures appear to be textually motivated.

5. THE MAE (224–329)

THE TEXT: The mae means the section before a larger part. It is a transition between the kudoki and the odoriji in this piece. The mood of the text returns to one of vengeance as Gorō recalls the eighteen years since his father's death. He will not let his enemy get away. His ardour is so strong that it will push back the very winds that might impede him as if they were butterflies (his costume is embroidered with butterflies). This section is played by the two tsuzumi as well as voices and shamisen.

THE SHAMISEN MUSIC

TABLE 46: *Outline of the shamisen part for the mae of* Gorō

I	II	III	IV	V	VI	VII	VIII
1	224–228	5	2 3	bF♯	GF♯	b F♯	D
2	229–232	4	4	gf♯	cb	f♯ b	D

I	II	III	IV	V	VI	VII	VIII
3	233–241	9	4 4 1	ab′	gf♯	b′ f♯	C
4	242–249	8	8	ab′	bA	b′ b	D
5	250–256	7	3 (3–1)	AFAb	Ee	b e	U
6	257–264	8	4 4	ef♯	EF♯	f♯ F♯	C
7	265–273	9	4 5	ce(f♯)	cb	e b	C
8	274–277	4	4	df♯	GF♯	f♯ F♯	D
9	278–286	9	4 5	bAb	f♯cb	b b	S
10	287–295	9	5 4	ef♯	Ab	f♯ b	D
11	296–302	7	5 2	DE	cb	E b	U
12	303–310	8	8	de	FE	e E	D
13	311–316	–	optional	de	ebe	e e	S
14	317–320	4	4	ebe	e	e e	S
15	321–329	9	3 2 4	gf♯	eb	f♯ b	D

SUMMARY OF TABLE 46

I & II. There are 15 shamisen phrases.

III. The frequency of each type of phrase length is as follows:

- 3 eight bars
- 3 four bars
- 5 nine bars
- 2 seven bars
- 1 five bars
- 1 optional (see below)

IV. The motivic divisions are:

- 5 undivided
- 1 symmetrical
- 8 asymmetrical
- 1 optional

V. Opening movements are as follows:

- 8 LN
- 2 UN
- 2 S
- 1 4th
- 2 skip up to PC

VI. Cadence formulas are as follows:

- 2 LN
- 8 UN
- 3 S
- 1 4th
- 1 PC to LN

VII. The pitch progressions are as follows:

E leads to B or F♯

B leads to E or F♯

F♯ leads to E or B

VIII. The general directions of lines are:

2 U
7 D
3 S
3 C

In addition to the normal four- and eight-bar phrasing one finds a large number of nine-bar phrases. The first such phrase (233) seems to be an eight-bar phrase with one bar added to accommodate the drum call, which is very important to the setting of the tempo of the subsequent measures. The next three examples seem to entail the addition of one measure in order to complete brief antiphons between the voice and shamisen or to finish a section of heightened speech. The remaining example (321) is the final cadence of the section which is treated rather freely. These phrases cause the number of asymmetrical phrases to rise. The optional example is found at measure 314. This measure is repeated as many times as is necessary for the actor to complete his stage action. The first shamisen player watches him and gives the signal when to proceed. In concerts it is usually repeated once.

The number of means used to open and close phrases is reduced in this section as more standard methods take precedence, the lower neighbor dominating the beginnings and the upper neighbor the endings. Pitch progression remains as before and the downward trend of the lines is still evident.

The very opening of the mae is accompanied by ōzatsuma patterns. This is in keeping with the recitative quality of the vocal part. The music of the interlude (233–41) is used by the actor to remove his sandals. He disengages one foot at measures 233–34 and kicks the sandal backward to a waiting stage assistant at measures 235–36, repeating the process for the other foot in the next four bars. The drum calls help to set the tempo for this movement.

Phrase 6 (257) shows the use of both the raised and lowered version of one note of a scale within one phrase. The subsequent phrase is a striking example of the use of the tritone to maintain the melodic tension at a point when rhythm and the density of notes have both been removed.

The special function of ōzatsuma patterns is illustrated again in phrase 8 (274). As soon as the voice returns to heightened speech the shamisen stops its normal melodic procedure and uses the pattern kakeji. The final cadence of the section should be noted as one of the standard nagauta half-cadence patterns.

TABLE 47: *Outline of the vocal part for the mae of* Gorō

I	II	III	IV	V	VI	VII	VIII
1	224–228	5	2 3	spoken			
2	229–232	4	4	spoken			
3	233–241		tacet				
4	242–248		tacet				
5	249–256	8	4 4	bAb	de	b e	U
6	257–264	8	4 4	ef♯	GF♯	f♯F♯	D
7	265–273	9	4 5	c-(f♯)	cb	(b)f♯ b	D
8	274–277	4	4	spoken			
9	278–285	8	4 4	spoken			
10	287–295	9	2 3 4	ef♯	Ab	f♯ b	D
11	296–302	7	7	DE	Ab	E b	U
12	303–311	9	5 4	de	DE(D)	e E	D
13	312–316		tacet				
14	317–320	4	4	de	de	e e	S
15	321–329	9	3 6	ef♯	Ab	f♯ b	D

SUMMARY OF TABLE 47

i & ii. There are 12 sung phrases.

iii. The frequency of each type of phrase length is as follows:

> 3 eight bars
> 3 four bars
> 4 nine bars
> 1 seven bars
> 1 five bars

iv. The motivic divisions are:

> 4 undivided
> 3 symmetrical
> 5 asymmetrical

v. The opening movements of lines are as follows:

> 6 LN
> 0 UN
> 1 S
> 1 skip down to PC
> 4 spoken

vi. The cadence formulas are:

> 6 LN
> 2 UN
> 4 spoken

vii. The pitch progressions are similar to those of the shamisen.

viii. The general directions of lines are:

```
2   U
5   D
1   S
4   spoken
```

The vocal line of this section is noteworthy for its more extensive use of the standard lower neighbor progressions and types of phrase beginnings and endings. There has been an increasing tendency in this direction with each section. The number of unusual patterns has been reduced to one. The four lines of heightened speech are an imitation of the kabuki declamatory style. Though they have no definite pitch, there is a tendency for each line to begin in a middle range, rise at the points of accent, and drop at the end. In concert performances the end of the last declamation (284–85) is sometimes retarded. Because of this the voice begins the next line alone, followed by the shamisen. This is the reverse of the normal procedure though not exceptional (see measure 265).

THE HAYASHI MUSIC: During the opening declamatory section the ō-tsuzumi enters with the noh pattern uke-mitsuji, while the ko-tsuzumi plays mitsuji. This is in keeping with the recitative quality of this phrase, as the patterns used are basic, rather neutral ones in the noh. This is one of only two noh-style drum sections in the entire piece, as there are no further drum-accompanied recitatives in the composition.

The drums support the rhythm of the removal of the sandals (232–40) and help to set the pace by the length of their drum calls. From this point until the cadential kashira at measure 323 these drums support the rhythm of this masculine dance with kabuki chirikara rhythms. Note the dramatic use of a different style of drum call at measure 311 as a transition into the use of double stops in the shamisen.

SUMMARY OF THE MAE

Instrumentation: Shamisen, voices, and the tsuzumi are used.

The vocal-shamisen line: Nine-bar phrases are particularly exploited along with the usual quadruplex units. Both parts show an increase in the use of lower neighbor to pitch-center movements at the start of phrases. Upper neighbor to pitch-center cadences are more common in the shamisen while the lower neighbor remains predominant in the voice part. The declamatory passages in the voice are accompanied by ōzatsuma patterns in the shamisen. A downward trend in lines is seen in both parts.

Pitch progressions: The overall progression is B-E-F♯ (as a fifth of B)-E-half cadence in E. No new pitch relations are found.

Tempo and rhythm: After the opening recitative the tempo increases. The drums begin with one noh pattern but use kabuki-style rhythms for the remainder of the section.

General remarks: The change in mood in the text is matched in the music by a change in melodic style (toward the conventional) and a more forceful instrumentation. Direct relations between the music and the choreography can be found.

6. THE ODORIJI (330–465)

THE TEXT: The text in the odoriji returns to the topic of the love of Shōshō and Gorō. The words say that no matter how the nightingale in the bush may sing it is still left to envy the plum tree in the garden. This is meant to convey the difficulty of the human love affair. The spring winds send gently the news of their famous love. In a passage full of double meanings and puns the poem states that when day breaks there is much dew on the violets and other plants. This also reads that the lovers wake wet with the dew of love as proof of their sincerity. The text further comments how good is their love affair of the Naka district.

This section begins in a new tuning, ni-agari, and with a new instrumentation. The voice and shamisen are now coupled with the bamboo flute and the taiko. The tsuzumi join the ensemble later (371).

THE SHAMISEN MUSIC

TABLE 48: *Outline of the shamisen part for the odoriji of* Gorō

I	II	III	IV	V	VI	VII		VIII
1	330–338	9	4 5	F♯	ef♯	f♯	f♯	U
2	339–346	8	4 4	f♯	bA	f♯	b	D
3	347–352	6	2 4	F♯Abc	bF♯	F♯	F♯	C
4	353–356	4	4	GbGF♯	CB	F♯	B	D
5	357–365	9	2 2 2 3	b'gf♯	ef♯	f♯	f♯	C
6	366–371	6	6	gf♯	f♯	f♯	f♯	S
7	372–375	4	4	ec(b)	EF♯	b	F♯	C
8	376–383	8	2 6	ecef♯	cb	f♯	b	C
9	384–391	8	4 4	bF♯	F♯c	b	(b)	C
10	392–397	6	(1–2) 3	ecb	GF♯E	e	E	D
11	398–402	5	5	A-b	cb	(b) b		C

I	II	III	IV		V	VI	VII		VIII
12	403–408	6	3	3	ecef♯	ef♯	f♯	f♯	S
13	409–418	10	10		b'gf♯	ef♯	f♯	f♯	S
14	419–428	10	6	4	f-fe	f♯ec	e	f♯(b)	D
15	429–437	9	4	5	gf♯e	bc	e	b	C
16	438–444	7	4	3	cb	bF♯	b	F♯	C
17	445–454	10	6	4	b'gf♯	f♯	f♯	f♯	S
18	455–458	4	4		ef♯g	ec	(f♯	b)	C
19	459–464	6	6	(1)	ecb	ceb	b	b	S

SUMMARY OF TABLE 48

i & ii. There are 19 shamisen phrases.

iii. The frequency of each type of phrase length is as follows:

3 eight bars
3 four bars
3 nine bars
3 ten bars
5 six bars
1 five bars
1 seven bars

iv. The motivic divisions are:

7 undivided
4 symmetrical
8 asymmetrical

v. The opening movements are as follows:

3 LN
9 UN
2 S
1 4th
2 skip down from PC
1 skip up from PC
1 unresolved dissonance

vi. The cadence formulas are as follows:

5 LN
4 UN
2 S
2 4th
1 PC to LN
1 PC to UN
1 skip down to PC
3 unresolved dissonance.

vii. The pitch progressions are primarily between F♯ and B with E appearing mostly in the middle section.

viii. The general directions of lines are:

1	U
4	D
5	S
9	C

One of the striking features of this section is the return to a variety of phrase lengths. These create a more subtle, less predictable line. The long nine- and and ten-bar lines are excellent support for the lyricism inherent in the topic of the text. This feeling of lyricism is also enhanced by the shamisen cadence structure. The change from the hon-chōshi to the ni-agari tunings begins with the testing of the new middle-string pitch, F♯. The music then moves between B and F♯ so that the latter becomes the fifth of the former. The shamisen, however, does not clearly rest on B until measure 382. For fifty-two bars the music cadences on fifths or unresolved tones so that the vocal line can flow easily over the rather sparse shamisen accompaniment. It should be added that this same unresolved quality to cadences makes it very difficult to decide with certainty the correct designation of phrase lengths.

The melodic movement of this section is also calculated to create an interesting line without interfering unduly with the vocal part. Such a variety of openings and cadences has not been seen since the kudoki. This is significant since the kudoki and odoriji are traditionally the most lyrical sections of a piece. Before leaving the shamisen music it should be noted that the final cadence pattern is the same as that used to close the mae.

THE VOCAL MUSIC

TABLE 49: *Outline of the vocal part for the odoriji of* Gorō

I	II	III	IV	V	VI	VII	VIII
1	330–338		tacet				
2	339–344	6	3 3	ef♯	cb(A)	f♯ b	D
3	345–352	8	3 5	AbF♯	EF♯	b F♯	D
4	353		tacet				
5	360–363	4	4	egf♯	cec	f♯ (b)	D
6	364–372	9	9	ef♯b′	ef♯(e)	f♯ f♯	S
7	373		tacet				
8	384–392	9	5 4	bGF♯	cbc	b b	C
9	393–397	5	5	bcb	F♯E	b F♯	D
10	398–403	6	2 4	cAF♯	Ab	(b) b	S
11	404–411	8	3 5	egb′	ef♯	f♯ f♯	C
12	412–419	8	5 3	gb′	ef♯e	b′ f♯	D
13	420–425	6	6	df	de	e e	S
14	426–429	4	4	gf♯	cbc	f♯ b	D

I	II	III	IV	V	VI	VII	VIII
15	432–437	6	3 3	ef♯	cb	f♯ b	C
16	438–444	7	4 3	AbF♯	bAF♯	b F♯	C
17	445–454	10	1 9	eg(f♯)	bef♯(e)	f♯ f♯	S
18	456–465	10	6 4	geb	Ab	(f♯)b b	S

SUMMARY OF TABLE 49

I & II. There are 15 sung phrases.

III. The frequency of each type of phrase length is as follows:

3 eight bars
2 four bars
2 ten bars
2 nine bars
1 seven bars
4 six bars
1 five bars

IV. The motivic divisions are:

5 undivided
2 symmetrical
8 asymmetrical

V. Opening movements are as follows:

5 LN
2 UN
1 S
2 skip up to PC
1 skip down to PC
1 skip down away from PC
3 unresolved dissonance (implied PC)

VI. Cadence formulas are as follows:

7 LN
2 UN
0 S
2 PC to LN
2 PC to UN
1 skip down to PC
1 unresolved dissonance

VII. The pitch progressions are between B and F♯. E is used once.

VIII. The general directions of lines are:

0 U
6 D
5 S
4 C

The vocal line is equally as varied as that of the shamisen in its use of different phrase lengths. Its phrase openings and endings are also varied though the lower neighbor to pitch-center cadences form a clearer majority. The three ambiguous opening movements and the five cadences which do not end on a pitch center are further indications of the importance of melodic dissonance to the style of lyric writing in nagauta.

THE HAYASHI MUSIC: As is traditional in odoriji sections, the opening percussion accompaniment is restricted to the taiko. The drum part is different from the one used in the michiyuki in several ways. First of all, it is not intimately connected with the flute part. The bamboo flute here is used to play a melismatic version of the basic vocal-shamisen melody and thus could not have the same connection with the taiko that the noh flute had in the michiyuki. Secondly, the drum does not begin with standard, named patterns but uses patterns unique to this piece. Finally, it can be seen that these unnamed patterns support rather than work against the rhythm of the shamisen line. The long rhythmic phrase in measures 345–51 is particularly useful in giving continuity to the fragmental shamisen line. One reason for this different orientation of the taiko may be the fact that the other drums are not present. Because of this the shamisen line does not have sufficient rhythmic strength to balance a truly independent taiko part. Even in this supporting role, however, one can notice considerably more independence in the rhythmic organization of the taiko than is found, for example, in the rhythms of the tsuzumi during the michiyuki section.

After the cadential kashira pattern (369–70) on the taiko, the tsuzumi enter playing a direct support for the shamisen rhythm which is answered by a taiko cadence. After this the tsuzumi carry on the support alone until measure 383. This overlapping of instrumentation is not unlike techniques found in Western orchestration. The ending section (383) also overlaps by the use of drum calls. The taiko now plays a kabuki pattern, *bungo sagari-ha,* followed by a kashira. A standard tsuzumi pattern (398–400) leads all the drums in to the higehiki pattern mentioned previously (page 84) as a suitable accompaniment for strong masculine gestures. Extremely masculine posturing (not, however, the specific higehiki movement) does occur at this point. The tsuzumi now take over the function of supporting the shamisen line, while the taiko for the first time since the michiyuki is free to set up a different rhythmic line. It does this with two repeats of the pattern abare (410–24). After a sudden stop in all three drums (424) they join together.

This is the first time that all three have been used as one unit, thus adding another sound to the nagauta instrumental vocabulary.

The relationship between the drums and the shamisen is also more involved. At measure 426 drums begin one of two eight-bar phrases (one beat to a bar). The shamisen at this point is in the middle of a ten-bar phrase replete with caesuras on melodically tense tones. The drum patterns are so arranged that each of these pauses in this phrase and the next are accompanied by strong rhythmic activity. The next melodic phrase begins (438) before the drum pattern ends (441). The last drum pattern, therefore, begins in the middle of the melodic phrase. The melody, however, is broken into so many small units that it is difficult to say precisely where each melodic thought ends. The discrepancy of the drum phrasing further complicates the problem. An added factor is the difference in the feeling of weak and strong beats in the two parts. For example, the drum pattern at 442 seems to go from strong to weak while the shamisen seems to do the opposite. The total effect of all these elements is a restless movement forward and a lack of the feeling of any firm cadences until the end. It reminds one of the similar lack of complete stops in many of the Bach inventions and fugues.

SUMMARY OF THE ODORIJI

Instrumentation: Shamisen, voices, bamboo flute, and taiko are used at the beginning. The tsuzumi enter later and join the taiko in a new relation at the end.

The shamisen-vocal lines: Both parts are characterized by a variety of phrase lengths and opening and closing patterns. The only comparable situation is found in the kudoki. Pauses in the shamisen accompaniment tend to be on unresolved pitches or half cadences.

Pitch progressions: The overall progression is from F♯ (as a fifth of B) to B. E appears briefly in the middle, and the final B cadence is made to sound like a half cadence in E.

Tempo and rhythm: The tempo is steady and moderate. The drum rhythms are varied but light at the beginning. The relations between the various percussion instruments and the shamisen become more complex as the section progresses. Kabuki named patterns are used in the drums, sometimes for choreographic reasons.

General remarks: Though this is a lyrical section one finds that the several factors mentioned above create a mood of restlessness beneath the vocal line. There is a greater variety of instrumental combinations in this section than before in the piece and the changes in tone color occur at closer intervals.

7-8. THE CHIRASHI AND DANGIRE (466–527)

THE TEXT: The final text says that no one compares with Gorō in his act of filial piety. Even in the future he will be honored like a saint. The words conclude with a little advertisement by saying that even now in prosperous Edo (Tokyo) the play about Gorō in the Asakusa district is crowded with spectators.

This section is scored for the full ensemble, with the noh flute being substituted for the bamboo flute.

THE SHAMISEN MUSIC

TABLE 50: *Outline of the shamisen part for the finale of* Gorō

I	II	III	IV		V	VI	VII		VIII
1	466–473	8	4	4	eb	eb	e	e	S
2	474–477	4	(3–1)		ce	ee	e	e	S
3	478–485	8	4	(3–1)	gf♯	ef♯	f♯	f♯	C
4	486–493	8	4	4	f♯gb′	cb	f♯	b	D
5	494–497	4	(3–1)		dc♯	c♯	c♯	c♯	S
6	498–505	8	4	(3–1)	f♯dc♯	F♯f♯	f♯	f♯	C
7	506–513	8	4	(3–1)	F♯f♯	F♯f♯	f♯	f♯	S
8	514–517	4	4		Bgf♯	cb	B	b	D
9	518–527	–	free		Bb′	AbF♯	B	b	D

SUMMARY OF TABLE 50

I & II. There are 9 shamisen phrases.

III. The frequency of each type of phrase length is as follows:

    5   eight bars
    3   four bars
    1   free

IV. The motivic divisions are:

    3   undivided
    5   symmetrical
    1   free

V. The opening movements are as follows:

    0   LN
    4   UN
    2   S
    1   4th
    1   skip up to PC
    1   skip down away from PC

vi. Cadence formulas are as follows:

$$
\begin{array}{ll}
3 & \text{LN} \\
1 & \text{UN} \\
4 & \text{S} \\
1 & \text{4th}
\end{array}
$$

vii. The progression between C♯ and F♯ has been added to the former procedures. The section seems to be divided into three areas; E, F♯, and B in that order.

viii. The general directions of lines are:

$$
\begin{array}{ll}
0 & \text{U} \\
3 & \text{D} \\
4 & \text{S} \\
2 & \text{C}
\end{array}
$$

This outline of the finale presents a new surprise. Instead of the variety of structures one has come to expect in this piece, the shamisen part reveals an extensive regularity. Only eight- and four-bar phrases are used, the last phrase really being an eight-bar phrase attenuated for cadential purposes. Symmetrical divisions suddenly take precedence (remember that the use of 3–1 in column IV indicates merely that there is a measure of silence in the phrase). The openings of phrases are still varied but the cadences are all of a more definite type. Four of the opening movements (phrases 1, 4, 6, and 8) begin with a pattern which outlines a fourth or fifth. The whole feeling throughout this section is one of pitch-center stability in contrast with the section just past. F♯ for the first time is firmly supported by the use of its fifth, C♯. The steady progression from E to F♯ to B and the strong cadences by no means weaken the general move- ment of the line, as there is a great amount of rhythmic activity both in the shamisen and the percussion.

THE VOCAL MUSIC

TABLE 51: *Outline of the vocal part for the finale of* Gorō

I	II	III	IV			V	VI	VII	VIII
1	470–477	8	4	(3–1)		de	ef♯	ef♯	U
2	478–485	8	4	4		gf♯	ef♯(e)	f♯ f♯	C
3	486–493	8	(1–3)	4		gb'f♯	cb	b' b	D
4	494–497	4	(3–1)			bc♯	c♯	b c♯	U
5	498–505	8	4	(3–1)		spoken			
6	506		tacet						
7	514–522	9	7	2		egf♯	f♯b	f♯ b	D
8	523–526	4	4			c♯Ab	Ab(A)	b b	S

ɪ & ɪɪ. There are 7 sung phrases.

ɪɪɪ. The frequency of each type of phrase length is as follows:

      4   eight bars

      2   four bars

      1   nine bars

ɪᴠ. The motivic divisions are:

      2   undivided

      4   symmetrical

      1   asymmetrical

ᴠ. The opening movements are as follows:

      6   LN

      1   spoken

ᴠɪ. The cadence formulas are as follows:

      3   LN

      1   UN

      1   S

      1   5th

      1   spoken

ᴠɪɪ. The pitch progressions are as follows:

      E leads to F♯

      B leads to C♯

      F♯ leads to B

      C♯ leads to F♯

ᴠɪɪɪ. The general directions of lines are:

      2   U

      2   D

      1   S

      1   spoken

      1   C

The vocal line also illustrates a return to a less varied structure. The four- and eight-bar phrases and the lower neighbor openings both contribute to the stability of the music, as do the cadences used. The short moment of heightened speech is not accompanied by an ōzatsuma pattern as is usual, but it is interesting to note that the pitch area is F♯, as this is one of the important pitch elements of such patterns. The final cadence surrounds the pitch center with the whole step above and below it. This is one of the standard movements used in final cadences. The whole step lower neighbor and half step upper neighbor are used also, for example, in phrase 7 (514), but the progression using the whole step above and below a pitch center is reserved for special cadences.

THE HAYASHI MUSIC: The tsuzumi in the chirashi begin by supporting the shamisen in their usual manner. The taiko and noh flute are once more locked together in a different rhythmic-melodic unit called sarashi. This pattern (466–87) has a different phrase structure than that of the shamisen and the other drums. It consists of a repeated five-bar group, a repeated two-bar group, and an eight-bar ending phrase. This makes a total length of twenty-two bars which, after a one-bar rest, is repeated with only one five-bar phrase at the beginning. The relation of these units to the tsuzumi and shamisen lines is shown in Table 52. The dots represent bars and the numbers indicate the length of each phrase unit. The tsuzumi and taiko agree only at three places, two of them being the beginning and ending phrases. The shamisen agrees at these two points also. For a short moment after the opening it is out of phase with both drum phrases, but the rest of the time it coincides with the tsuzumi part. By a judicious placing of rests these standard relationships have been maintained. The repeat of the tsuzumi patterns (485) occurs after twenty bars. Since the total length of the taiko pattern is twenty-two bars (plus a one-bar rest), the repeat of this pattern is set against the same tsuzumi part but starting at a different point. It is this kind of rhythmic counterpoint that creates one of the special, artistic qualities found in nagauta ensemble writing.

The dangire contains the only passage using ko-tsuzumi and shamisen alone. Sometimes a taiko and ō-tsuzumi part are added, though they are not used in the Tanaka school version.[4]

TABLE 52: *Phrase relationships in the chirashi of* Gorō

R = rest   • = bar

SHAMISEN	. . . .
TSUZUMI	. . . .
TAIKO	. . . .

SHAMISEN: 4 4 3 R4 4 4 4 3 R4 3 R

TSUZUMI: 4 4 3 8 R4 4 3 R4 3 R

TAIKO: 5 5 2 2 8 R5 2 2 8

The steadiness of the shamisen line allows the tsuzumi to play a much freer part than has hitherto been possible. It plays the noh pattern *otsu-uchikomi* and thus sets up a relationship not unlike that of the taiko to the shamisen as seen in earlier parts of the piece. This part adds excitement to the finale and main-

4 The ō-tsuzumi part can be heard on Nippon Columbia LP record BL 5003.

tains the important sense of rhythmic imbalance found throughout so much of this piece.

The dangire contains a standard dangire procedure in the
hayashi. The ko-tsuzumi and taiko coincide on the drum call
and beat. The taiko plays an attenuated kashira while the tsuzumi plays its special dangire pattern. All three drums play
a final beat before the last shamisen note. The noh flute also
enters at the very end with a dangire melody.[5]

SUMMARY OF THE CHIRASHI AND DANGIRE

Instrumentation: The full ensemble is used with noh flute.

The vocal-shamisen line: Both parts return to a four- and
eight-bar phrasing and stronger melodic structures. Standard
cadence patterns are used in both parts for the dangire.

Pitch progressions: The finale goes from E to F♯ to B. The
F♯ is supported for the first time by a strong C♯.

Tempo and rhythm: The tempo is more rapid. The two levels
of rhythmic activity found in the michiyuki return in this section to create their special form of tension for the finale. In the
dangire special cadence patterns are used by the drums.

General remarks: The return to regular phrasing in the voice
and shamisen and the use of stricter, named patterns in the
taiko and kabuki drumming in the tsuzumi produce a special
dramatic effect which contributes greatly to the excitement of
the finale. It should be remembered that this was originally a
dance piece.

It is now time to study the frequency of melodic types found
in this piece. The basic types for the shamisen and voice were
discussed in the last chapter. The reader is referred to that
discussion and to Examples 20 and 21 for the background of
the study that follows. We shall begin with Table 53 which
shows the types found in the shamisen part of *Gorō*.

TABLE 53: *Frequency of melodic types in the shamisen part of* Gorō

I	II	III	IV	V	VI	VII
3–B	98–A	14–B	109–D	11–B	38–E	1–B
34–B	160–E	23–E	132–C	280–B	72–E	6–F♯
89–B	162–A	39–A	233–A	293–B	522–E	102–B
157–B♭	173–A	56–E	237–A	304–E		217–F
165–F	306–A	149–A				261–C
206–C	326–E	154–E				399–F♯

[5] In dance versions of the piece a repeat of the sarashi pattern is sometimes added
to the end for dramatic effect.

I	II	III	IV	V	VI	VII
213–F	334–E	201–B				403–C
227–C♯	349–E	230–E				439–F♯
259–B	393–E	244–A				482–C
272–F♯	409–B	246–E				483–C
290–F♯	423–A	257–E				486–F♯
322–F♯	442–E	276–B				
355–F♯	445–B					
380–F♯	488–B					
433–F♯	498–F♯					
457–F♯	500–F♯					
491–F♯						
514–F♯						

I	II	III	IV	V	VI	VII
9–F♯	2–F♯		1–C	3–B		4–F♯
4–B	3–B	3–B	2–A	1–E	3–E	2–B
1–B♭	5–A	3–A	1–D			4–C
2–F	6–E	6–E				1–F
1–C						
1–C♯						

I	II	III	IV	V	VI	VII
18	16	12	4	4	3	11

The scalewise descending type I is found to be the most common pattern in this piece and its abbreviated form is next. In both types the patterns leading to B outnumber the other forms. The melodic type emphasizing the tritone (III) was the most common in *Tsuru-kame* but here it is tied with the ascending line (VII) for third place. Note that four of type VII begin on notes which will produce tritones with their final pitches. Type VI which was totally missing in *Tsuru-kame* is found three times here, all on the same pitch. Types IV and V, as in the previous piece, are relatively uncommon in *Gorō*.

Table 54 summarizes the use of vocal melodic types in *Gorō*. As in the shamisen, the descending type I prevails, though it must be remembered that the vocal types have a slightly different contour than those of the shamisen. The tritone type (III) is next in frequency though it should be noted that the close relation between types I and II gives at least that contour a clear majority. In type I the patterns moving toward F♯ are most frequent (starting on A), while types II and III tend to resolve to B (starting on E.) Type V is missing here but found in *Tsuru-kame,* while the opposite situation exists with type VII. The infrequency of upward directed lines has been noted before.

I	II	III	IV	V	VI	VII
5–A	11–E	96–A	36–F		6–F♯	300–E
8–D	90–A	128–E	100–C		11–B	450–B
16–A	136–A	145–A	158–G		198–B	
85–E	166–F♯	257–E	160–C		474–C	
139–E	209–A	259–B	349–G			
175–C	271–E	289–E	405–G			
178–A	321–E	341–E				
200–E	432–E	360–E				
214–C	448–E	425–E				
345–A	520–E	490–E				
365–G		514–E				
389–G						
413–G						
438–A						
443–A						
6–A	3–A	2–A	2–C		2–B	1–B
2–C	6–E	1–B	1–F		1–C	1–E
1–D	1–F*d*	8–E	3–G		1–F♯	
3–E						
3–G						
15	10	11	6	0	4	2

SUMMARY OF THE ANALYSIS

If all the summaries of the various charts are totaled, the results given below are obtained. The Roman numerals used refer to those found in the sectional charts. The smaller totals for the vocal columns in charts V, VII, and VIII are due to the presence of seven spoken passages in this piece.

I & II. There are 82 shamisen phrases and 64 vocal phrases.

III. The frequency of each type of phrase length is as follows:

shamisen	voice	
19	14	eight bars
17	13	four bars
1	0	fifteen bars
0	1	twelve bars
5	2	ten bars
11	7	nine bars
4	7	seven bars
9	10	six bars
5	3	five bars

shamisen	voice	
3	2	three bars
0	1	two bars
8	4	free
82	64	

IV. The motivic divisions are as follows:

shamisen	voice	
9	6	free
29	21	undivided
17	15	symmetrical
27	22	asymmetrical
82	64	

V. The opening movements of phrases are as follows:

shamisen	voice	
20	27	LN
26	7	UN
14	10	S
7	0	4th
2	1	PC to LN
1	0	PC to UN
12	12	others
82	57	

VI. The cadence formulas are as follows:

shamisen	voice	
14	31	LN
28	8	UN
18	1	S
6	2	4th
2	1	5th
6	6	PC to LN
2	2	PC to UN
6	6	others
82	57	

VII. Taking the seven divisions of the piece (the chirashi and dangire are one), root progressions are found as listed below. The numbers here represent the number of sections in which a progression is found and not the frequency of its appearance within each section.

shamisen	voice	
6	4	E to B
3	4	E to F♯
0	1	E to A
6	4	B to E
5	4	B to F♯

shamisen	voice	
1	1	B to C♯
1	0	B to A
6	5	F♯ to B
2	1	F♯ to E
1	0	F♯ to C♯
1	1	C♯ to F♯
1	1	A to E

VIII. The general directions of lines are as follows:

shamisen	voice	
12	5	up
33	28	down
17	16	static
20	8	curved
82	57	

Eight- and four-bar phrases are shown to be preferred in this piece as they were in *Tsuru-kame*. The choice of other lengths in *Gorō*, however, is more frequent. This may be the reason for the larger number of asymmetrical divisions in both the shamisen and vocal lines, though there are still many undivided phrases as seen in *Tsuru-kame*.

Upper neighbor to pitch-center movements are preferred in the shamisen part, while lower neighbor to pitch-center progressions dominate the vocal music. This differs from *Tsuru-kame* in the opening movements of the shamisen in which stationary passages were preferred. Another important difference in *Gorō* is the greater number of other, unusual melodic movements, particularly at the start of phrases.

The basic pitch-center progressions are to and from B and its upper and lower fifths, F♯ and E. The movement between E and F♯ is next in frequency. Movements to and from A or C♯ are rare.

Descending lines are again the most common in both parts. Curved lines often have a static quality in the sense that they frequently begin and end on the same pitch so one can see that the static line is also quite idiomatic.

The use of double stops in *Gorō* is relatively small. If one does not include the arpeggios used in the oki, there are a total of fourteen double stops in the piece. Nine of these are octaves, four on E and five on F♯, two are sevenths (312–14), and there is one each of unisons (5), fifths (25), and fourths (527).

Formally, one finds that *Gorō* is constructed along traditional kabuki lines. A clear distinction is made instrumentally between the michiyuki, kudoki, and odoriji. The style of music also changes in each section. The placement of the two tunings and appearance of A in the kudoki are also typical. The fact that the hon-chōshi tuning does not return causes the piece to end on a different pitch center than the one with which it began. This is rather common in kabuki-style pieces.

The amount and type of drum music used is also typical. The oki and kudoki are devoid of drum sounds and a majority of the percussion sections consist of kabuki-style patterns. The structure of the drum part of the finale varies considerably from that of *Tsuru-kame*. At the ni-agari the taiko is used alone, followed by a section in which it carries on a dialogue with the tsuzumi. Eventually, the three drums join, the taiko playing standard, named kabuki patterns while the tsuzumi carry on in chirikara fashion. During this section a contrast in phrasing with the shamisen occurs in a manner more reminiscent of the last of *Tsuru-kame*. In the finale the drums are not bound, however, by any eight-beat orientation but rather act against each other in a rhythmic counterpoint.

Word painting seems more evident in *Gorō* than in *Tsuru-kame*. The heightened speech section (224), however, uses ōzatsuma patterns, and C♯ and F♯ sounds just as is found in such passages in *Tsuru-kame*. It is at this point that one of the two noh rhythms of the piece appears in the drums for one short phrase.

Through the use of conventional timbres, tunings, and musical style changes this through-composed piece has been given a sense of unity and of formal progression. By exploiting the power of tense melodic tones and varying rhythmic orientations the form has been filled with music of great vitality and interest.

For over one hundred years *Gorō* has remained a favorite piece on stage and in the concert hall. It is one of the many pieces which represent the kabuki dance form in its flowering period and as such it is an excellent illustration of the artistic merit and also the limitations of traditional nagauta music.

CHAPTER ELEVEN

Conclusions

NAGAUTA has been represented as one of the most significant musical developments of the Edo period. It began in the early seventeenth century as one of the many shamisen genres and by the eighteenth century had become the basic music of the kabuki theatre. The first instrumental ensemble used in the kabuki had been three drums and a flute (the hayashi) borrowed from the noh-drama tradition. When this group was combined with the nagauta shamisen and singer, a new Japanese vocal-instrumental form was created. The addition of the bamboo flute and the occasional support of off-stage instruments completed the instrumental resouces of this music.

This study has shown that one important factor in the understanding of this music is an awareness of the presence of stereotyped melodic patterns. These are of four types. The first group are melodies borrowed from other shamisen genres. Most of these were acquired from the lesser music forms of the kabuki which have since been replaced by nagauta or some other present form of kabuki music. In most cases these melodies have been completely absorbed in the new music and only the shamisen music historian is aware of their origin. Some of them, however, are known as vestiges of older music and are deliberately used in compositions to evoke the mood of the original source. This is particularly true when an older piece is rewritten as a nagauta composition.

The second type of stereotyped melody consists of the so-called forty-eight ōzatsuma-te. These might be considered as a subtype of the first group since they are all derived from the repertoire of a defunct shamisen music, ōzatsuma-bushi. This particular set, however, is clearly distinguished from other melodies. Each pattern has a name and the entire set is used only for specific purposes which are the accompaniment of recitatives and heightened speech sections or the creation of rubato cadences. This group also has a tendency to concentrate in recitative sections on patterns centering around certain pitch areas, in the transcriptions of this study, F♯ and C♯. Despite the rather specific nature of these melodies it is not always possible to make a clear distinction between some of them and certain melodies derived from other genres. This is due to the extensive melodic borrowing practiced by all the various styles of shamisen music. Because of this the same melody may be listed differently in two nagauta pieces depending on the particular sources used by the composers involved. The ōzatsuma patterns, nevertheless, are the most clearly defined of the standard melodies.

The third type of stereotyped melodies is a group which can be called repertoire-wide leitmotives. These are used to signify special moods, places, or people. A majority of these patterns have grown out of the off-stage music tradition. These may have a known origin in some other form of music and may be used in the manner of the first type of melodies mentioned above. Their use in nagauta, however, is distinguished by the special connotations of their appearance in relation to the text of the piece.

The final group consists of the standard melodic procedures as shown in the two detailed analyses. This group does not have any known historical connection. Rather, it is the result of a gradual solidification of nagauta style. Of the seven types each found in the voice and the shamisen lines, the descending lines were shown to take precedence in the two pieces studied. This direction was slightly modified in the vocal part by a preliminary diatonic step upward before the skip down. The shamisen line in particular showed a preference for the use of patterns which emphasized the drop of an augmented fourth.

The use of the augmented fourth as an important melodic component is part of the general approach to melody construction in nagauta, which this study has presented as being based upon a fundamental concept of melodic consonance and dissonance. Under this system certain pitches are given the quality of pitch centers by the frequent support of their upper and lower neighbors and their fifths. These principal tones have been defined as being melodically consonant, requiring no further resolution. All other pitches are conceived of as melodically dissonant, since they seek resolution into one of the consonant ones. The delaying of such resolutions constitutes a major element in the sense of motion found in nagauta melodies. It was found, for example, that whenever the shamisen part became sparse or less rhythmic it had a tendency to dwell more often on these dissonant tones. When the vocal part was not using one of the standard melodic types it was constructed almost exclusively of undulations between a principal tone and its dissonant neighbors. The foregoing study suggests that the use of this consonance-dissonance principle may be the most important single element in the construction of nagauta melody.

It should be added that the professional Japanese musician, while not overtly aware of the tendencies noted, is trained to think of the various stereotyped patterns mentioned above as standard procedures rather than specific melodies. He is able to recognize and remember each pattern in its permutations as found in particular pieces. This may account for some of the amazing feats of memory displayed by nagauta shamisen players.

The two analytic chapters (IX and X) showed that there was a preference in both the shamisen and voice for four- and eight-bar phrasing but that a variety of other types occurred. Because of the overlapping nature of the two parts these phrases did not always coincide. The noh-derived composition, *Tsuru-kame*, showed a greater tendency toward this regularity than the kabuki dance piece, *Gorō*. This is due in part to the eight-beat orientation of noh music and to the fact that the drum music, being primarily noh-derived, tended toward such even phrasing.

On a statistical basis progressions from lower neighbors to pitch centers are the most prevalent in the vocal part, while the shamisen uses primarily static progressions or movements from upper neighbors to pitch centers.

Using the pitches of the transcription as a basis, the general movement between pitch centers themselves has been shown to follow a general path between E, B, and F♯ with an occasional A or C♯ center being used for a short time. Both the yō and in form of a scale is not uncommon. This usually is the result of a melodic change in direction: that is, the second and fifth notes of scales tend to be raised in ascending passages and lowered in descending ones. The sophistication of nagauta melody writing, however, is such that it would be a mistake to presume that one could predict the structure of every case. One can only note tendencies.

It is in the drum music that one finds the most fascinating applications of the principle of stereotyped patterns. Drum music derived from the original noh-hayashi tradition was shown throughout this study to be very carefully and consistently organized around "tonic" patterns which lead through a series of other patterns, chosen and placed according to definite rules of progression, and end with specific cadential formulas. The particular patterns chosen varied according to the original source used: that is, if a nagauta drum section was borrowed from a standard noh piece, the special order of the patterns of that piece was adopted. It is hard to reduce all these patterns to one series. One could, perhaps, reduce the taiko music to certain basic patterns. Kashira and tsuke-gashira usually open a noh-style phrase. Kizami is considered to be the basic pattern for the rest of the music, though it is often interrupted by the interpolation of oroshi, hane, or taka-kizami. When the cadence approaches it is signaled by the use of uchikomi and uchikiri, which lead into a final kashira pattern. The basic pattern for the two tsuzumi is tsuzuke, though mitsuji or ji are frequently substituted for it. Kan-mitsuji is the normal beginning pattern for the ko-tsuzumi, while uchidashi is found in the ō-tsuzumi part. Various forms of the uke and ji pattern groups, particularly uke-hashiri and nagaji, are found during the body of a drum section. The cadence is approached through the patterns musubi and uchikomi, and the closing pattern is kashira.

These laws of progression have been presented here as possible substitutions for the concepts of harmony and chord progression often noted as absent from shamisen music. Here is a system of definite starting points and goals with a deliberate choice of various means of traversing the distance between them. This is identical in spirit with the laws of harmonic progression used in the West. The critical difference is that the Western laws refer to vertical pitch complexes while the Japanese rules deal with conjunct horizontal rhythmic units.

It is only when these laws are coupled with an understanding of the two non-melodic units of nagauta that the full significance of this knowledge becomes clear. These two units are the pair of tsuzumi drums and the taiko and noh flute. The noh flute has been called a non-melodic instrument because of two factors. First, the notes it plays are never similar to the melody of the shamisen nor do they have any specific pitch relationship to it. Secondly, it has been shown that when this flute is used in conjunction with the taiko the two are considered as one unit and even in lessons the one part is seldom learned without the other.

Taking, then, these two units in their relations to the shamisen part, one finds situations in which the tsuzumi are playing kabuki patterns and the taiko and flute are playing noh patterns. The former phrase with the shamisen and support its rhythm while the latter do not. The "out of phase" group, however, is following one of the prescribed orders of pattern progression mentioned above. At the cadences there is a use of closing patterns in all parts.

When the tsuzumi play noh patterns they likewise cease to support the shamisen rhythm directly and follow a definite pattern to the cadence. The analysis of *Gorō* showed that there may even be sections of kabuki patterns in which all three drums are out of phase with the shamisen. In other words, except when the tsuzumi alone support the melody with kabuki patterns, there is always some instrument or unit of instruments playing contrary to the rest of the group. This creates tensions which demand release. The release occurs at the cadence. The manners in which these cadences are left and approached are standardized.

In Western music the basic functions of harmony are to color the line, create tensions (beyond those inherent in the melody) which drive the music onward, and help in the creation of formal designs. These harmonies have a standardized form of approaching and leaving cadences and a general, though flexible, order of progression. It is the contention of this study that the same type of functions, following analogous standardized orders of progression, are found in what could be called the third unit of nagauta music. The first unit is the melodic group: the voice, shamisen, and the bamboo flute when it is used to embellish the vocal line. The second unit is the rhythmic group which is defined here as any combination of percussion instruments which directly supports the rhythm of the shamisen line. The third group cannot be called harmonic since they play no chords, but in lieu of harmony they provide a sense of orderly progression from tension to release. Sometimes this third unit consists of flute and taiko, at other times it is purely percussive. If one accepts the noh-flute music as basically coloristic and rhythmically oriented, one might say that this group plays a second level of rhythm. The effect one hears, however, is not so much that of any resultant rhythm but rather of a forward driving motion. Therefore, it would seem better to call this group the dynamic unit, not in the sense of dynamics which become loud or soft but in the connotation of dynamism, that quality in things which gives them a sense of motion and action.

In most Western art music there are three essential elements: melody, rhythm, and harmony. If one accepts the double function of the hayashi, nagauta can also be said to have three elements: melody, rhythm, and dynamism.

Besides the laws of tension and release another important

principle in art is that of unity and contrast. The West is particularly noted for its extensive development of thematic ideas along these lines. The law also applies, among other places, to the principles of form and of orchestration. Development of a single motive in one piece is almost unknown in nagauta. It has been noted already, however, that there is a large group of standard melodies which can be permutated throughout the entire repertoire.

Formally, nagauta is organized along lines of contrast more in keeping with Western concepts. The seven basic units of the kabuki dance form (the oki, michiyuki, kudoki, odoriji, chirashi, and dangire) have been shown to contrast each other in the kind of instrumentation used, the mood of their music, and often, as shown by analysis, the specific style of melodic writing employed. Because of the dramatic orientation of nagauta one cannot always predict the specific elements which will appear at each moment in the piece. Nevertheless, one can expect a lack of percussion in the kudoki; the ni-agari tuning and use of the taiko and bamboo flute in the odoriji; a tendency toward quickening tempos, shamisen interludes, and more drum music in the chirashi; and standard cadence patterns in all the parts during the dangire. It is doubtful that one could expect to find a greater number of predictable items in any art music of even the most traditional type.

Kabuki dance form is not the only form used. The studies in Chapters III and IX have shown that there are several possible mixtures of forms. When a piece is derived from a noh drama it will usually incorporate some of the formal elements of that play. Thus, such terms as issei, ageuta, or the name of some noh-dance interlude will be interpolated into the nagauta music. The treatment of the music, as was shown in *Tsuru-kame,* is occasionally inspired by noh music rather than being a direct imitation of it. Jiuta form with its alternation of vocal sections and instrumental interludes is also used in nagauta, particularly in the more modern pieces.

The compositional process of nagauta also developed in a manner different from that of the modern West. Because of the great number of standard procedures which were common knowledge among the practitioners of nagauta, it was possible for each specialist to compose his own part and still produce a piece that sounded unified and logical. While this system of community composition created some genuine masterpieces during the flourishing days of this music, it has created very serious obstacles to the further development of the art. The great problem that nagauta composers face today is how to separate the essentials of their music from the hackneyed elements and create a new music exploiting fresh ideas set within the matrix of these essentials. Perhaps the special inter-relation of so many traditional techniques makes such a develop-ment impossible. At present there is no indication that anyone is deeply aware enough of the problem to struggle with it. Modern nagauta tend to be a mixture of traditional techniques and generally ineffectual imitations of the Western orchestral sound ideal. This study has shown, however, that nagauta, at the height of its development, was a mature, highly organized shamisen genre worthy of a place among the art musics of the world.

APPENDIX

Titles and Locations of Nagauta Compositions Studied

FOR THOSE who may wish to become better acquainted with nagauta the following list of modern notations and recordings has been provided. In general, only one notation and one recording have been listed, although seventy-eights are still manufactured in Japan and some nagauta pieces are available in that form. This list is valid as of the summer of 1961.

The recording call letters signify the following companies, speeds, and sizes:

B: Nippon Columbia, 78, 10″   LKD: King, 33, 12″
CL: Nippon Columbia, 33, 10″   LR: Nippon Victor, 33, 10″
EP: Nippon Columbia, 45   NK: Nippon Victor, 78, 10″
EV: Nippon Victor, 45   OR: Nippon Victor, 78, 10″
JHO: Toshiba, 33, 12″   SB: Nippon Columbia, 45
JL: Nippon Victor, 33, 10″   SP: King, 78, 10″
JLH: Toshiba, 33, 10″   WL: American Columbia, 33, 12″

COMPOSITION	NOTATION	RECORDING
Adachi ga Hara	Yoshizumi, VI–4	—
Aki no Irogusa	Yoshizumi, III–1	CL–51
Asazumabune	Bunka, 3351	LKD–12
Ataka no Matsu	Yoshizumi, IV–3	CL–48
Ayame Yukata	Bunka, 3320	CL–43
Ayatsuri Sambasō	—	CL–65
Azuma Hakkei	Yoshizumi, III–3	CL–13
Dōjōji (see *Kishū Dōjōji* and *Musume Dōjōji*)		
Echigojishi	Yoshizumi, III–5	CL–6
Funa Benkei	Yoshizumi, VII–1	—
Geikizaru	Yoshizumi, II–9	CL–47
Genroku Hanami-odori	Yoshizumi, II–8	CL–25
Gojōbashi	Bunka, 3338	SP–D4164–66
Gorō Tokimune	Yoshizumi, 1–5	LR–507, JHO–1015

COMPOSITION	NOTATION	RECORDING
Hanaguruma	—	—
Hana no Tomo	Yoshizumi, I–6	—
Hanami-odori (see *Genroku Hanami-odori*)		
Haru no Uta	Yoshizumi, VIII–12	—
Hashi Benkei	Yoshizumi, III–8	CL–53
Hinazuru Sambasō	Yoshizumi, II–1	—
Ise Ondo	Bunka, 346	—
Kagamijishi	Bunka, 3332	B–217–23
Kanda Matsuri	Yoshizumi, VIII–7	JHO–1010
Kanjinchō	Yoshizumi, V–3	JL–504, CL–35
Kanjo	Yoshizumi, II–5	B–116–18
Kibun Daijin	Yoshizumi, VIII–6	—
Kikuju Kusazuribiki	Bunka, 346	—
Kimi no Niwa	Yoshizumi, II–13	OR–246–49
Kishū Dōjōji	Yoshizumi, V–6	—
Kuramayama	Yoshizumi, I–9	JL–11
Matsu no Midori	Yoshizumi, II–12	EV–4007
Mitsumen Wankyū	—	—
Miyakodori	Yoshizumi, III–7	CL–18, EV–4018
Mochizuki	Yoshizumi, VII–7	—
Momiji Gari	—	—
Mugen no Kane	—	—
Musume Dōjōji	Yoshizumi, IV–4	JLH–1001
Ninin Wankyū	Bunka, 344	SP–D4040–44
Oharame	—	CL–5
Oimatsu	Yoshizumi, II–2	CL–60, LR–509
Renjishi	Yoshizumi, IV–1	JHO–1024
Sagi-musume	Yoshizumi IV–8	CL–71, JHO–1003
Sambasō (see *Ayatsuri Sambasō, Himezuru Sambasō,* and *Shita-dashi Sambasō*)		
Shakkyō	Yoshizumi, V–5	JHO–1001
Shigure Saigyō	Yoshizumi, V–4	CL–82
Shita-dashi Sambasō	—	CL–61
Shizu Hata Obi	Yoshizumi, III–9	—
Suehirogari	Yoshizumi, I–2	JHO–1019
Sukeroku	Yoshizumi, III–4	CL–43, JHO–1005
Takasago Tanzen	Bunka, 3342	CL–67, NK–3096–98
Tokiwa no Niwa	Yoshizumi, IV–6	—
Tomoyakko	Bunka, 3334	CL–12, JHO–1013
Tsuchigumo	Yoshizumi, III–2	WL–5110
Tsui no Amigasa	Bunka, 3364	—
Tsunayakata	Yoshizumi, V–2	CL–98
Tsuru-kame	Yoshizumi, I–10	CL–40, JL–509

COMPOSITION	NOTATION	RECORDING
Uki Daijin	Yoshizumi, VIII–4	—
Urashima	Yoshizumi, I–11	CL–4
Utsubozaru	Yoshizumi, VI–7	CL–90
Wakana-tsumi	Yoshizumi, I–8	—
Yōrō	Yoshizumi, VIII–5	—
Yoshiwara Suzume	Bunka, 3326	CL–46
Yuya	Yoshizumi, VI–2	—

Bibliography

DICTIONARIES AND ENCYCLOPEDIAS

Geinō Jiten (Dictionary of the Theatre Arts). Edited by the Kokugeki Kōjōkai. Tokyo: Tōkyō-dō, 1953. 795 pp.

Hōgaku Buyō Jiten (Dictionary of Japanese Dance Music). Compiled by Atsumi Seitarō. Tokyo: Fuzambō, 1956. 459 pp.

Koji Ruien (Selected Ancient Texts). Gotō Ryōichi, ed. Tokyo: Ruien Kankōkai, 1931. Vols. 43 & 44 (music and dance).

Nōgaku Yōkyoku Daijiten (Dictionary of Noh Singing). Shōda Shōjirō, ed. Tokyo: Yoshikawa Kobunkan, 1935. 669 pp.

Ongaku Jiten (The Music Dictionary). Shimonaka Yasaburō, ed. Tokyo: Heibon-sha, 1955–57. 12 vols.

Yōkyoku Taikan (A Collection of Noh Singing). Sanari Kentarō, ed. Tokyo: Meiji Shoin, 1930–31. 7 vols.

Yōkyoku Zenshū (A Complete Collection of Noh Singing). Nogami Toyoichirō, ed. Tokyo: Chūōkōron-sha, 1935. 6 vols.

BOOKS AND ARTICLES

Asakawa Gyokuto. "Kibun Daijin," *Nihon Ongaku*, No. 74 (July, 1954), pp. 12–15, and No. 75 (Aug., 1954), pp. 11–14.

—— "Meriyasu Godai" (Five Origins of the Word Meriyasu), *Nihon Ongaku*, No. 84 (May, 1956), pp. 13–15.

—— "Nagauta," *Hōgaku no Tomo*, 1 (Jan., 1956), pp. 31–34.

—— "Nagauta Hayashi ni tsuite," (About Nagauta Hayashi) *Nihon Ongaku*, Part I, No. 41 (Aug., 1951), pp 6–7. Part II, No. 43 (Oct., 1951), pp. 11–13.

—— *Nagauta Hikikata, Utaikata* (The Playing and Singing of Nagauta). Tokyo: Daidōkan, 1936. 300 pp.

—— "Nagauta no Keishiki" (Nagauta Form), *Hōgaku no Tomo*, Part I, No. 2 (Feb., 1956), pp. 31–34. Part II, No. 3 (March, 1956), pp. 32–35.

—— *Nagauta no Kiso Kenkyū* (A Basic Study of Nagauta). Tokyo: Hōgaku-sha, 1955. 288 pp.

—— "Nagauta no Rekishi" (The History of Nagauta), *Hōgaku no*

Tomo, Part I, No. 11 (Apr., 1956), pp. 24–27. Part II, No. 12 (May, 1956), pp. 24–27. Part III, No. 13 (June, 1956), pp. 23–26.

Atsumi Seitarō. See *Hōgaku Buyō Jiten* above.

—— *Kabuki Buyō* (Kabuki Dance). Tokyo: Sōgen-sha, 1956. 129 pp. illus.

—— *Kabuki Nyūmon* (A Kabuki Manual). Tokyo: Tōkai-shobō, 1948. 419 pp.

—— "Kabuki Ongaku Kōza" (Lectures on Kabuki Music), *Nihon Ongaku*, Nos. 5–8, 10, 12–23, 36, 37 (June, 1946–May, 1950).

Ernst, Earle. *The Kabuki Theatre*. London: Secker & Warburg, 1956. 269 pp. illus.

Halford, Aubrey S. & Giovanna M. *The Kabuki Handbook*. Rutland & Tokyo: Tuttle, 1956. 190 pp.

Hibbett, Howard. *The Floating World in Japanese Fiction*. London: Oxford University Press, 1959. 232 pp.

Hiroshi Anda. "Sangengaku" (Shamisen Music), in *Geinōshi no Kenkyū*. Ema Tsutomu, ed. Tokyo: Hoshino Shoten, 1934. pp. 109–25.

Hood, Mantle. *The Nuclear Theme as a Determinant of Patet in Javanese Music*. Groningen: Wolters, 1954. 323 pp. illus.

Iba Takashi. *Nihon Ongaku Gairon* (An Outline of Japanese Music). Tokyo: Koseikaku Shoten, 1928. 999 pp.

Ikeda Kojirō. *Nagauta Shōshi* (A Brief History of Nagauta). Vol. I of *Hōgaku Sōsho*. Tokyo: Nagauta Ginreikai Shuppan-bu, 1930. 71 pp.

Kanetsune Kiyosuke. *Nihon no Ongaku* (Japanese Music). Tokyo: Hattori Shoten, 1913. 508 pp. 40 pages of music.

Kawatake Shigetoshi. "Kabuki no Ongakuteki Enshutsu" (The Musical Production of Kabuki), in *Taō Ongaku Ronsō*. Kishibe Shigeo, ed. Tokyo: Yamaichi Shobō, 1943. pp. 175–92.

—— *Kabuki-shi no Kenkyū* (A Study of Kabuki History). Tokyo: Tōkyō-dō, 1943. 680 pp.

Keene, Donald. *The Battles of Coxinga*. London: Taylor's Foreign Press, 1951. 205 pp. illus.

Kikkawa Eishi. "Samisen and Samisen Music," *KBS Bulletin*, No. 6 (June, 1952), pp. 5–6.

—— *Hōgaku Kanshō* (The Appreciation of Japanese Music). Tokyo: Hōbunkan, 1952. 442 pp.

Kineya Eizō. *Nagauta no Utaikata* (The Singing of Nagauta). Tokyo: Sōgen-sha, 1932. 2 vols.

Kineya Tokichirō. *Nagauta no Sōhō* (Nagauta Accompaniment). Tokyo: Kōundō, 1932. 140 pp.

Kō Yoshimitsu. *Ko-tsuzumi Nyūmon* (A Manual of Ko-tsuzumi Drumming). Tokyo: Nōgaku Shorin, 1953. 121 pp.

Koizumi Bunfu. *Nihon Dentō Ongaku no Kenkyū* (A Study of Traditional Japanese Music). Tokyo: Ongaku no Tomo-sha, 1959. 253 pp.

Konakamura Kiyonori. *Kabu Ongaku Ryakushi* (A Short History of Dance Music). Tokyo: Meiji Shoin, 1906. 1st ed. 1893. 2 vols.

Lane, Richard. "Saikaku's Five Women," in *Five Women Who Loved Love*. Ihara Saikaku. Trans. by Wm. Theodore de Bary. Rutland & Tokyo: Tuttle, 1956. pp. 231–64.

Machida Kashō. "Japanese Music and Dance," in *Japanese Music and Drama in the Meiji Era*. Komiya Toyotaka, ed. D. Keene and E. Seidensticker, trans. Tokyo: Ōbun-sha, 1956. pp. 329–448.

—— *Nagauta no Utaikata to Hikikata* (Nagauta Singing and Playing). Tokyo: Hōki Shoten, 1934. 330 pp.

—— *Rajio Hōgaku no Kanshō* (Appreciation of Japanese Music by Radio). Tokyo: Nihon Hōsō Shuppan-kyōkai, 1950. 327 pp.

—— *Shamisen Seikyoku no Senritsukei no Kenkyū* (A Study of Stereotyped Melodies in Shamisen Music). Mimeographed supplement to meetings 42–47 of the Tōyō Ongaku Gakkai, Tokyo, 1955. 6 vols.

Malm, William P. "A Short History of Japanese Nagauta Music," *Journal of the American Oriental Society*, Vol. 80, No. 2 (May, 1960), pp. 91–92.

—— "An Introduction to Taiko Drum Music in the Japanese No Drama," *Ethnomusicology*, Vol. 4, No. 2 (May, 1960), pp. 75–78.

—— *Japanese Music and Musical Instruments*. Rutland & Tokyo: Tuttle, 1959. 299 pp. illus.

—— "Japanese Nagauta Music," *Festival of Oriental Music and the Related Arts*. Los Angeles: University of California Press, 1960. pp. 33–36.

—— "The Rhythmic Orientation of Two Drums in the Japanese No Drama," *Ethnomusicology*, Vol. 2, No. 3 (Sept.,1958), pp. 89–95.

May, Elizabeth. *Japanese Children's Music Before and After Contact with the West*. Berkeley: University of California Press, in press.

Minagawa Tatsuo. "Japanese Noh Music," *Journal of the American Musicological Society*. Vol. 10, No. 3 (Fall, 1957), pp. 181–200.

Miyake Kōichi. *Fushi no Seikai* (The True Understanding of Melody). Tokyo: Hinoki Shoten, 1955, 1st ed. 1951. 135 pp. 100 pages of music.

—— *Jibyōshi Seikai* (The True Understanding of Noh Rhythm). Tokyo: Hinoki Shoten, 1954. 223 pp.

—— *Shidai kara Kiri made no Utaikata* (Noh Singing from Start to Finish). Tokyo: Hinoki Shoten, 1952. 270 pp.

Mochizuki Taiinosuke. "Nagauta Hayashi Hayawakari" (A Quick Understanding of Nagauta Hayashi), *Shamisengaku*, (Jan., 1935–July, 1936).

—— "Nagauta Hayashi no Taii" (A General View of Nagauta Hayashi), *Shamisengaku*, (Feb.–Apr., 1937).

Nakagawa Aihyō. *Sangengaku-shi* (A History of Shamisen Music). Tokyo: Dainippon Geijitsu Kyōkai, 1941. 1,016 pp.

Peri, Nöel. *Essai sur les Gammes Japonaise*. Bibliothèque Musicale de

Musée Guimet. . . . Series 2, No. 1. Paris: Geuthner, 1934. 70 pp.

Piggott, Francis. *The Music and Musical Instruments of Japan*. London: B. T. Batsford, 1893. 230 pp.

Sanjō Shōta. *Nihon Ongaku no Chōshi no Hanashi* (A Discussion of Japanese Musical Scales). Tokyo: Koseikaku Shoten, 1932. 374 pp.

Sassa Seisetsu. *Edo Nagauta*. Tokyo: Hakubunkan, 1926, 1st ed. 1878. 260 pp.

Shimofusa Kanichi. *Nihon Minyō to Onkai no Kenkyū* (A Study of Japanese Folk Songs and Scales). No. 75 of *Ongaku Bunko*. Tokyo: Ongaku no Tomo-sha, 1954. 105 pp.

Shively, Donald H. "Bakufu versus Kabuki," *Harvard Journal of Asiatic Studies*, Vol. 18, Nos. 3–4 (Dec., 1955), pp. 326–56.

—— "Notes on the Word Kabuki," *Oriens*, Vol. 10, No. 1 (1957), pp. 144–49.

Sieffert, René. "Mibu-kyōgen," *Bulletin de la Maison Franco-Japonaise*, New series 3 (1953), pp. 119–51.

Sunaga Katsumi. *Japanese Music*. Tokyo: Maruzen, 1936. 65 pp.

Takano Tatsuyuki. *Nihon Kayōshi* (A History of Japanese Songs). Tokyo: Shūju-sha, 1926. 1,090 pp.

Tanabe Hisao. *Edo Jidai no Ongaku* (Music of the Edo Period). Tokyo: Bunkyō Shoin, 1928. 306 pp.

—— *Nihon no Ongaku* (Japanese Music). Tokyo: Bunka Kenkyū-kai, 1954. 337 pp.

—— *Nihon Ongakushi* (Japanese Music History). Tokyo: Yūzankaku, 1932. 310 pp.

—— "Shamisen Ongaku no Hassei yori Gendai made" (Shamisen Music from its Growth to the Present Time), *Hōgaku no Tomo*, (1955–). A monthly feature.

Tanaka Denzaemon. "Kabuki Hayashi Yōroku" (A Digest of Kabuki Drum Music), *Hōgaku no Tomo*, (Apr., 1958–), irregular feature.

Tōyō Ongaku Gakkai. "Shamisen no Kenkyū" (A Study of the Shamisen), *Tōyō Ongaku Kenkyū*, No. 14 (1958). pp. 1–131. English summaries.

Waley, Arthur. *The No Plays of Japan*. New York: Grove Press, 1957; 1st ed., 1920. 319 pp.

Zeami. *Kadenshō*. Iwanami Bunko No. 171. Tokyo: Iwanami Shoten, 1927. 110 pp.

MUSIC COLLECTIONS AND ORIGINAL SOURCES

Kabuki Sōshi Emaki. Tokyo: Kōko Gakkai, 1911. Photostatic reproduction in scroll form.

Kineya Mishichi, ed. *Shamisen Bunkafu, Nagauta*. Tokyo: Hōgaku-sha, 1925–1958. Individual printings of a majority of the nagauta repertoire.

Kō Yoshimitsu. *Kō-ryū Ko-tsuzumi Seifu*. Tokyo: Nōgaku Shorin, 1955. 163 pp.

Komparu Sōichi. *Komparu-ryū Taiko Zensho*. Tokyo: Hinoki Shoten, 1953. 322 pp.

Kunijo Kabuki Ekotoba. Commentary by Ogura Chikao. Kyoto: Kyoto University Library, 1951. Reproduction of scroll in book form, 20 pp. 4 pages of text.

Mochizuki Tazaemon. *Nagauta Hayashi Tetsuke*. Tokyo: Mochizuki-ryū Fuhon Seikyūkai, 1929. 6 vols.

Morita Misao. *Yōkyoku-mai Hyōshi Taisei*. Osaka: Yoshida Yōkyoku Shoten, 1915. 71 pp.

Nishino Torikichi. *Collection of Japanese Popular Music*. Tokyo: The Kaiseikan, 1916. 10 vols.

Senga Harumitsu. *Ko-tsuzumi no Shiori*. Tokyo: Ejima Ihei, 1907. 3 vols.

Tanaka Satojirō. *Ko-tsùzumi Fuhon*. Mimeographed scores of nagauta hayashi parts for various pieces as played by the Tanaka school. 6 vols.

Tazaki Nobujirō. *Kadono-ryū Ō-tsuzumi Kaitei*. Tokyo: Hinoki Taiko-dō, 1925. 80 pp.

Yoshizumi Kōjūrō. *Nagauta Gakufu*. Tokyo: Nakamura Tōji, 1926–1934 (?), Nagauta in Western notation. 6 known examples.

Yoshizumi Kosaburō. *Nagauta Shin-keikobon*. Tokyo: Hōgaku-sha, 1955.' 8 vols.

Index and Glossary

IN THIS glossary-index all major music terms are defined briefly and musicians identified. Many terms have several meanings but they are defined here only as used in the text. Japanese characters have been included whenever possible except in the case of cities, period names, and historical persons. Long marks appear on all Japanese words. Melodic and rhythmic patterns are indexed by their general class name and only the most common subtypes appear in the index (thus, *jo* is listed but not *tobijo*). In listing nagauta pieces the date of the composition consulted is given though other versions may exist. Note that most references to Western music are of a comparative nature.

In the index "fig." refers to a figure, "ex." means an example, "pl." is a plate, "fn." is a footnote, and "t." is a table. In general, the table is indicated if that is the only appearance of that term on the page. If it is also in the text the table is not listed. The letter "f." means that there is a further reference to the subject on the following page and "ff." means that there are references for several pages.

Transcriptions

Contents

Note on the Notations Used

THE PHILOSOPHY and sources of the following transcriptions have already been discussed in the Preface and on page 117. It is necessary here only to add an explanation of the special symbols used and to comment on certain technical matters.

The special symbols appearing in the vocal part are as follows:

～～～	A wide vibrato
⌊×	A tone of indefinite pitch, heightened speech
+	A tone slightly higher than tempered pitch
−	A tone slightly lower than tempered pitch

The special symbols appearing in the shamisen part are as follows:

∨	An upstroke with the plectrum
⌒	A left hand pizzicato
×	A tone stopped by the left hand
♫	A finger slide
♪	An indefinite pitch

The following symbols appear in the flute part:

+	A tone slightly higher than tempered pitch
−	A tone slightly lower than tempered pitch
╱	A glissando

The specific execution of the sounds produced on the ko-tsuzumi are explained on page 76. The symbols used to represent them are as follows:

λ	*ta*
⌊×	*pon*
ɔ̧	*chi*
↓ɔ	*pu*

The sounds produced on the ō-tsuzumi are explained on page 76. The symbols used to represent them are as follows:

Y   *tsu*

φ   *chon*

The strokes of the taiko are explained on page 77. In the transcriptions a stem up indicates the right stick and a stem down indicates a left stick. The size of the stroke is shown by one of the following symbols:

♩   small

♩   medium

♩   large

♩   more strongly accented large strokes

The words appearing below the drum parts are the drum calls. Similar interjections are occasionally found below the shamisen player's line. A number in parentheses above the drum lines indicates the number of a stroke in a particular drum pattern. Such a number is used only when the specific passage is discussed in the text of the book. Drum symbols or calls appearing in parentheses are optional.

The texts in the transcriptions do not contain long marks. The Japanese texts for the two main pieces appear at the end of each transcription. Capitalization of the texts in the transcriptions is based primarily on the musical rather than the poetical form.

Finally, it should be noted that measure numbers appear every ten bars. The barring of free measures is based on the original notation of the shamisen part. The octave and basic pitch chosen for the voice and shamisen parts are in keeping with standard Japanese practice.

CORRECTIONS

Please make the following corrections in the scores: page 288, measure 648, the first shamisen note is E, not G; page 284, measure 590, the ho in the ko-tsuzumi is an eighth beat later; page 299, measure 16 is divided between the third and fourth scores.

Tsuru-kame

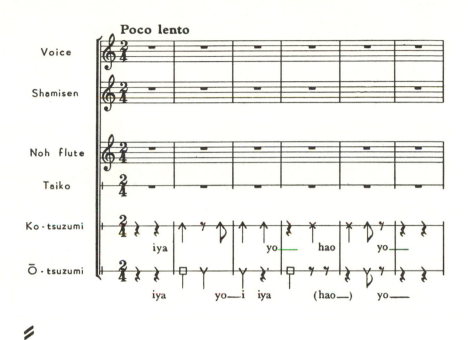

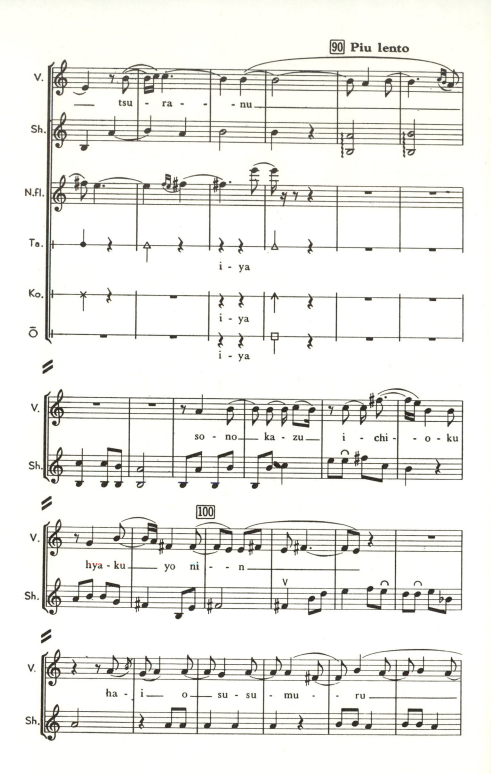

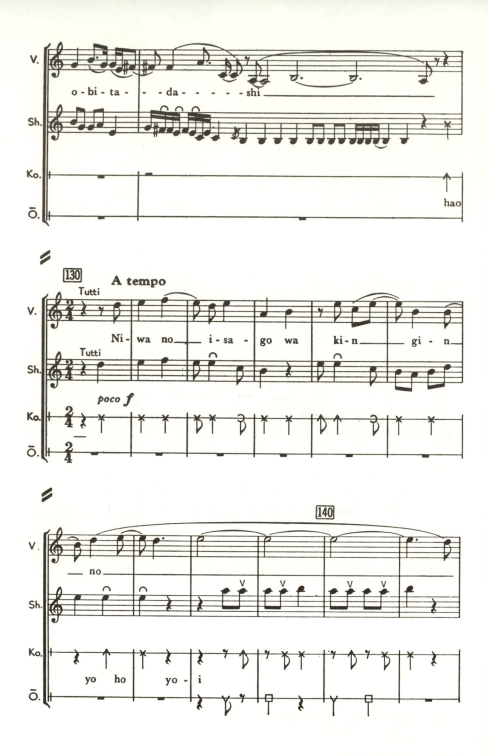

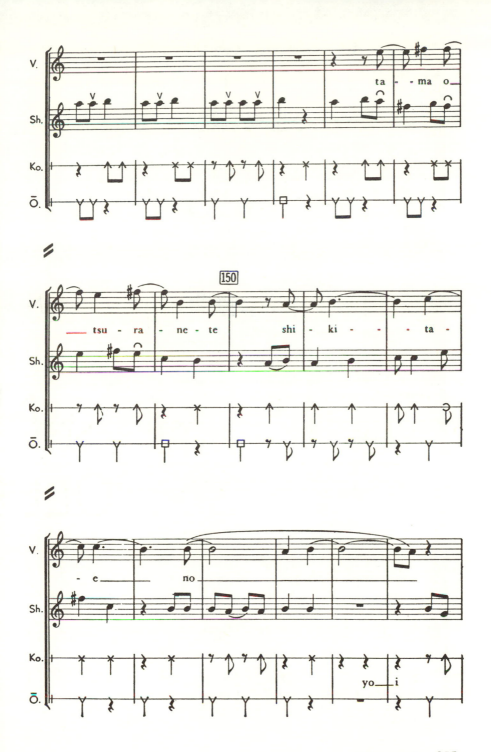

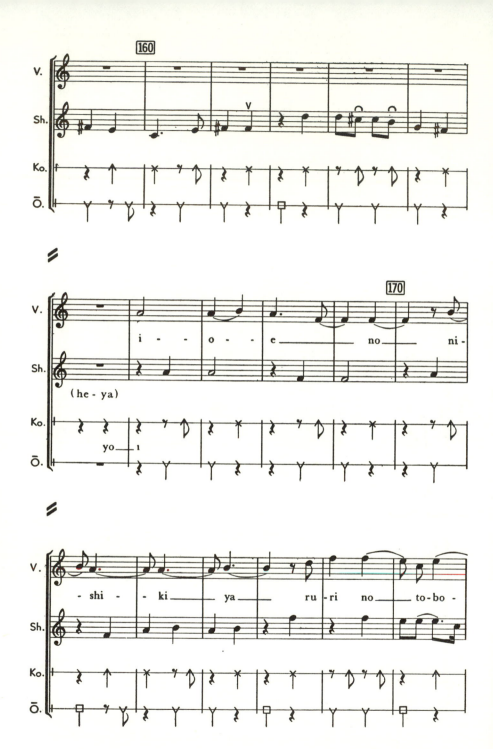

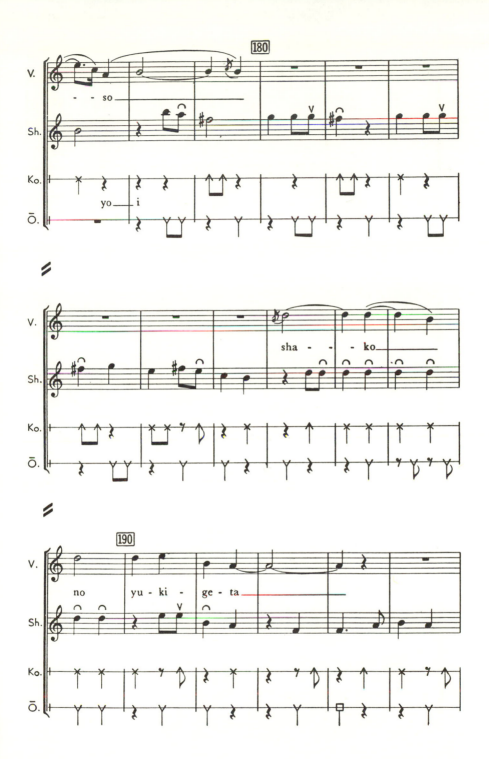

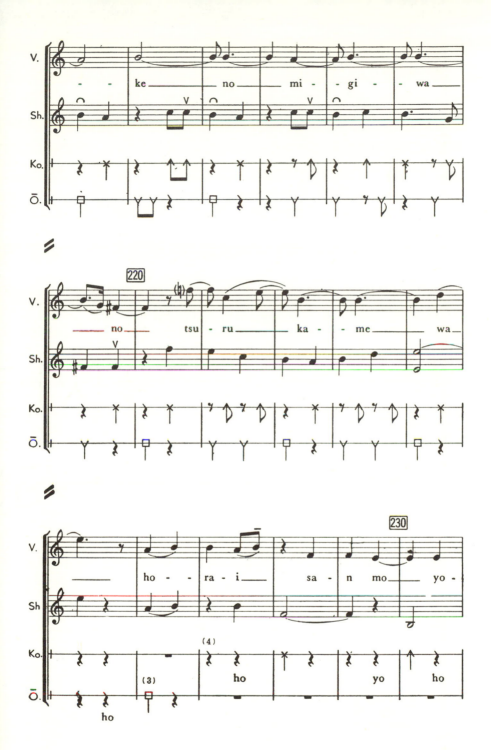

Rubato

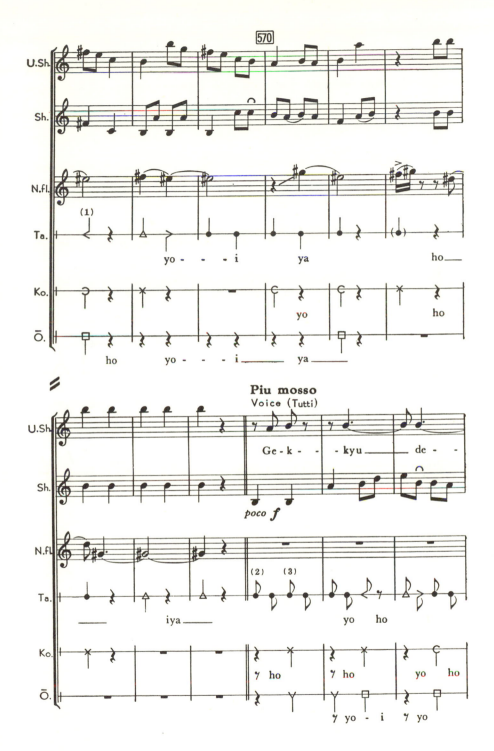

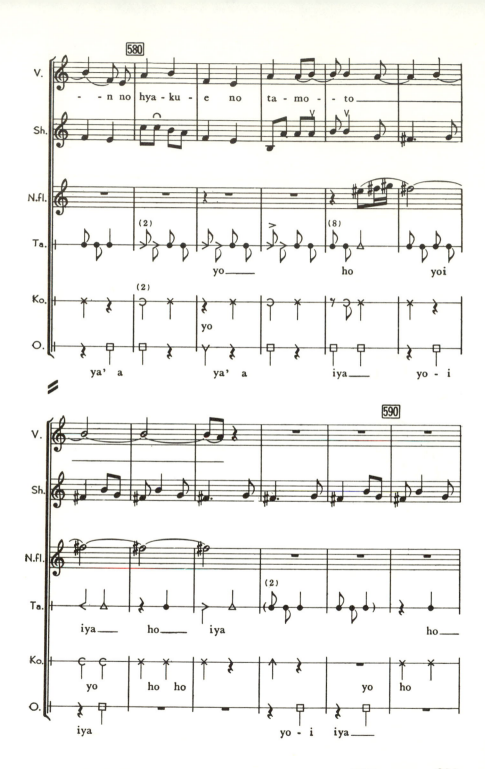

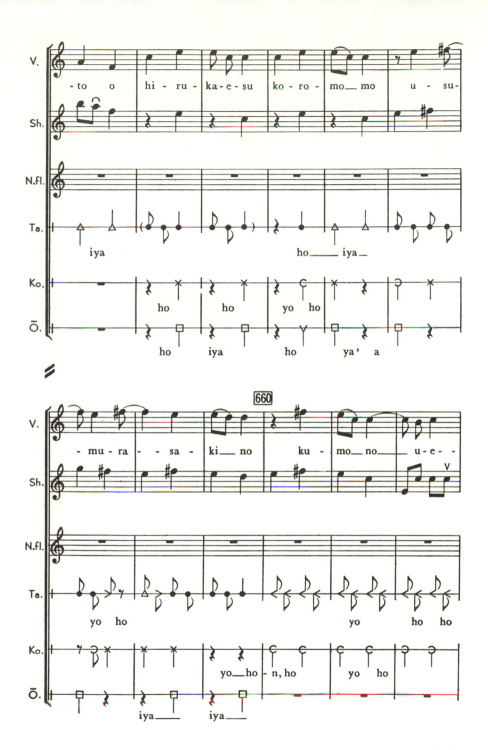

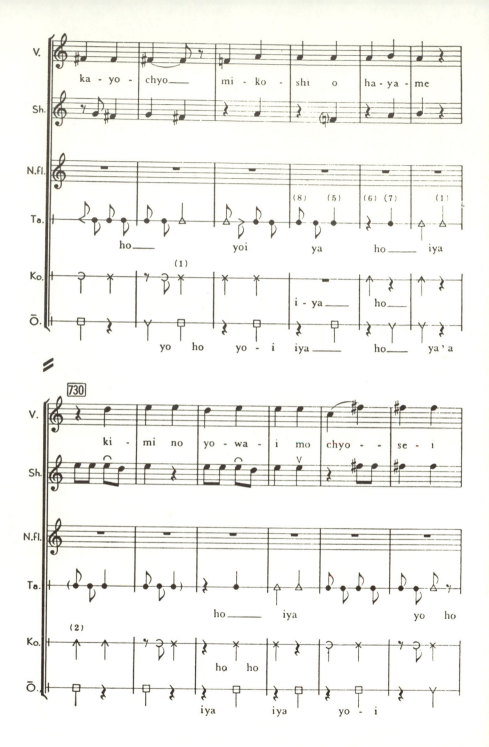

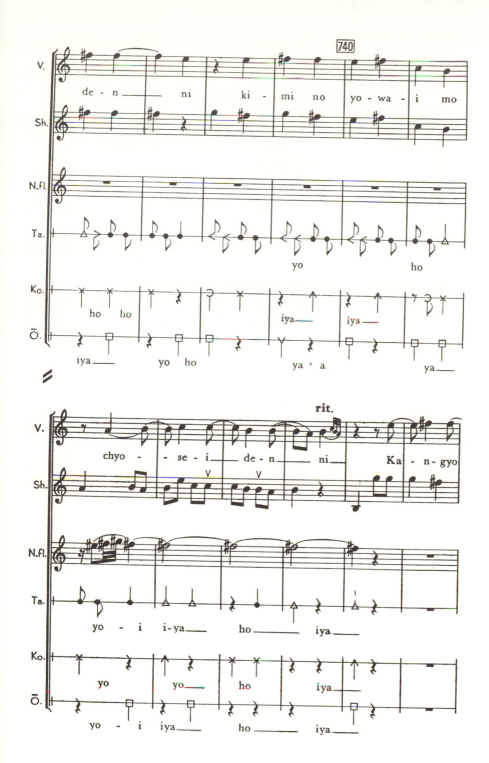

鶴亀

夫青陽の春になれば、四季の節會の事初め、不老門にて日月の、光りを君の、

叡覧にて、百官卿相袖を連ぬ、其數一億百餘人、拜を進むる、萬戸の聲、一同

に、拜する其音は、天に、響きて、夥し、庭の砂は金銀の、玉を連ねて敷妙

の、五百重の錦や瑠璃の扉、硨磲の行桁、瑪瑙の橋、池の汀の鶴龜は、蓬莱山

も餘所ならず、君の惠みぞ、有がたき、如何に奏聞申すべき事の候、奏聞とは

何事ぞ、毎年の嘉例の如く、鶴龜を舞はせられ、其後月宮殿にて舞樂を、奏せ

られうずるにて候、ともかくもはからひ候へ、龜は、萬年の齡を經、鶴も、千

代をや重ぬらん、千代のためしの數々に、何をひかまし姫小松、よはひに比ふ

丹頂の、鶴も羽袖をたをやかに、千代をかさねて舞遊ぶ、みぎりに、しげる呉

竹の、みどりの龜の幾萬代も池水に、棲めるも安き君が代を、仰ぎ奏でて鶴と

龜、齡を授け奉れば、君も御感の餘りにや、舞樂を奏して舞たまふ、月宮殿の

白衣のたもと、月宮殿の白衣の袂、色々妙なる花の袖、秋は時雨の紅葉の羽袖、

冬は冴え行く雪の袂を、翻す衣も薄紫の、雲の上人の舞樂の聲々に、霓裳羽

衣の曲をなせば、山河草木國土豐に、千代萬代と舞たまへば、官人駕輿丁御輿

を早め、君の齡も長生殿に、君の齡も長生殿に、還御なるこそ芽出度けれ

* The Japanese text, following that of the scores in use today, uses traditional rather than modern orthography

Gorō Tokimune

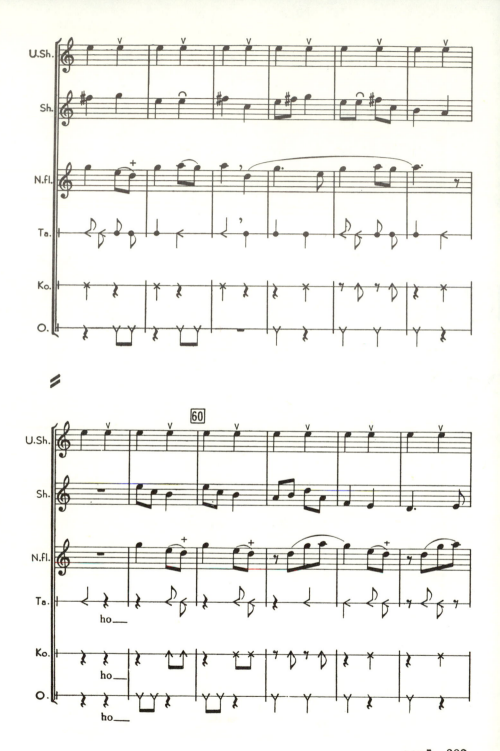

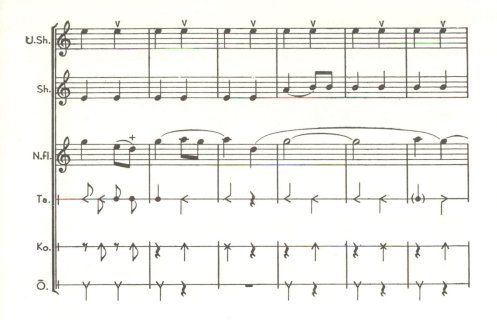

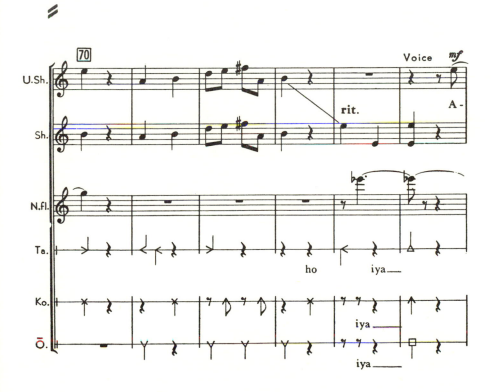

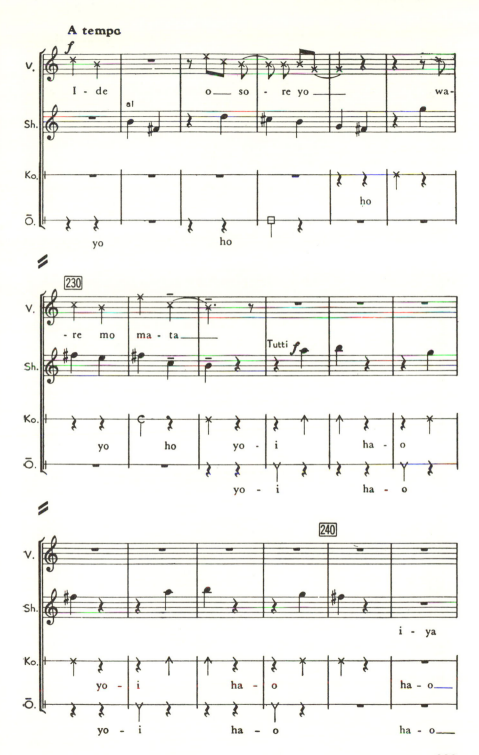

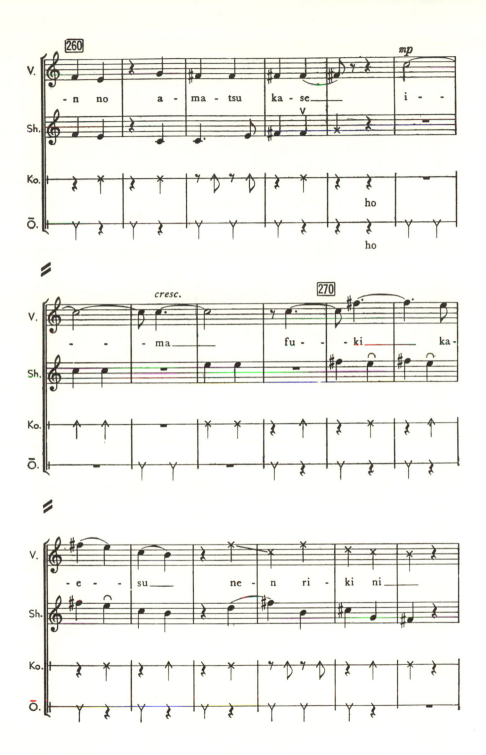

Japanese Text of *Gorō Tokimune**

五郎(時致)

さる程に、曾我の五郎時致は、倶不戴天の父の仇、討たんずものと撓みなき、

彌猛心も春雨に、濡れてくるわの化粧坂、名うてと聞きし少將の、雨の降る夜

も雪の日も、通ひくくて大磯や、廓の諸分のほだされ易く、誰に一筆雁の傳て、

野暮な口舌を返す書、粋な手管につい乗せられて、浮氣な酒によひの月、晴れ

てよかろか晴れぬがよいか、兎角霞むが春の癖、いで、オヽそれよ、我も亦、

何時か晴らさん父の仇、十八年の天津風、いま吹きかへす念力に、遁さじ遣ら

じと勇猛血氣、その有様は牡丹花に、翼ひらめく胡蝶の如く、勇ましくもまた

健氣なり、藪の鶯氣まゝに啼いて、羨ましさの庭の梅、あれそよくくと春風

が、浮名立たせに吹き送る、堤の菫鷺草は、露の情に濡れた同士、色と戀との

實くらべ、實浮いた仲の町、よしやよし、孝勇無双の勲は、現人神と末の代

も、恐れ崇めて今年また、花のお江戸の浅草に、開帳あるぞ賑はしき

* The Japanese text, following that of the scores in use today, uses traditional rather than modern orthography.

The Forty-eight Ōzatsuma-te

I. JO (序): SEVEN TYPES

II. KAKARI (かかり): FIVE TYPES

1. Kakari

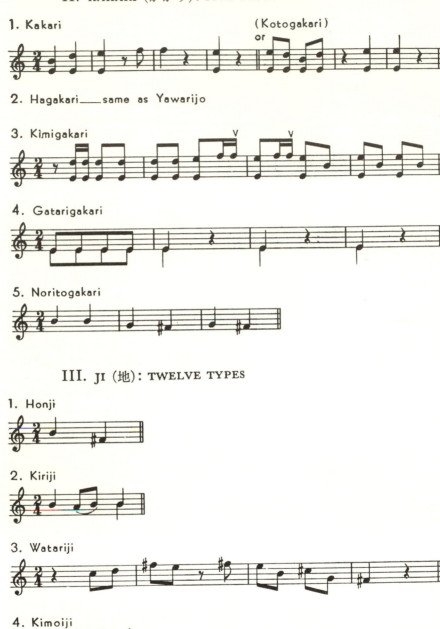

(Kotogakari)
or

2. Hagakari____same as Yawarijo

3. Kimigakari

4. Gatarigakari

5. Noritogakari

III. JI (地): TWELVE TYPES

1. Honji

2. Kiriji

3. Watariji

4. Kimoiji

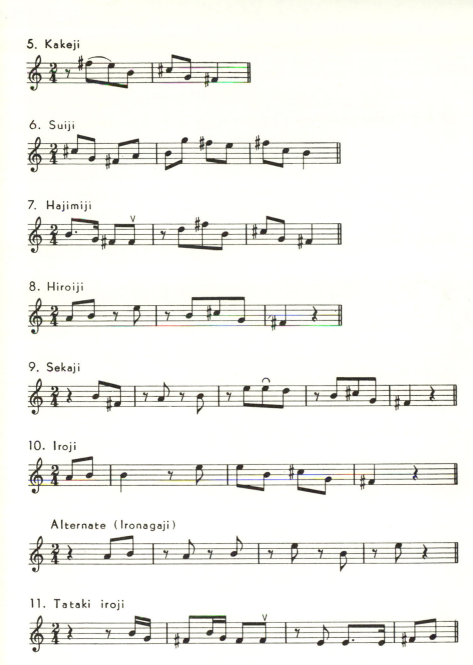

5. Kakeji

6. Suiji

7. Hajimiji

8. Hiroiji

9. Sekaji

10. Iroji

Alternate (Ironagaji)

11. Tataki iroji

12. Tataki yawarigi iroji

IV. TE (手): SIX TYPES

1. Honte

2. Honte oshigasanu

3. Riyaku honte

4. Hikiren

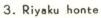

5. Ryoukete

6. Ritsu ukete (compare with honji)

V. SANJŪ (三重): FOUR TYPES

1. Sanjū

2. Sanjū gaeshi

3. Dangire sanjū

4. Riyaku sanjū

VI. TATAKI (たたき): TWO TYPES

1. Tobi tataki

accel.

2. Ryo tataki

tempo ad lib.

VII. OTOSHI (落し): SIX TYPES

1. Otoshi

2. Omotoshi

3. Koto otoshi

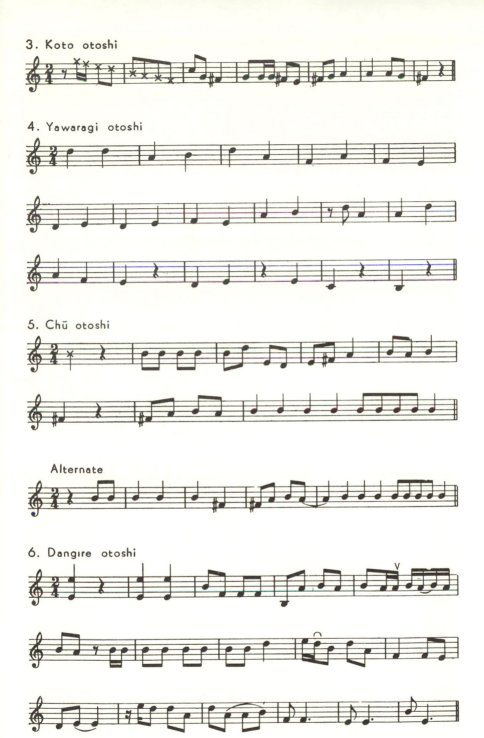

4. Yawaragi otoshi

5. Chū otoshi

Alternate

6. Dangire otoshi

VIII. MUSUBI (結び): FOUR TYPES

1. Ryo musubi nagashi

2. Ritsu musubi nagashi

3. Watari musubi

4. Koto watari musubi

IX. DANGIRE (段切れ): TWO TYPES

1. Dangire

2. Riyaku dangire

"Kyōgen-gakko"

"Kusabue" from *Shigure*

"Inakabue" from *Utsubozaru*